THE
Ultimate
CAT
BOOK

THE
Ultimate
CAT
BOOK

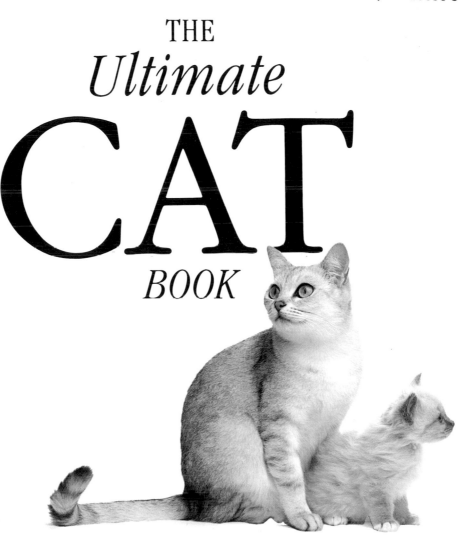

DAVID TAYLOR

DAPHNE NEGUS
CONSULTING EDITOR

COMMISSIONED PHOTOGRAPHY BY
DAVE KING • JANE BURTON

SIMON AND SCHUSTER
New York London Toronto Sydney Tokyo

A DORLING KINDERSLEY BOOK

Simon and Schuster
Simon & Schuster Building
Rockefeller Center
1230 Avenue of the Americas
New York, New York 10020

Simultaneously published in Great Britain by
Dorling Kindersley Limited,
9 Henrietta Street, London WC2E 8PS

Project Editor
Maria Pal

Project Art Editor
Liz Black

Editors
Elizabeth Eyres
Elizabeth Nicholson

Designers
Martyn Foote
Christian Sevigny

Managing Editor
Vicky Davenport

Managing Art Editor
Colin Walton

Typeset by Printronics, Covent Garden, London
Reproduced by Colourscan, Singapore
Printed in Italy by A. Mondadori, Verona

1 3 5 7 9 10 8 6 4 2

Library of Congress Cataloging in Publication Data
Taylor, David, 1934-
    The ultimate cat book : a unique photographic guide to more than
100 international breeds and varieties : with practical information
on cat care, behavior, development, and much more / David Taylor ;
Daphne Negus, consulting editor ; photographs by Dave King and Jane
Burton.
      p. cm.
    Includes index.
    ISBN 0-671-68649-6
    1. Cats. 2. Cat breeds. 3. Cats — Pictorial works. I. Negus,
Daphne. II. King, Dave. III. Burton, Jane. IV. Title.
SF442. T38 1989
636.8 — dc 19
                                     89-6097
                                      CIP

Contents

The Essential Cat

One of the most finely designed of hunting carnivores, the cat has been refined over the ages to become the creature we know today. Unlike the gregarious canine carnivore, the cat has taken the road to individuality and self-reliance. It hunts alone, using its well-honed arts of stealth, ambush, and lightening foray. There is little difference between the domestic feline and its wild relatives, and so we see in our pet cat a character that it shares with the wild cats of the Scottish forests and the tigers that haunt the mangrove forests of Bangladesh.

The cat displays the disdain, nobility, and *hauteur* of the knight errant or samurai, and like them is a polished exponent of the martial arts. At the same time, the cat is ever elegant and neat in all its movements. Whereas the dog is prone to humble fawning before human friends, the cat gives love and friendship more cautiously and on an even-handed basis. A cat's respect and affection must be earned. The friendship of a cat is no less firm than that of a dog, it is just more considered.

Behind the handsome face and piercing gaze of the cat there is always that tantalizing, inscrutable something, the exotic and secret center that harks back to an ancient connection with sacred cults and the black arts. Cats, I think one can say, are truly *magic*.

Origins and Domestication

The early mammals

About sixty-five to seventy million years ago, the close of the great age of the dinosaurs was witnessed by a new and rather insignificant sort of animal that, to any observer at the time, might have seemed to bear little promise of success in the evolutionary stakes. These were the first mammals: small, tree-climbing, long-nosed, insect-eating and not very bright. As the millennia passed, these primitive mammals took different pathways of development. Some became herbivores, whereas others preferred to concentrate on a diet of meat, in the form of other animals. These latter, meat-eating mammals, were the earliest ancestors of the cat.

The evolution of creodonts

The first carnivorous mammals, called creodonts, had long bodies, short legs, and clawed feet. Although their brains were very small, they were sufficiently developed to have forty-four teeth for killing and chewing. The creodonts went on to evolve into a whole spectrum of predators, some as big as a wolf or even a lion. However, their relatively low intelligence led to a gradual decline which ended in their extinction ten million years ago. Before the creodonts died out, one of their forms gave rise to another new kind of animal, the miacid, which, although a small, shy forest-dweller, had that important ace card for survival up its sleeve: a much

bigger brain. As time passed, all the modern carnivores, including the canids (dogs, wolves, and foxes) and the viverrids (mongooses, genets, and civets) evolved from the miacids. It is likely that the cat family sprang from the ancient civet species.

Forty million years ago, an animal that was half civet, half cat, called *Proailurus,* made its entrance. It had long legs and a tail, but unlike true modern cats was a plantigrade (it walked placing all its footbones flat on the ground). Twenty-five million years ago the first nearly true cat appeared, which walked almost as a digitigrade, that is on the tips of its toes. This creature, *Pseudoailurus,* possessed the dentition of a true cat with "stabbing" canine teeth.

The family tree of the cat shows how the modern cat family is divided into three branches. The domestic cat is part of the Felis group.

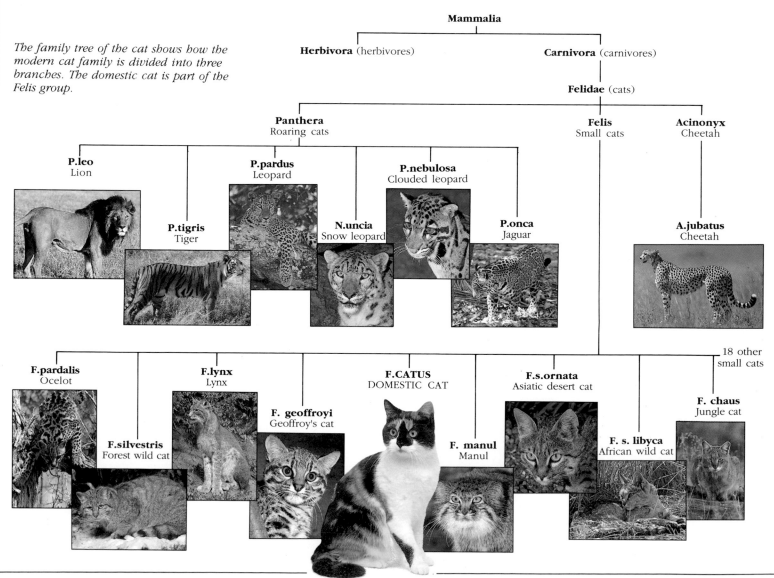

The spread of the domestic cat

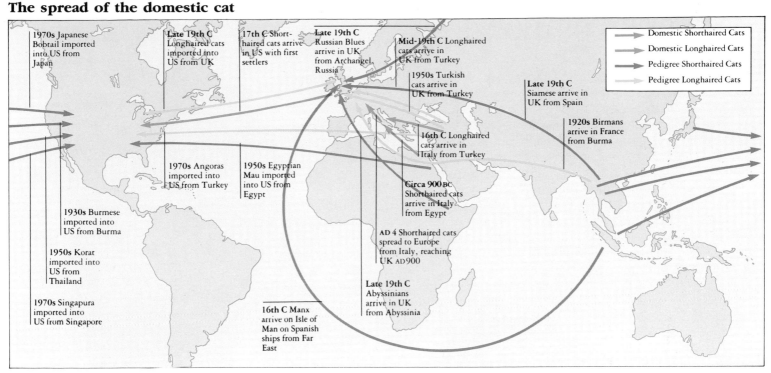

1970s Japanese Bobtail imported into US from Japan

Late 19th C Longhaired cats imported into US from UK

17th C Shorthaired cats arrive in US with first settlers

Late 19th C Russian Blues arrive in UK from Archangel, Russia

Mid-19th C Longhaired cats arrive in UK from Turkey

1950s Turkish cats arrive in UK from Turkey

Late 19th C Siamese arrive in UK from Spain

1920s Birmans arrive in France from Burma

16th C Longhaired cats arrive in Italy from Turkey

1970s Angoras imported into US from Turkey

1950s Egyptian Mau imported into US from Egypt

Circa 900 BC Shorthaired cats arrive in Italy from Egypt

1930s Burmese imported into US from Burma

1950s Korat imported into US from Thailand

AD 4 Shorthaired cats spread to Europe from Italy, reaching UK AD 900

1970s Singapura imported into US from Singapore

16th C Manx arrive on Isle of Man on Spanish ships from Far East

Late 19th C Abyssinians arrive in UK from Abyssinia

Domestic Shorthaired Cats
Domestic Longhaired Cats
Pedigree Shorthaired Cats
Pedigree Longhaired Cats

The map above shows how the shorthaired domestic cat traveled from Egypt — long before the birth of Christ — and through Europe. Longhaired cats, on the other hand, came from Iran and Afghanistan.

The first "real" cats

At last, about twelve million years ago, the first true cats began to stalk the earth, and their fossil remains show that there was soon a wide range of felines to be found. The Tuscany lion, smaller than a modern lion and perhaps more closely related to the leopard, roamed Northern Italy and Central Europe along with lynxes and giant cheetahs. Giant tigers were living in China, and giant jaguars prowled the forests of North America. But there were also smaller species of wild cat like the manul and Martelli's wild cat. The latter is now extinct, but the manul is still found in parts of Asia.

Martelli's wild cat lived all over Europe and in parts of the Middle East. It faded out perhaps a little less than one million years ago, but it was arguably the direct ancestor of the modern small wild cats from which domesticated cats were later to be developed. Among its descendants was *Felis silvestris*, which padded into the picture between six hundred and nine hundred thousand years ago. It spread all over Europe, Asia,

and Africa and gave rise to three main types, the Forest wild cat (*Felis silvestris*), the African wild cat (*Felis silvestris libyca),* and the Asiatic desert cat (*Felis silvestris ornata*). It is from the African wild cat, with the Asiatic desert cat perhaps contributing something, that the domestic cat is thought principally to be descended.

Domestication

As with so many other keystones of human civilization, the domestication of the cat appears to have its origins in the Middle East. African wild cat bones have been found in the cave dung heaps of ancient man. Did he hunt cats just to eat them, or did he perhaps also rear and tame wild kittens to be companions and to control the pests that threatened his hard-won grain stores? There is evidence that man the hunter admired and envied the hunting skills of the wild cats and perhaps began to venerate the creatures he would dearly have loved to imitate in the skills of the chase.

Certainly, the Ancient Egyptians both employed cats as guardians of grain stores and worshipped them as gods, and it is to Egypt that we can trace the original source of the non-pedigree domesticated cat as we know it.

The Ancient Egyptians revered their cats and went into mourning when they died. The cats were then mummified and taken to the temple of the cat god, Bast. Large numbers of these mummies have survived, enabling modern scientists to identify this first domestic species of cat as *Felis libyca.*

From Egypt, Phoenician traders took cats into Italy, and from there they spread slowly across Europe. By the tenth century, domestic cats had arrived in England, although they were still rare. The first colonists in their turn took cats with them to the New World.

Longhaired cats probably have an ancestry stemming from countries even farther to the east. It is likely that modern Persians descended from the wild cats of Iran and Afghanistan, which in turn may have developed from the longhaired manul of Central Asia.

Although cats have been domesticated for at least five thousand years, the concept of selectively breeding cats and producing pedigrees did not catch hold until the mid-nineteenth century. This is in strong contrast with domestic dogs, which have for centuries been selectively bred to perform a wide variety of specific and disparate tasks.

The Design of the Cat

Cats, like humans, dogs, and giant pandas, are mammals and possess anatomical features common to mammals such as hair and mammary glands that produce milk for their young. The basic body pattern of mammals is the same, and so cats have tissues and organs that are fundamentally no different in structure or function from those of human beings. However, just as humans are upright, omnivorous primates with unique specializations, so the body of the cat displays structural adaptations that suit its role as a quadruped, and a carnivorous predator.

The adult cat weighs between six to twelve pounds (two and five kilograms). The heaviest cat on record was a thirteen-year-old female tabby from Cumbria in Great Britain that topped eighteen kilograms (forty pounds). The smallest of the wild cats, the Rusty-Spotted cat of India and Sri Lanka, rarely exceeds one-and-a-half kilograms (three pounds) in weight.

Flexibility

The cat has a most elastic body. The backbone or spine is held together by muscles (rather than by ligaments as is the case in man), and this makes the back very flexible. The cat's shoulder-joint design permits the foreleg to be turned in almost any direction. In fact, looked at in automobile terms, the "suspension" of the feline model gives a near perfect "ride".

Another factor that enhances flexibility in the cat is that it has up to twenty-six more vertebrae than the human

backbone. Also, unlike the human being, the cat lacks a clavicle or collarbone, having instead just a small scrap of clavicle tissue deep in the breast muscle. A full collarbone would broaden the chest and both reduce the cat's ability to squeeze through restricted spaces and limit the length of its stride. In humans, the collarbone enables the fore-arm to be lifted outward. As this movement is not required by the cat, it is unnecessary for it to have this extra bone.

The feline body is capable of unrivaled fluid movement.

Lions and tigers work out in just the same way as the domestic cat.

The supple and luxurious stretching of a cat may be a form of concentrated exercise that benefits the animal in a similar way to human isometric workouts.

The "cross-hand climb" of a typically athletic and ingenious cat.

The brain

As you would imagine, the parts of the cat's brain associated with the senses are well developed, as befits a skilled hunter that depends upon its detection mechanisms. On the other hand, the "intelligence" areas in the frontal lobes are much simpler than in primates such as the ape or human or other highly intelligent animals like the dolphin.

The intestines

The cat is a more highly specialized carnivore than the dog and it possesses an alimentary tract designed purely for meat eating. Consequently, the cat's intestines are proportionately shorter than those of the omnivorous human or dog. Interestingly, the intestines of domestic cats are somewhat longer than those of wild cats — probably because our pets have become used to, and fond of, more varied and to some extent less meaty food.

The teeth and skull

The cat has twenty-four milk teeth and thirty permanent teeth, sixteen in the upper jaw, and fourteen in the lower. These include canine, or fang, teeth for biting, and specialized blade-like carnassial molar teeth for shearing flesh. The canines in the wild animal are the main killing instrument. To give strength to the

The most conspicuous features of the mouths of many carnivorous animals, such as the cat, are the canine (fang) teeth.

feline bite, the cat has short, sturdy jaws worked by powerful muscles that are anchored on reinforced arches of bone placed strategically on the skull.

The skull is notable also for its well-developed bone structures, which include large auditory bullae (echo chambers). These contribute to the cat's sensitivity in hearing such delicate sounds as the scurrying of a mouse or the rustling of a bird among the leaves.

Body shapes

Although domestic dogs come in all shapes and sizes, domestic cats have not yet been produced with much in the way of anatomical extremes. There are three main body shapes: the cobby, the muscular and the lithe. The cobby cat is a solidly built individual with short, thick legs, broad shoulders and rump, and a short, rounded head with a flattish face. The muscular body type has medium-length legs, with shoulders and rump that are neither wide nor narrow, and a medium-length, slightly rounded head. The lithe cat is lightly built with long, elegant, slim legs, narrow shoulders and rump, and a long, narrow, wedge-shaped head.

Balancing Acts

Cats, as we all know from watching the tom next door effortlessly negotiate the length of the garden fence, have a wonderful sense of balance. The main reason for this is the speed of the cat's muscle reaction to remarkably fast messages sent from the eyes and balancing organs in the inner ear by way of the brain. The animal is ultrasensitive to changes in its position, and communicates any alteration to the muscles and joints far faster than a human being.

The use of the tail

It is thought that the cat's tail acts as a counter-balance in much the same way that a tightrope walker uses a long pole. The principle is simple: for example, if a cat is walking along a narrow wall or fence and decides to peer over in one direction, thereby shifting its center of gravity, it will automatically move its tail in the opposite direction, re-establishing its body's center of gravity and keeping itself from falling off.

The tail also acts as a counterweight when the cat is making quick turns while running at high speed. Watch a cheetah going flat out after a zig-zagging gazelle. At each turn, the tail is swung away from the direction of the body to give split-second stability on the "cornering." It seems logical that the cheetah, the champion sprinter among cats, should have such a long tail.

When jumping, a cat's tail is often said to act as a sort of rudder, but it is nevertheless true that cats with very short tails like lynxes or manx cats still jump exceedingly well.

The Art of Falling

When a cat falls through the air, its eyes and specialized structures within the inner ear transmit information to the brain on the position of the head in relation to the ground. As the head changes position or is subjected to changes in acceleration, crystals and liquid inside the inner ear are affected, and this movement is detected by sensitive hairs. In milli - seconds, the brain receives the signal and sends ultra-fast nerve commands to the head to put it "square" with the ground. The rest of the body aligns with the head, and the cat ends up in a position perfectly prepared for landing.

The domestic cat has all the balancing skills of its wild cousin, the leopard.

A cat can be perfectly at ease on a narrow perch. The tail is used as a counterweight as the cat begins to lean forwards.

A newborn kitten is born with the inner ear mechanism fully developed, but because its eyes haven't yet opened, it cannot see. Since perfect balance requires a combination of eye and inner ear messages, a kitten's righting reflex isn't operational until its eyes open.

Recently it has been found that cats that fall from tall buildings don't suffer injuries in exactly the way you might expect. As you would predict, the rate of cat injuries increases steadily the higher the story from which the animal falls — up to seven stories in height. But above that height the rate of fractures inflicted actually decreases! The reason for this appears to be that, after falling for a distance of about five stories, the average-sized cat reaches maximum speed, the so-called terminal velocity of a falling body. At this point the cat's inner ear system is no longer stimulated by acceleration and the speed is constant. The cat therefore relaxes and spreads its legs so that its body and limbs take advantage of maximum air resistance — much in the same way that a freefall parachutist stabilizes his descent.

Relaxed limbs are less likely to fracture so, strange as it may seem, a cat falling from a ten-story-high window ledge may well fare better than one tumbling a mere three stories. (Please do *not* try to prove what I say by experimenting with your pet!).

I well recall incidents of this kind happening when I was a student in Scotland. In the summer, cats would bask on the narrow window ledges of the old tenement apartment buildings, until the owners closed the windows and launched the cats into space. They would fall distances of

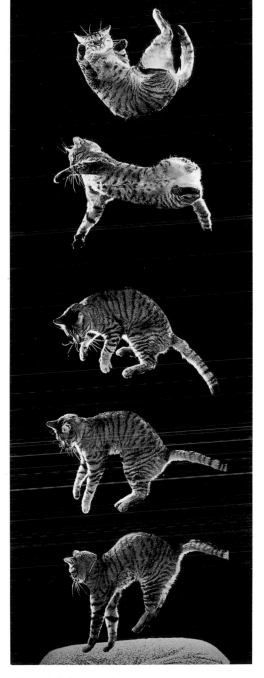

An older kitten begins to show the characteristic, superb co-ordination of its species.

Still a wobbly walker, this fifteen-day-old kitten has not yet attained the balancing abilities of its parents.

The righting reflex:
Serial photographs of a cat falling a short distance onto a soft cushion, show the change in body position and preparation for landing initiated by the eyes and inner ear.

two to five stories, and many of them survived the descent and landed in the correct position. However, because cats have relatively weak neck muscles, they could not hold back their heads, so their chins hit the ground with some force. One of my commonest accident cases in those summer days was to treat the midline fractures of the lower jaw that resulted.

The Cat in Motion

The movement of a cat must match its role as a hunter, often of fast moving and agile prey. The cat's body must provide rapid acceleration, a burst of high speed and nimbleness in order to change course smoothly and to cope with variations in the terrain. It must be silent and allow for attacks with paws or bites with jaws while the cat is still in motion. It must also permit athletic leaps and jumps. The cat's particular build is perfectly designed to achieve all this.

Walking

Because the feline predator must save its strength for the brief dash of the final charge, it has learned how to conserve energy at other times.

An accomplished jumper: the cat first crouches, tipping back its pelvis and bending the three joints of the hip, knee and ankle.

The cat therefore walks with minimum expenditure of energy. It places its feet in a diagonal pattern, left hind foot followed by right fore-foot followed by right hind foot and finally left forefoot. The fore- and hind limbs do not move simultaneously, but slightly out of phase, with the hind one moving slightly in advance of the fore.

The animal's center of gravity is set toward the head, with the fore-limbs supporting the frame and actually exerting a slightly retarding effect. The push forward comes from the hind legs.

As mentioned earlier, true cats have digitigrade feet; they walk on the tips of their toes. Such an arrangement, comparable with the human athlete who sprints along on the tips of his or her toes, is ideal for running.

These joints have little or no lateral mobility and are designed to take strong forces acting in one direction only — down the body.

Running

The cat is a sprint specialist, a Carl Lewis rather than a Sebastian Coe. When it runs its limbs are totally extended in the air. While the fore-feet are on the ground, the highly flexible spine bends like a spring allowing the rear end to continue moving forward in an uninterrupted fluid fashion. This system enables a cat to increase its speed by stretching its trunk fully and lengthening its stride, rather than increasing the number of times the feet hit the ground. At the gallop the retardation forces exerted by the contact of limbs with the ground completely disappear.

When the muscles contract, the hip, knee and ankle joints are rapidly extended, propelling the body sharply forward.

All cats qualify for the finals in athletics, especially in jumping. The gold medal goes to the wild caracal or desert lynx which often catches birds by leaping into the air to a height of several feet and knocking them down with its paws. These kittens, while not in quite the same league, display similar general abilities.

While domestic cats can cover about three times their own body length per cycle at full speed (around 50 kph or 31 mph) the cheetah can briefly attain 112 kph (70 mph) and perhaps a little more. It is interesting that the cheetah has unique grooves on the pads of its feet that act like the tread of a tire in giving the animal grip when sprinting, and particularly when changing direction at high speed. Other cats, including domestic ones, have tough, but "treadless" pads.

The arrangement of the limbs of the cat shows adaptations for running, with long feet and relatively short bones near to the chest. The absence of a collarbone and the narrow chest are features which facilitate twisting and turning and give the animal a longer stride.

Climbing

The powerful back and hind leg muscles of the cat make it an efficient climber. The fore limbs, stretched forward with their hooked and extended claws, act like a mountaineer's crampons. If they can get a grip, the clawed hind feet will power the body swiftly upward to another hold. Most climbs begin with an initial leap to gain height.

Good as they are at going up, cats are not any great shakes at coming down! The muscles of the hind limbs cannot be employed to hold the weight of the body back, and the claws curve the wrong way. That is why cats frequently find themselves stuck up trees or are seen letting themselves slither down, rear end first, in rather ungainly and haphazard fashion, relying on their claws to stop them making too undignified a landing.

Exercise

Curiously, cats stay in trim without having to spend any time working out in a gymnasium or jogging round the park. The luxurious stretching which all cats indulge in may somehow provide all the exercise necessary to keep the animals in tip-top condition.

A complete lack of conventional exercise, combined with gross over-feeding by doting humans eventually produces obesity, but this generally does not bring with it the ill-health and curtailed life one would expect in dogs and their owners. Cats seem to have mastered the secret of a life of leisure.

Going up is easy and elegant, but coming down can be positively awkward.

The spongy pads of the feet, tough skin, also act as shock absorbers when the cat lands.

When landing, the shock is withstood by the feet, wrist and ankle bones, which are arranged so that there is little possibility of sideways "wobble."

15

The Senses

Hunting animals depend on their acute senses for the detection of prey, and the domestic cat retains all the perceptual abilities used by the tiger that prowls the jungle at night.

SIGHT

The cat's eye is constructed in much the same way as that of a human being, but there are important modifications that enable the animal to do things we cannot.

Night vision

It is often said that "cats can see in the dark." Not so. In a totally blacked-out room, a cat can see no better than you or me. What it *can* do is gather the faintest quantities of light in its surroundings. Even on a moonless night the sky is never completely empty of light. Faint starlight or the pale reflections of high cloud are always present, and the cat's eye is designed to gather and use such minute scraps of luminosity.

It uses an ingenious though logical method in the form of a "mirror" placed behind the light-sensitive retina. This "mirror" is composed of up to fifteen layers of glittering cells and is called the *tapetum lucidum*. Faint light-beams enter the

The typical flash of the special mirror (tapetum lucidum) *in cats' eyes that improves night vision. The odd-eyed cat on the right emits two different-colored flashes.*

eye, and pass through to hit and stimulate the light receptor cells of the retina (rods and cones). They then carry on past to be reflected by the "mirror" so that they contact the rods and cones for a second time. This "double dose" multiplies the effect of the light and increases the feline night vision immensely.

We know that domestic cats can make clear visual discrimination at one-sixth of the light levels required by human beings. But obviously, as I have said, the "mirror" cannot work where there is zero light.

The shining of the mirror is what produces the characteristic golden or green gleam of a cat's eye in the dark. ("Tiger! Tiger! burning bright, in the forests of the night", William Blake's famous lines, were perhaps inspired by this phenomenon.) Human eyes do not gleam in the dark: the red glow of our pupils that is occasionally seen in flash photographs is produced by blood vessels behind the human retina.

Visual field

Another advantage for cats is that they have a wider angle of view than we possess. We have a visual field of about 210 degrees of which 120 degrees is binocular. Cats have a total visual field of 285 degrees, 130 degrees of which is binocular.

The 130 degree binocular vision of the cat is another hunting adaptation that allows the animal to judge depth and distance with accuracy. In practice, there is more to judging distance than merely having binocular vision, and cats can be shown to be not quite as good as humans at estimating range. Humans make up for a somewhat narrower field by far more extensive eye movements, permitted by the larger area of white that surrounds the cornea and iris.

In very bright light, the cat's pupil is a vertical slit with a pin-hole at either end. As illumination decreases, the pupil dilates until, at its widest, it can gather every scrap of available light.

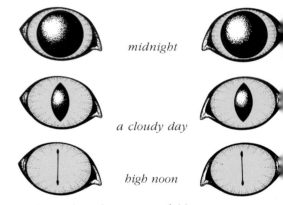
midnight

a cloudy day

high noon

A cat's pupils at three stages of dilation, in different light conditions.

How the eye works

The pupil of a cat's eye, like that of other mammals, constricts in bright light and dilates in dim conditions, but the actual shape of the pupil varies among different feline species. Bigger wild cats possess broadly oval pupils, the puma has a round pupil, and only members of the genus Felis (including the domestic cat) have a vertical slit pupil. The virtue of having a slit pupil lies in its ability to close more efficiently and more completely than a circular pupil. This serves to protect the ultra-sensitive retina. Total closure never in fact occurs — a minute pin-hole remains open at each end of the slit.

The rods on the cat's retina give good night vision and are sensitive to low light levels. The cones provide resolving power. The feline eye contains relatively more rods and fewer cones than a human's. It can therefore see better in dim light but

A cat reveling in a bed of catnip is enjoying its scent which (surprisingly) stimulates a sexual reaction.

isn't able to discern fine detail quite as well as we can.

Cats focus like we do, by changing the shape of the lens through the involuntary control of tiny muscles. This process, which is known as "accommodation", can either bow the lens to bring close objects into focus, or flatten it to concentrate on objects further away. Man and cat share equally good powers of focusing.

Color vision

Does your cat quietly admire the lavender-shaded new curtains or grit its teeth at the first showing of your youngster's psychedelic T-shirt? In short, do cats see in color? They do possess cones of at least two and possibly three kinds, and in human beings, cones undoubtedly play a major part in color vision.

Scientists believe that although cats can see color it means absolutely nothing to them! The eyes distinguish colors but the brain does not interpret them. This almost philosophical distinction between seeing and perceiving is important, for it has been demonstrated that cats can, with difficulty, be trained to understand colour. In general, however, cats do not use color perception — it is not an essential part of their normal life and plays no part in hunting a mouse or approving a bowl of favorite food.

SMELL

Smell is another very important feline sense. Cats have in the region of nineteen million specialized "smelling" nerve endings in the membrane lining their noses, as compared with only five million in humans (although a long-nosed dog, such as a fox terrier, has about one-hundred-and-forty-seven million). On the other hand, tigers are supposed to have little or no sense of smell — which is surprising in an animal that is known for its hunting abilities.

A cat's nose is particularly sensitive to odors containing nitrogen compounds. This permits the animal to reject food that is going "off" or rancid, when it gives off chemicals rich in nitrogen.

One particular olfactory delight of cats, of course, is the plant catnip (*Nepeta cataria*). The reason why your cat is attracted to this garden herb, in which it may well roll and sprawl ecstatically, is that it happens to contain an essential oil which is chemically closely related to a substance excreted by a queen in her urine. As you might guess, toms are "turned on" by catnip more than queens or neutered toms. Catnip, to a cat, is very sexy vegetation! Another plant, valerian, can produce a similar response.

Recognition by smell is far more important in the feline than it is in humans.

Flehming

Many carnivores, including some cat species, make a curious, lip-curling, nose-wrinkling grimace known as "flehming". This is believed to bring some odors into contact with a little-understood organ that lies at the front of the roof of the mouth and that consists of a tiny pouch lined with receptor cells similar to the "smell" receptors of the nose.

This structure, called Jacobson's organ, seems to be involved with both smell and taste. It exists in a rudimentary and non-functional state in man but is functional in cats, although only weakly so in the domestic cat. It can be observed at its best in the mouth of a snake, where it analyzes "smell molecules" delivered by the flicking forked tongue. In cats the Jacobson's organ seems to come into play mainly in connection with odors of a sexual nature.

The characteristic "flehming" grimace of the cat. This is believed to be a way of enhancing the senses of smell and taste.

TASTE

Cats, as we know, tend to be fussy eaters, and are more gourmets than gourmands. Whereas dogs quite readily share a human diet and often adore the odd cookie or candy bar, cats don't generally have much of a sweet tooth.

As pure carnivores, why should they? Many cats cannot digest sugar and get diarrhea if they consume much of it. Perhaps the fact that they do not have a sweet tooth is a natural aid to avoiding sugar. The reason for the difference between canines and felines appears to be that while dogs have "sweet" receptors in the taste buds of their mouth, cats don't. It was once thought that, whereas dogs definitely did have nerve links between tongue and brain that can carry "sweet" messages, cats did not. Now we know that a few "sweet"-bearing nerves do exist in domestic cats, and the numbers seem to be on the increase! I suppose that the breeding of cats that share the homes and habits of their human companions is reinforcing the persistence of such structures, and perhaps one day all pet cats will be toffee addicts!

Moving on from theorizing to the reality of some of the strange things that cats eat, as discussed later in the chapter on diet, the flat-headed cat (*Felis planiceps*) has a liking for sweet potatoes. One assumes it must be able to taste the sweetness. I know that tigers in Manchuria love to eat sweet nuts (shells and all), berries, and fruit in the autumn, and in Malaysia they are keen on durian fruit. Many domestic cats I have known, particularly Siamese and Burmese, have had a sweet tooth. One of mine adored raisins and another regularly went crazy for slices of juicy tangerine.

Day-old kittens have a well-developed sense of taste but, as with humans, the acuity fades gradually with age. A temporary loss of the ability to taste, with accompanying loss of appetite can occur in cats with respiratory disease, just as our taste buds are affected by a bad cold in the head.

Fastidious feeders, cats have a well-developed sense of taste, but one that is not as wide-ranging as ours.

HEARING

The cat's second most important sense is its hearing, and with thirty muscles working each external ear, as compared with six in man, it can turn its ears precisely to locate sound. This ear-turning is done far quicker by a cat than by a dog.

The outer ear is more than just a funnel for collecting sound waves and channeling them down to the ear drum. Its shape is not as simple as the round Victorian ear trumpet, but is irregular and asymmetrical. This shape, combined with the ear movements, produces variations in the quality of received sound that allow the cat to localize its source with precision. A cat has the ability to discriminate between two sounds separated by an angle of five degrees with an accuracy of around seventy-five per cent.

Range

At high frequencies, the cat's hearing (and the dog's) is far more acute than ours. A cat can hear sounds up to two octaves higher than the highest note we can hear, and that is half an octave higher than the best a dog can do! In the high-frequency range, where one may expect to find the high-pitch noises produced by small prey animals, the cat exhibits particular sensitivity. It has great powers of discrimination between notes in this range, being able to distinguish one-fifth to one-tenth of a tone in difference between two notes. The large echo chambers in the skull play an essential part in magnifying sounds for the purpose of analysis by the feline ear and brain.

Most cats learn to recognize, without any training, words uttered by the human voice. They will respond to their name, a call to dine, and so on, but their vocabulary never grows as large as that which can be learned by dogs.

The intent gaze and pricked ears of a hunter which relies on keen senses.

Hearing loss

As in human beings, age brings its toll upon the hearing of cats. Their sensitivity to high notes reduces quite quickly with the passing of the years, often beginning to decline as early as three years of age and usually showing marked loss by the time that the cat reaches four-and-a-half.

Senility and diseases of some kind may result in a cat becoming completely deaf. Ear infections and

The newborn kitten is blind and rather deaf. It depends mainly at this stage on its sense of touch.

blockage with wax generally respond well to prompt treatment by the veterinarian. White cats, particularly ones with blue eyes, have a tendency to deafness induced by a rogue gene in their make-up that causes shriveling of the inner ear structure. This type of deafness is not amenable to therapy. In general, cats cope extremely well with deafness when it occurs.

TOUCH

The sense of touch is highly developed in our fireside friend. The function of cats' whiskers, however, is not fully understood. They obviously have something to do with touch, and removing them can distinctly disturb a cat for some

Possessing a skin rich in touch-sensitive nerve endings, the cat is a supremely tactile individual.

time. There is no substance in the belief that a cat's whiskers protrude on each side to a distance equal to that of the animal's maximum width, so enabling it to gauge whether or not it can pass through a given space without touching anything or making a give-away noise when stalking prey.

But in the dark, a cat's whiskers are immensely sensitive and rapid-acting antennae. Their owner uses them to identify things that it cannot see. Scientists have suggested that if a cat's whiskers touch a mouse in the dark, the cat reacts with the speed and precision of a mouse-trap. Other scientists speculate that the cat may bend some or all of its whiskers downward when jumping or

bounding over the ground at night. Certainly the little desert jerboa uses two of its whiskers to do this — its downward-pointing whiskers are used to detect stones, holes or other irregularities in the animal's path. Even when the jerboa is going at full speed, it can take avoiding action, while in the air or on the ground, by changing the direction of its body in a split second. Maybe cats use their whiskers in some similar way.

Reaction to tremors

Apart from touch, cats are highly sensitive to vibrations. Like some other species, they may give warning of a coming earthquake. There were widespread reports of strange behavior by house cats in the ten to fifteen minutes preceding the disasters at Agadir, Skopje, Chile and Alaska in the 1960s. It seems the animals can detect the first tremors, which are imperceptible to human beings. Peasants on the slopes of Mount Etna keep cats as early warning devices. When their drowsing tom ups and makes for the door hell-for-leather for no apparent reason, the human occupants follow hot-foot.

This hyper-sensitivity to vibration is probably allied to the widely held belief that cats are capable of extra-sensory perception, and that they can pick up "vibrations" of a kind not detected by the five normal senses. It is in fact impossible to say whether or not cats are "psychic" in this way, although it is easy to guess why they have gained this reputation.

The acuteness of the feline senses allows the animals to react to occurrences of which the relatively blunt-edged human brain is unaware. This fact, coupled with the inscrutable "knowing" look of its features, no doubt played a large part in the growth of the belief that a cat possesses a supernatural dimension and communicates with strange forces, which many still believe is so today.

Ragdoll

Devon Rex

Black-and-White Bicolor Persian

Red Self Persian

The whiskers of pedigree cats, like those of fashionable young men, are nowadays mere vanities. These specialized hairs do, however, have a function in enhancing the cats sense of touch, although how they do so is not fully understood.

Behavior

"The Cat he walked by himself, and all places were alike to him."
(Rudyard Kipling)

The cat is a less sociable animal than the dog, and only the lion among wild cats shows much gregarious activity. However, cats are not totally self-sufficient or indeed anti-social creatures. Proud and aloof they may be, but they possess the ability to form close friendships with man. This is true not only of the domestic cat but also of some of its wild relatives such as the African wild cat. Tigers, lions, leopards, and pumas that are reared in circuses often dote on their trainers and handlers with as much apparent affection as any pedigree Siamese. Between cats there is very often much affection and what must pass for love.

Close affection between cats is often demonstrated.

SLEEP

Cats do a wide variety of things in their daily lives, but, as befits specialist hunters that must conserve their energy for brief, high-performance bursts of activity, they delight in rest and relaxation. Taking "cat-naps" of a few minutes at a time, they total about sixteen hours of sleep out of twenty-four, and are the greatest sleepers among mammals. They out-drowse even the rather dozy Giant Panda, which is active for about fourteen hours per day. Why the cat requires so much sleep, we just don't know.

It goes without saying that cats enjoy their naps and are masters in selecting the warmest and most sheltered spot in the garden, or the cosiest nook indoors.

While they sleep their brains continue to work at a basic level, recording and analyzing stimuli coming in from their surroundings. In deep sleep, surprisingly, the brain remains as active as it is when awake, and the senses continue to scan for the first signs of danger. At the first alarm, the cat's nervous system, which is ever-alert, rouses the body muscles instantaneously. Experiments have been done in which external stimuli are completely removed, and the cat is put into a darkened, sound-proof, odor-free room. When its brain-wave activity is recorded it is found that the mental processes gradually wind down to a minimal, body-maintenance level. There is apparently no spontaneous thought; as the cat lies there it doesn't compose poetry, recall with relish past dinners or fantasize about the young queen in the house next door. This is quite different to what is found in human beings placed under similar conditions. They proceed from trains of spontaneous thought to suffering hallucinations and other mental aberrations.

Like ours, the cat's sleep pattern embraces periods of both deep and

Although not as social an animal as the dog, the cat does form close and affectionate relationships with human beings.

light sleep. Seventy per cent is light and thirty per cent is deep. The phases alternate, with evidence of dreaming during the deep phases. You can tell that your cat is dreaming when, in a similar way to dogs, its paws and claws may move, its whiskers twitch, its ears flick and in some cases, it actually makes noises.

HUNTING

The cat is a natural carnivorous predator, but it is not a completely instinctive hunter. The urge to hunt successfully is induced and honed by competition and demonstration; the skills are learned by observation, and trial and error. Cats are not born good bird-catchers, for example — in fact until they have thoroughly practiced the art over and over again,

Naturally cats are experts at cat-napping.

Just like a tiger, the domestic cat displays the phases of the feline hunter's attack: the slink run, the final charge and the pounce.

they are downright bad at it.

Learning from mother and other cats is essential, and a good teacher makes a good pupil. The offspring of non-hunting cats rarely make good hunters themselves. There may also be a genetic factor. The cat's hunting technique is inherited originally from its forest-dwelling ancestors, for whom ambush was more rewarding than the chase.

Hunting technique

Once the cat has located a suitable victim by means of its senses, it begins to approach slowly and cautiously, using every bit of available cover. Next, to cross any open space, it travels forward rapidly in a movement known as the "slink-run," its body pressed close to the ground to reduce its outline. The slink-run is broken by pauses when the cat stops and stares intently at the prey.

After several such runs and pauses, the cat reaches a patch of cover nearest to the prey from where the final attack can be launched over a relatively short distance. Here it "ambushes": lying crouched, eyes glued to the prey, hind feet making treading movements as if revving up for the charge, and tail-tip twitching in feverish anticipation.

Suddenly the final attack is mounted. The cat breaks cover and shoots forward, body still held fairly close to the ground. When it is within striking distance, it raises its fore parts and leaps on to its prey. While the forepaws pin down the victim, the hind feet act as anchors planted solidly on the ground.

The lynx and the leopard lurk close beneath the skin of our domestic cat, even in play.

The kill

Now comes the kill. If the prey starts to struggle, the cat may release it briefly and then repeat the final attack in order to get a better grip. Alternatively, it may throw itself on to its side, keeping hold with the forepaws but releasing the hind paws in order that they can rake powerfully, claws extended, at the victim.

The killing bite of a cat, domestic tabby or jungle tiger, is a remarkably well-organized affair. All felines tend to use a neck bite. The prey is usually killed by dislocation of the vertebrae in the neck.

It is fascinating to note that the distance between the left and right fang teeth of a cat is the same as the distance between the neck joints of its usual prey. A domestic cat has its fang teeth aligned for dislocating the neck of a mouse, and the tiger is designed to do the same to its favorite meals, deer and wild pig.

There are special nerves linked to the fang teeth of the cat that sense in the twinkling of an eye when the points of the teeth are perfectly positioned over the neck joints of the prey. These nerves then send ultra-fast messages to the brain, which responds in turn by sending messages to the jaw muscles, instructing them to close at an unusually high speed and thereby perform the dislocation. The neck-bite of a cat is a brilliant "computer-controlled" process.

Learning to hunt

Domestic queens, like the females of other feline species, teach their kittens how to perfect their killing techniques in a graduated series of lessons. First, the queen carries

This growing kitten begins to practice its hunting skills on a toy bird.

home prey that she has killed and eats it in the presence of her offspring. A little later she leaves killed prey for the kittens to eat, and then finally, when they are two-and-a-half to three months old, she brings home live prey, presents it to her young and lets them kill it. She does not help them to make the kill, but if the prey escapes from them, she will catch it and re-present it so they can try again. Similar behavior has been recorded in, for example, cheetahs and tigers.

It is competition among the litter mates that, by raising their excitement and enthusiasm, stimulates kittens to make their first neck-bite kills. The learning process is delicate; if no kills are made during the developmental period, the cat finds it difficult if not impossible to learn how to do it later. A hand-reared kitten denied the opportunity to make its first kill at the right time in its development will grow into a non-killer that shows little interest in mice or other small prey.

Domestic cats will swipe at anything that moves, but the hunt proper is reserved for small creatures such as mice, birds, and, (worth remembering), pets such as hamsters.

I don't know whether the story of a ginger tom hunting down, killing, and eating a tiny Chihuahua dog that lived in the house next door is apocryphal or not. It is not true to say that cats are better hunters if they are kept hungry, nor that neutered cats are worse mousers than unneutered ones. Plump and well-fed cats are often the best guardians of granaries and food stores. What makes a good, rather than a merely competent, mouser is what makes one human a champion athlete — inborn and probably inherited talent. The instinct of the domestic cat is to hunt, almost for hunting's sake, unlike the bigger wild cats that tend only to hunt in order to fill their stomachs.

Coping with a hunting cat

The successful hunter bears the spoils proudly to his home, and the cat is frequently no exception. Brimming with satisfaction, it delivers a dead mouse or young rabbit to your door, or actually deposits it on the carpet at your feet. Don't scold or try to punish your pet; it is just showing affection towards someone "in the family" by giving a present. Wild cats do it as a social gesture, and you should feel honored to be so highly thought of. Try to dispose of the gift as promptly and hygienically as possible — though your cat will find it difficult to understand why you dash out to the trash can with the mouse held by its tail between finger and thumb, instead of settling down to eat it!

Those cats that do learn through practice how to catch wild birds can cause havoc among your garden's feathered visitors. Site all bird feeding devices that you may have in the open so that your cat is denied cover for stalking. Fitting a bell to the cat's collar can be useful as a warning to birds, but I have known cats that still manage to catch birds despite having been "belled". One in particular actually scooted along on three legs holding the bell pressed silently to its throat by a forepaw.

Don't be alarmed if your cat insists on catching and eating flies. It's just another form of the hunt and it will not, as is sometimes claimed, "make the cat grow thin." Flies can carry disease bacteria or parasite eggs, but the risk is low and not worth worrying about.

Domestic cats exhibit great skill in hooking fish out of shallow ponds as I, and my goldfish, know to our cost. Some wild species, such as the fishing cat, flat-headed cat and jaguar, are even better fish poachers. Big cats such as the lion and tiger tend to eat their meals while lying crouched down, probably to hide their meal from predators, but domestic cats prefer to sit neatly on their haunches or remain standing.

The feral cat (a domestic cat returned to the wild) eats a diet similar to that of its small wild cat relatives — small rodents, other mammals up to the size of a hare, birds up to the size of a hen, insects and, when available, lizards.

PLAY

Play is a most notable feline activity, and wild cats play with as much eager enthusiasm as their domestic relatives. Because play is generally most pronounced in animal species where the young pass through a relatively prolonged period of "childhood", carnivores, including cats, are among the most playful of mammals. Naturally, the young play more than the adults.

It is impossible to define *purely*

This cat proudly returning with its trophy is interested in hunting for its own sake.

playful activity, that is behavior which is only to be observed as a form of recreation. For the cat, play blends naturally into rehearsal of the serious skills and behavior patterns involved with hunting, killing, fighting, and escaping. When kittens chase one another, the roles of pursuer and pursued switch frequently as the youngsters learn the essentials of a predator's life. With no prey available, somebody has to take on the part of the mouse — just as happens in children's games such as cops and robbers or cowboys and Indians.

Although the games may be played with much verve and excitement, the essential principle of play is never lost — bites and scratches are never carried out at full force and injuries are very rare. Because the end point of a real hunt, the kill, does not happen in kittens' play, the various pre-kill phases of hunting and combat tend to be repeated over and over again with an animal playing, in quick succession, the roles of aggressor or defender, rival or prey.

However, there is never any component of fear or distress in any of the players. Indeed, one notable feature of feline play is the exuberant exaggertion of many of the movements in the playing. It is impossible to escape the conclusion that the animals, apart from learning, derive real fun and enjoyment from their sporting. Play relieves the frustrations of not being able, for some reason or another, to hunt. This is why cats sometimes play "cruelly" with live prey for some time before killing it. In the wild, cats hunt often

Reminiscent of two young lions in ritual combat, these domestic kittens practice their ancient arts.

and kill sometimes, whereas in the domestic situation, food (the kill) is readily available and hunting opportunities are scarce. So, to satisfy the age-old urge and inbuilt adaptations to hunt, the cat will stretch the "hunting phase" when it does come across a suitable victim.

The cubs of some cat species rehearse in play certain features of adult behavior that are specific to their kind. The youngsters of the black-footed cat and of the leopard, for instance, love to somersault as they play. This is a way of practicing the technique, needed by relatively light predators

This little kitten is completing a mock attack in identical fashion to the real thing, as practiced by a tiger.

attacking much heavier prey, of clutching with forepaws, raking with hind claws and rolling over with their victim without losing their grip. Even more striking (literally) is the way cheetah cubs rehearse on one another the typical paw slap with which they will later fell a Thomson's gazelle.

Benefits of playing

All this practice, practice, practice, in play develops the young cats' experience of the external world and its physical laws. Through play, they learn how to time a punch; how far to jump to land on a moving object; how fast they must run in order to

Even very mature cats may play from time to time.

intercept their prey, and other useful lessons of this kind.

For adult domestic cats, as well as for wild cats kept in zoos, play also relieves frustration and can increase their contentment and interest in life. For these cats, food is regularly provided, without the need for a thrilling (and, in the wild, often fruitless) chase, so their powerful hunting instincts surface instead in the form of play. Such playing actually makes the animal more keen to eat, and makes what might otherwise be a monotonous and predictable meal more fun.

The moral of this is that you should play with your cat regularly. The playing of the domestic cat is not only a demonstration of hunting rituals, but is also useful in exercising and strengthening the growing cat.

Intelligence and Communication

A cat is a very intelligent creature — as a usually solitary, self-reliant hunter it has to be. It has to learn to calculate, to solve problems, and to be versatile. It is rather a waste of time discussing the comparative intelligence levels of various animal species. People often do it, but they

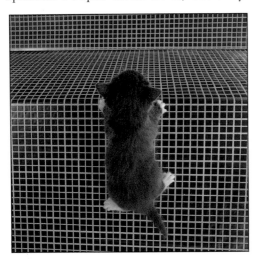

Just as the human eye and brain can be deceived by tricks of perspective so can those of the cat. This little kitten, on a glass sheet covering a design which makes it look like a table edge, is peering down and hesitating prudently at the apparent corner.

have no reliable yardstick with which to measure this quality we call "intelligence." Cultural differences even between the various groups or races in a single species, *homo sapiens,* are notorious for distorting the results of "intelligence tests." And this is the only species with which we can truly communicate by means of a common language!

An imperfect but at least objective method has been to compare brain weight with length of spinal chord. This gives a ratio that roughly indicates how much brain controls how much body. The human ratio is 50:1, a monkey's 18:1 and a cat's 4:1. But does this permit us to say that a human being is over ten times more intelligent than a cat?

Learning and memory

Cats do learn well, and for many of life's activities they must learn rather than rely on instinct. Hunting is not instinctive but learned from observation, as is the use of a litter tray. In the latter case the teacher is either the mother cat or a human companion.

Such learning by example merges with the ability to be positively trained. Cats can be trained to perform tricks, though they do not respond well to coercion (even though I admit that some circus big cats in the old days were "tamed" by unacceptably cruel methods). They are easier to train by rewards, but even so, cats don't show the eagerness to be trained that we see in dogs. Despite a plentiful source of attractive rewards in the form of tasty titbits, they will only co-operate if they feel in the mood. You can't buy cats — that's part of their independent nature.

The feline memory is well developed, and most domestic cats learn such useful knacks as tapping on window panes to gain entrance, opening a door by jumping for the latch, finding their way home or

This cat has learned enough to know both where prey might be found and how to get it.

coming to the call of a familiar voice.

Essentially cats live for themselves. They have no "work ethic" like some dogs, rodents or birds, and they will only work to attain a definite end — finding food for example. That apart, they adopt a rather aristocratic view of life and learn early on to expend energy only as necessary.

Sixth sense

Do cats possess a sixth sense? It has often been claimed so. There certainly is an air of mystery about the cat's personality and demeanor. Do cats perhaps know things hidden from us, sense things we cannot?

I believe that the cat has super-efficient natural senses that can detect things we cannot. When a cat suddenly raises its hackles when you are alone with it in the house, it isn't because it has seen a ghost, but because it is reacting to sounds or vibrations you cannot pick up. This ability evolved primarily as a means of survival, by providing an early warning system. The world must reveal far more to the highly sensitive cat than to less well endowed creatures like ourselves.

Social behavior

Although cats are lone hunters, they are not anti-social. Indeed, they have intricate social interactions with their own kind. Furthermore, there is a complex feline society which, in the case of the domestic cat, forms an infra-structure to human civilization.

Inscrutable it may be, but the cat can communicate with its fellows in a variety of ways, such as those illustrated on the facing page. There are four principal methods:

• Vocalization: The cat's repertoire is plaintive mews, seductive purrs, incensed wails and irate screeches.

• Body language: Facial expressions are emphasized by the markings which "make up" the features. Body postures or tail positions are also enhanced by coat markings.

• Touch: Cats communicate by rubbing noses, pressing bodies against, or grooming others.

• Scent: Using their sensitive noses, they identify other cats by their scents, sniffing one another's heads and beneath tails, where odor-making glands are situated. They also mark out territory with scent "markers".

Vocalization: This little kitten is saying that it feels short of attention. Some are more "polite" in their demands than others.

Body language: A pose that speaks louder than words of this cat's desire for its dinner — something its owner can ignore at his or her peril.

Rubbing: Sensuous rubbing to indicate love and affection is one of the most attractive feline methods of communication.

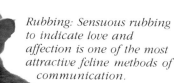

Friend or foe? The sense of smell is just one of the senses that is aroused when two cats meet. The complicated process of determining if a new "introduction" is friendly or not involves all of the cat's methods of appraisal.

A defensive cat: This cat stands with an arched back, usually with its body turned at an angle to the aggressor. The pupils are wide open, the ears are flattened to the head, the mouth is open with the teeth showing, the fur of its back is bristling and the tail, also bristling, is arched. It makes hissing, spitting sounds.

An aggressive cat: The animal is poised to strike with its ears pricked and furled back, the pupils of its eyes closed to a slit, the whiskers bristling forward, the mouth wide open with the lips curled back into a snarl, and the tail low, bristling and swishing to and fro. Its fur is smooth and it makes growling and spitting noises.

A submissive cat: This animal, which is definitely not spoiling for a fight, is communicating its submission and pacific intentions by means of its posture. It cringes close to the ground with enlarged eye pupils, flattened whiskers and ears, a mouth which may be open and silent or half open and emitting a pitiful distress call. The body fur is flattened to the skin and the tail is thumping the ground.

This tense meeting concerns ownership of the tree trunk — which is clearly part of one cat's territory.

Look at the map of your town. Depicted there is the framework of civilized society — humble homes, great houses, meeting places, common land and a network of thoroughfares. But that map is also the plan of the town's feline society, superimposed invisibly upon the man-made geography. The feline citizens also have an ordered division of the land for various purposes and like ours, their society has its social strata, top cats in feline Nob Hill and proletarian pussies on the other side of the tracks.

Your cat, unless of course it is kept

"Top Cat" he may be, but this battered tom shows the scars of his constant battles for supremacy.

permanently indoors, is part of the cat community in your local neighborhood with a precise, though not necessarily unchanging, position in the hierarchy. It, like all other members of the community, must abide by rules and rituals that are laid down in a very precise way. All the cats in the neighborhood community know one another and their positions in society. A newcomer taking up residence is only allotted a position and territory after fighting for it.

The cat hierarchy

Cat society is essentially organized as a matriarchy. The unneutered queen with the most kittens reigns at the top of the pecking order. When she is neutered, however, her social

status slumps. Males take their place in the community in macho fashion by using brawn over brains. The meanest, toughest toms battle for power and prestige. Success in combat determines a tom's social niche. The organization is rigid, and a cat only occasionally loses its place by being vanquished by an up-and-coming young blade.

Unlike the position with monkeys, deer, or seals, dominant toms don't necessarily acquire large harems of queens. Queens seem to be very civilized and don't automatically give courtship rights to the all-conquering thug. Often queens will prefer as suitors toms situated well down the pyramid of power — shades of Lady Chatterley! Interestingly enough, top tom cats do however rule the biggest chunks of territory and it seems that, as with the landed gentry of days gone by, land rather than sex is the key to social status in feline society.

Neutered toms are always at the bottom of the social ladder, the feline equivalent of Skid Row. An entire tom begins to lose his position in the community as soon as he is castrated. After the operation, the amount of male sex hormone, testosterone, declines in the blood and the pungent masculine odor of his urine fades. As this process continues, he descends rung by rung down the social ladder.

It isn't that neutered toms cannot fight, but rather that they lose their aggression. To his peers, the neutered tom's weakening scent is a potent signal, which is interpreted, I suppose, as effeminacy. In the world of tom cat *mafiosi*, you have to smell "butch" to be "one of the boys"!

Territorial areas

Cats are territorial — they "own" patches of land. Even an "indoor cat" has its territory — a particular part of the room or a favorite chair. Where several cats live in a household, indoor territorial rights gradually merge until all the cats jointly possess the house and mutually defend it against feline outsiders.

Outdoors, all cats, no matter how lowly they may rank in society, have some territory. Females and neuters hold fairly small properties, but ones which they nevertheless fight harder to defend than any grandee tom with a vast estate. The problem for the top toms is that the large areas of territory that they own are difficult to defend around the clock, if they are to be able to grab forty winks. A dominant tom in a country area with a sparse cat population may rule fifty

This punch to the jaw is the opening move in a fight to determine which cat comes top in the "pecking order."

This cat is marking a tree trunk with urine. Such "visiting cards" can sometimes also be left on furniture or even people's legs (to their embarrassment).

Scratching as a way of marking territory is done by many feline species, including the domestic cat and the tiger.

Leaving scent by rubbing against a solid object is yet another way of staking a claim to it.

or more acres while in the city a "property" may be as small as a back yard. Within a property the cat, like a human landowner, has its favorite spots for catching the sun, sleeping or keeping a lookout.

The territory is marked as belonging to its owner in three main ways. The cat may spray the boundaries with urine (sometimes a tom may spray you —in which case you should be flattered that he sees you as a fixture in his estate). The second method is scratching (to leave visible and sweat-scented marks). Another way of territory marking is to rub a solid object with the head, which transfers scent from sebaceous glands in the skin.

If you have to move, you can help your cat establish its new terrritory by discouraging other cats and breaking up fights. Soon the "locals" will yield up the piece of land considered by the community to be appropriate to your pet's agreed social standing.

Public territories

Outside the private territories land is organized on a "municipal" basis. There are hunting grounds, meeting places and no-man's-lands; the latter might typically be places occupied by dogs. There is a formal network of

walkways or roads that link all these places, skirting privately owned feline territories and non-cat areas. Some pathways are private to a particular cat. Others are communal. Some can be used at certain hours of the day by cat A and at other times by cat B, C and so on. This system avoids conflict. "Main roads" have their traffic rules. For example, any cat moving along a main pathway has automatic and undisputed right of way over any other cat, whatever its social standing, approaching on an intersecting sidepath.

Meeting grounds are used for what can only be described as "cat clubs". Toms and queens gather from time to time to sit in these places in peaceful groups three to twenty feet (one to six metres) apart. Although meetings may involve the mating of a queen in season, normally the gatherings have no sexual overtones. We don't really know why cats assemble like this. It seems to be an important part of their social life and perhaps they exchange information, news and gossip by some means. Or maybe they just, like the best of human friends, simply and silently enjoy one another's company.

Cat clubs are one of the things that

are missing in the life of a cat kept permanently indoors. A solitary indoor cat may become lonely and bored and turn to bad behavior, like chewing carpets and urinating in forbidden spots. In such cases veterinary advice should be sought.

This is a group of feral cats in their "clubhouse." Such conclaves, usually very peaceful, are not understood by biologists.

Breeds

The blue-blooded, pedigree cat is an aristocrat, but one with a family tree that goes back little more than a century, and which has its roots in much humbler soil. Over a hundred different breeds and varieties of *Felis catus* are officially recognized world-wide, and they can be divided into five principal categories — Persians or Longhairs, other longhaired cats, British Shorthairs, American Shorthairs, and Oriental or Foreign Shorthairs. Although some are "natural" breeds that were originally indigenous to a particular country, the large majority are the result of carefully designed breeding programs that began with the selection of the best examples of run-of-the-mill, *mongrel,* cats.

Some breeds are descended from mere chance, genetic mutations that suddenly appeared among otherwise "orthodox" litters and would, by the evolutionary rules of natural selection, have perished because of the disadvantages bestowed by the mutation, had not man for purely esthetic reasons, nurtured the off-beat line. That it should have taken no more than one hundred years to develop the spectrum of feline aristocracy is due to the relatively short gestation period, rapid maturing and often generous litter sizes of the cat. Today, national associations in each country (the Cat Fanciers' Association in the US) lay down the standards that pedigree cats are judged by, and also register kittens.

Coat Types

A cat's fur is its crowning glory and is a source of insulation. In the wild, a cat's coat color serves as camouflage and is related to its natural habitat. Chance color mutations and selective breeding have produced the variety of coats seen in today's pedigree cats. Types of coat, like color, also developed to suit habitat — the more rugged the climate, the thicker the coat.

Types of tipping
Tipping may be very light or extend down the hair almost to the root. A ticked coat has hairs that are banded.

1. Untipped
2. Shell
3. Shaded
4. Smoke
5. Ticking

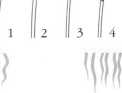

1 2 3 4 5

Coat varieties
The three types of hair in a cat's coat are the topcoat or guard hairs (gray), the bristly awn hairs (blue) and the soft, curly down hairs (pink).

Persian: A dense coat with very long guard hairs (up to 12.5 cm or 5 in); thick down hairs.

Maine Coon: Long guard and down hairs like the Persian, but shaggy and uneven.

Turkish Angora: Guard and down hairs very long, but finer and less profuse than the Persian.

American Wirehair: This coat has guard, awn, and down hairs, all very curly, even coiled.

British Shorthair: The guard hairs are about 4.5 cm (2 in) long, the awn hairs are sparse.

Sphynx: Almost hairless, no guard or awn hairs, but a few down hairs on face, tail, and legs.

Cornish Rex: Very short, curly awn and down hairs, all of similar length.

Devon Rex: Guard, down, and awn hairs, all very short and curly.

The domestic cat (like the wild cat) is basically tabby in marking, but selective breeding has produced a wide array of new "self" or solid colors as well as new patterns – from lilac, and chocolate, to smoke, and cameo, and many more. These are just some of the many possibilities.

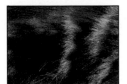

British Blue Shorthair

Turkish Angora

Russian Blue

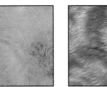

Lilac-point Siamese

British Tortoiseshell Smoke Shorthair

Abyssinian (Red)

Lilac Oriental Shorthair

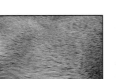

Abyssinian (Ruddy)

Tonkinese

British Black-tipped Shorthair

British Red Tabby Shorthair

Korat

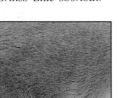

British Black Shorthair

British Blue-Cream Shorthair

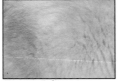

Exotic Colorpoint Shorthair

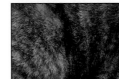

British Tortoiseshell Shorthair

British Silver Spotted Shorthair

Black Smoke Persian

Maine Coon

Cornish Rex

Blue Persian

British Black-and-White Bicolor Shorthair

British Tortoiseshell-and-White Shorthair

Blue-Cream Persian

Eye Types

The color of a cat's eyes is controlled genetically. This color is produced by the iris, which has pigment cells that carry particles of black, brown, or yellowish coloring matter. Where no pigment exists, as in albino cats, the iris is red-pink because all the color comes from the blood vessels. Blue eyes are not due to the presence of blue pigment but to the reflected light being "scattered" from a faintly black-pigmented layer of the iris. Green eyes similarly possess no green pigment, but achieve their stunning appearance by scattering reflected blue light, which then passes through a layer of yellowish pigment. The wide range of eye colors found in the cat depends on the amount of pigment and the degree of light-scattering. Some of the many possible variations are illustrated below.

Eye shapes
The three basic shapes of a cat's eye, as shown here, are round (Persian type), almond-shaped, and slanted. However, there are other variations and some cats have a combination.

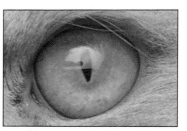

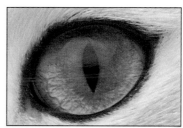

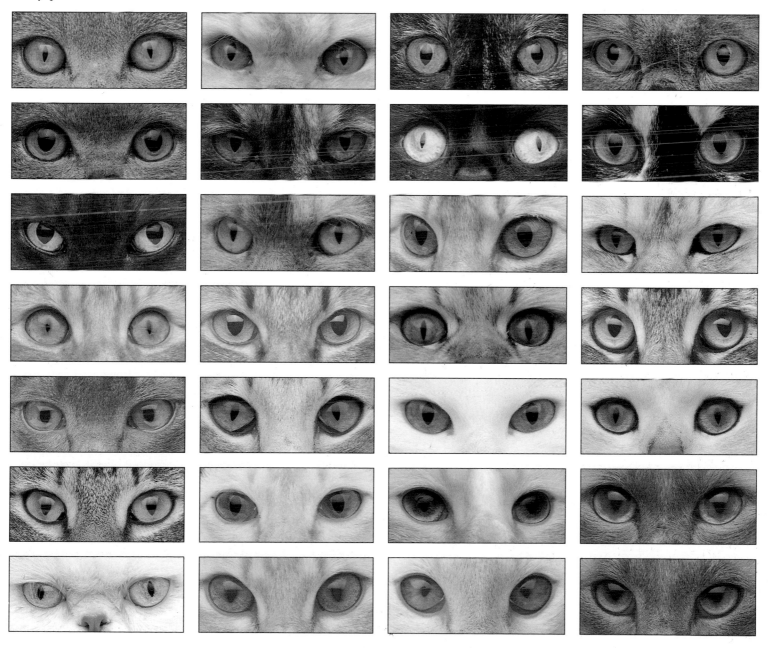

Longhaired Cats

Most wild cats are equipped with fur of short or medium length (Pallas's cat or Manul is the longest haired among the wild felines), and all domestic cats in Europe were originally shorthaired. Longhaired cats may have developed in cold countries such as Russia where there was need for a long coat, but it seems likely that they probably arose from spontaneous mutations which were then perpetuated through interbreeding.

By the late sixteenth century, they had arrived in Europe, according to some accounts brought back by the Italian traveller Pietro della Valle, from Asia Minor. Most of today's longhaired pedigree cats, however, are descended from cats brought to Britain from Turkey and Persia in the late nineteenth century.

Most longhaired cats are of the exotic-looking Longhair type popularly known as Persian. In the US these cats are formally classified as Persian, with the colors listed as varieties. However, in Britain, they are called Longhairs and each color is classified as a separate breed.

All Longhairs of Persian type have a cobby (sturdy and rounded) body with a round face and head, short, thick legs, a short nose, and large, round eyes. They also possess an exceptionally full coat. This is known as a double coat because it consists of two types of hair — long, soft, woolly undercoat hairs and slightly longer, coarser guard hairs, which can be as much as five inches (twelve centimeters) long in some show specimens. There are several longhaired cats that aren't of the Persian type. These cats have various origins, but most come from cold climates where a long coat is useful. On the whole, their coats aren't as woolly or as full as those of Persians, which makes them easier to groom. They differ from Persians in other ways too: they are slimmer, longer in the body and leg, and have narrower faces. Examples of these are the Balinese, Angora, Norwegian Forest Cat, and Maine Coon.

Although the coat of a longhaired cat is its pride and joy and is often extra long around the head where it forms an attractive ruff, there is one major disadvantage to this glamorous upholstery. Most longhaired cats moult all year round, and thus demand regular daily grooming to prevent matting and fur balls.

Balinese
A cat that is basically a longhaired Siamese, it has the same long, slim, body and wedge-shaped head. The fur is medium in length and gloriously soft.

Persian
The classic longhaired cat. It has the characteristic sturdy, rounded body that is described as "cobby", a round face and head, a short nose, round eyes, and short, thick legs. The fur is long and luxuriant, consisting of long, soft, woolly undercoat hairs that are covered by slightly coarser guard hairs.

Norwegian Forest Cat
A naturally-evolved, and extremely rugged breed, the *Norsk Skaukatt*, as it is known in its native country, has a medium build and a double coat consisting of water-resistant guard hairs covering thick underfur.

Ragdoll
The Ragdoll is an example of a large, muscular, cat, with fur that is long but not as full as a Persian. Another feature that sets this breed apart is its tendency to relax all its muscles when picked up or handled.

Turkish Angora
One of the original longhaired breeds, the Angora is slim and long-bodied, with a long, wedge-shaped head and silky, medium-long fur that is much easier to groom than a Persian's. It is a breed that is quite disimilar to any other.

Black Persian

ALTHOUGH THE BREED has a distinguished history stretching back to the sixteenth century, and was one of the first to be given official recognition, the Black Persian is a relatively rare animal. The difficulties of producing a pure black, unadulterated by any rustiness or smokiness, has made good specimens much prized. The coat needs particular care and attention: damp may lend the fur a brownish tinge, and over-exposure to the sun is likely to give a bleached appearance.

History
Early Black Persians often exhibited Angora traits, which have now been successfully bred out. World War II interrupted breeding programs in Europe, but not in the US, where a Black Persian has been voted Cat of the Year a record three times.

Temperament
The Black Persian makes a loyal and affectionate companion, although it can be suspicious of strangers. It is said to be more lively than its white counterpart.

Varieties
There are no varieties of Black Persian.

To keep the coat of the Black Persian in this sort of immaculate condition requires an owner dedicated to grooming.

EARS
Small and round-tipped.

Ear tufts

Full cheeks

EYES
Should be large, round, and deep orange or brilliant copper in color.

FACIAL CHARACTERISTICS
Black Persian

BODY
Solid and stocky, with a low carriage.

TAIL
Short and fluffy, carried straight and low.

Black Persian
A true original, this natural breed is one of the oldest.

HEAD
Round and broad, with a snub nose that should have a black nose pad.

Good breadth across shoulders

Long guard hairs

Full neck ruff

COAT
The fur must be a gleaming coal-black, without a single white hair, rustiness, or any kind of marking. Kittens may legitimately have temporary shading or white speckles; these should disappear after eight months or so.

Deep chest

LEGS
Short, thick and well covered with fur.

FEET
The paws should be large and round, with black paw pads in Great Britain and black or brown in the US.

Soft undercoat

White Persian

To its devoted followers, the White Persian combines all the virtues of its type: glamor, a noble expression, fur that is silky to the touch, and a sweet, tranquil nature. Nor, apart from daily grooming, does it need any special care.

History
Although pure white cats of the Angora type were the first longhaired cats to be introduced into Europe as long ago as the sixteenth century, the modern White Persian is of Victorian origin. It was developed by crossing Angoras with Persians. The breed was first shown in London in 1903, and has increased in popularity ever since, particularly in the US.

Temperament
White Persians are fastidious cats who take great pride in their appearance, regularly cleaning themselves. They are calm and affectionate, and make a superb pet for those confined indoors — a classic salon cat.

Varieties
Varieties are defined by their eye color: these cats can be blue-eyed, orange-eyed or odd-eyed (one blue, one orange). The blue-eyed variety is genetically predisposed to deafness. In odd-eyed cats, deafness may be apparent on the blue-eyed side.

EARS
Should be neat and small with rounded tips, set far apart and low on the head.

Ear tufts

Brilliant blue eyes

EYES
Large, round and full. Color should be brilliant blue, orange or copper, with both eyes having an equal depth of color.

HEAD
Should be round and broad with a snub nose and a pink nose pad.

FACIAL CHARACTERISTICS
White Persian

COAT
The fur is lush and silky, and should form an immense neck ruff. The color needs to be a pure, glistening white.

TAIL
Short and bushy, carried uncurved and generally at an angle lower than the line of the back.

BODY
A typical, sturdy, cobby type.

LEGS
Sturdy, short, and thick.

FEET
The paws should be large and round with pink pads.

Blue-eyed and Orange-eyed White Persians
Both longhaired and shorthaired white cats have varieties that are categorized by eye color.

Cream Persian

BEFORE THE STANDARD was modified, this luxurious animal was required to be the color of thick, whipped cream, a description that suits perfectly the glamorous good looks of the breed.

History

The first longhaired Cream probably originated from an off-white variety of the early Angoras. Later, accidental matings between Blue and Red Persians, or else Tortoiseshells and Red Tabbies, produced some pale individuals that were not taken seriously by British breeders, who nicknamed them "spoiled Oranges", a reference to the fact that Red Persians were known as Oranges. American breeders were, wisely, not so dismissive of the cream-colored cats, and began to develop the variety. Breeding in Great Britain did not begin in earnest until the 1920s.

Temperament

An even-tempered and friendly cat.

Varieties

There are no varieties.

EARS
Small and round-tipped.

Full cheeks

EYES
Large and round; should be rich copper in color.

HEAD
Broad and round with a snub nose.

Pink nose pad

FACIAL CHARACTERISTICS
Cream Persian

Cream Persian
Probably because they tend to have small litters, Creams are less numerous than most other breeds of Persian.

COAT
The fur is dense and silky. The American standard stipulates a color of buff cream; in Britain shades range from buttermilk through rich cream to pale honey.

TAIL
Short and bushy.

BODY
A sturdy, cobby type.

Color of coat must be sound to the roots

LEGS
Sturdy and short.

FEET
The paws are large and round and should have pink pads.

Blue Persian

The male Blue Persian tends to be larger than the female.

O F ALL THE PERSIANS, the Blue's popularity has been the most enduring. One hundred examples of the breed were entered in the 1899 London Cat Show, and today there are special shows in Britain devoted solely to Blues. Carefully controlled breeding has ensured that the Blue most closely represents the standard laid down for Persians, and as a result it is frequently used to improve the type of other color varieties.

History

Although longhaired blue cats have featured in artists' impressions for several centuries, and were well known in Renaissance Italy, the modern variety did not come into its own until the late nineteenth century. The breed probably originated from crossbreeding between Black and White Persians, and early examples showed tabby markings. The foundation of the Blue Persian Society in Britain in 1901 gave the breed considerable prestige, which was further enhanced by the patronage of Queen Victoria.

Temperament

The Blue Persian has a well-deserved reputation for being calm, considered, and above all gentle.

Varieties

There are no varieties.

TAIL
Short and fluffy.

Tail is usually carried straight and low

Blue Persian

The "blue" that gives the breed its name is in fact a dilute form of black that may more accurately be described as blue-gray.

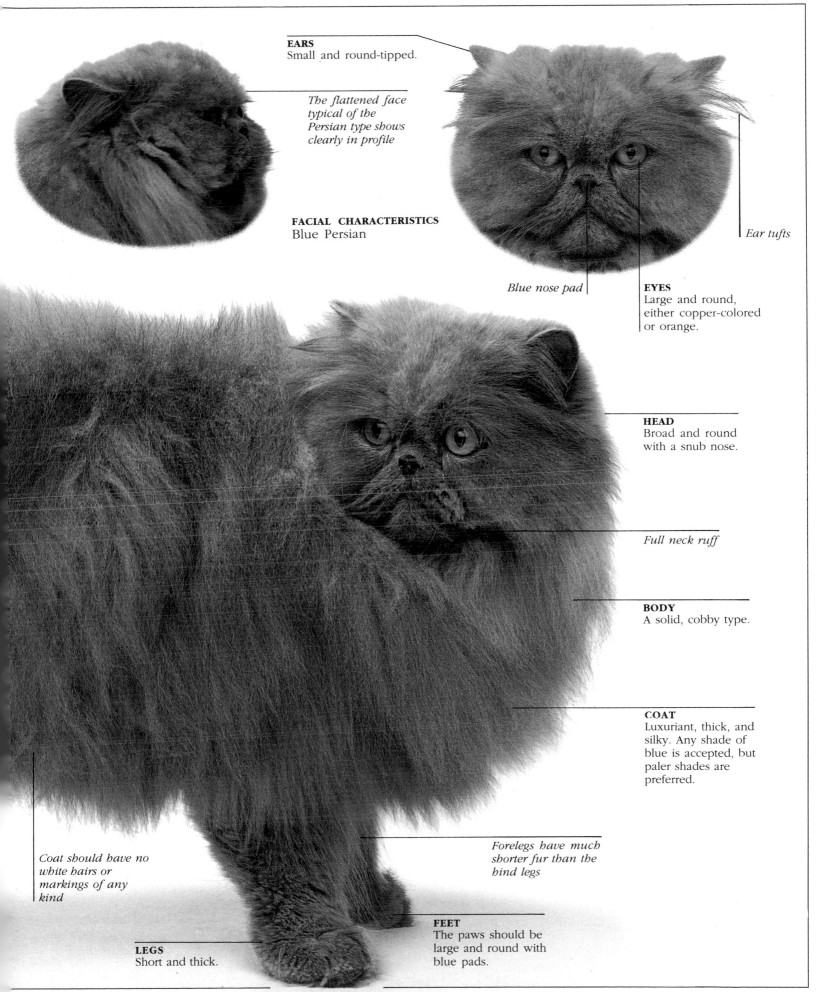

EARS
Small and round-tipped.

The flattened face typical of the Persian type shows clearly in profile

FACIAL CHARACTERISTICS
Blue Persian

Ear tufts

Blue nose pad

EYES
Large and round, either copper-colored or orange.

HEAD
Broad and round with a snub nose.

Full neck ruff

BODY
A solid, cobby type.

COAT
Luxuriant, thick, and silky. Any shade of blue is accepted, but paler shades are preferred.

Forelegs have much shorter fur than the hind legs

Coat should have no white hairs or markings of any kind

FEET
The paws should be large and round with blue pads.

LEGS
Short and thick.

Red Persian

IT IS RARE to come across a perfect example of this striking, flame-colored cat. In practice, most have some tabby markings, particularly on the face, legs, and tail. Elsewhere, the long coat helps to make the markings less evident. Within a litter there may be some kittens that are Red and others that are Red Tabby.

Peke-face Persian
A variety that has caused much debate, it has a nose that is ultra-snub, and set back in a furrowed muzzle. There is a distinct horizontal indentation between the eyes, which are particularly prominent.

History
Oranges, as Red Persians were originally known, were being shown in Britain as early as 1895. In the early 1930s, a German breeder produced some excellent examples of the breed, but unfortunately his stock was destroyed during World War II. The breed remained rare in Britain during the 1940s, but a revival of interest and selective breeding have ensured the Red Persian's continued presence on the show bench.

Temperament
Polite and friendly, the Red Persian makes a highly decorative and pleasant companion.

Varieties
Peke-faced Reds and Red Tabbies sometimes appear as spontaneous mutations in otherwise normal litters of Red kittens. These varieties are controversial because the extreme, squashed, facial features may cause breathing difficulties as well as skin problems.

EARS
Small and round-tipped.

Fine ear tufts

EYES
Large, round, and brilliant copper in color.

HEAD
Broad and round with a snub nose. The nose pad should be brick-red.

FACIAL CHARACTERISTICS
Red Persian

The lips and chin should be the same color as the coat

BODY
A solid, cobby type.

Red Persian
One of the hardest types to breed for exhibition, good examples of Red Persians are few.

COAT
Fur is silky and lush, and should be a deep orange-red color with no shading or tabby markings.

FEET
The paws are large and round with pads that are brick-red in color.

LEGS
Short and thick-set.

TAIL
Short and fluffy, usually carried straight and low.

Blue-Cream Persian

A COAT THAT is a pleasing mixture of mottled cream and pale blue-gray has ensured this breed's enormous popularity. The way in which color genes are inherited means that male Blue-Cream Persians are rare, and almost invariably sterile.

EARS
Small and round-tipped.

Ear tufts

EYES
Large and round; color should be deep, brilliant copper or orange.

Blue nose pad

FACIAL CHARACTERISTICS
Blue-Cream Persian

History
The result of mating Blues and Creams, longhaired blue-cream cats appeared in litters in the early days of pedigree breeding. They were not accorded official recognition in Great Britain, however, until as late as 1930.

Temperament
The Blue-Cream is considered more outgoing than many Persians, but is equally affectionate and amenable.

Varieties
There are no varieties, although the US standard differs. Whereas in Great Britain a gentle intermingling of the two colors is desired, in the US the blue and cream should form clearly defined patches.

TAIL
Short and bushy, usually carried uncurved and lower than the line of the back.

BODY
Very solid and cobby.

HEAD
Broad and round, with a snub nose.

COAT
The color should be a soft mixture of pastel shades of blue and cream.

Silky, dense fur

Blue-Cream Persian
The best examples of this breed have a build that is a near-perfect example of the cobby Persian type.

Toe tufts

FEET
The paws are large and round; the color of the pads should be blue.

LEGS
Short and thick.

Chinchilla Persian

Unlike the rodent chinchilla, which has a dark undercoat tipped with white, this cat sports the reverse coloration, giving it a distinctly sparkling appearance. Its luxurious coat requires meticulous grooming to show it to best advantage.

History
The Chinchilla is one of the earliest man-made varieties, and was given its own class at Crystal Palace in 1894. It is thought to have evolved from crossbreeding a range of Persians, most notably Silver Tabbies, and was at first much darker, frequently lavender-tinted, and more heavily marked than the modern form. The pursuit of a paler coloration weakened the European stock, which was further depleted during World War II. American types were imported to improve the variety, which is now strong and healthy.

Temperament
Chinchillas are sometimes said to be more temperamental than other Persians, but generally have the same affectionate, calm disposition.

Varieties
There is one variety, the Shaded Silver, that has long been recognized in the US and is gaining recognition in Great Britain.

EARS
Small and round-tipped.

EYES
Large and round; color should be emerald green or blue-green, outlined in black or dark brown.

Ear tufts

Brick-red nose pad

HEAD
Round and broad with a snub nose outlined in black or dark brown.

FACIAL CHARACTERISTICS
Chinchilla Persian

Chinchilla Persian
A coat that has the sheen of precious metal has earned this variety the popular name of Silver Persian in the US.

TAIL
Short and bushy, normally carried uncurved, below the line of the back.

COAT
The fur is dense and silky. The color should be snow white, with black tipping.

BODY
Less cobby than usual for a Persian, with a finer bone stucture.

More delicate in appearance than the typical Persian, the Chinchilla is nonetheless a robust, hardy, individual — as this typically playful pose illustrates.

LEGS
Short, thick, and furry.

Shaded Silver Persian
It is more difficult to breed this variety than the Chinchilla, because the standard requires heavier, darker tipping to form a mantle shading down the face, sides, and tail.

FEET
The paws are large and round with pads that should be black in color.

Cameo Persian

L IKE THAT OF THE CHINCHILLA, the Cameo's attractiveness stems from the contrast between its white undercoat and its tipped guard hairs, which can be red, cream, tabby, or tortie.

History
A breeding program for Cameos was established in the US during the 1950s. Originally produced from Smoke and Tortoiseshell pairings, Cameos can now count other colors in their lineage.

Temperament
Languorous and amenable.

Varieties
The extent to which the tipping is distributed along the length of the Cameo's hair shaft varies to produce different and dramatic coats. Shell varieties have short colored tips that give a subtle misty effect, Shaded Cameos have longer colored tips that glint against the white, and Smoke varieties have such long tips that the white undercoat cannot be seen until the cat moves.

COAT
The fur is silky, thick, and dense. The color must be white with cream tips.

BODY
A typical cobby type.

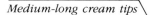

Medium-long cream tips

TAIL
Short and bushy, carried uncurved, usually lower than the line of the back.

LEGS
Short and firm.

Varieties	Markings	Eyes
Red Shell Cameo	Short red tips	Copper
Red Shaded Cameo	Longer red tips	Copper
Red Smoke Cameo	Longest red tips	Copper
Cream Shell Cameo	Short cream tips	Copper
Cream Shaded Cameo	Longer cream tips	Copper
Cream Smoke Cameo	Longest cream tips	Copper
Blue-Cream Cameo	Intermingled tipping in two colors	Copper
Tortie Cameo	Black, red, cream tips	Copper
Tabby Cameo	Cream, red tips	Copper

Cream Shaded Cameo Persian
The nearly matching coat and eye color of the Cream Shaded create an irresistible combination. As in all varieties, the deepest color should be confined to the mask, along the back, and on the legs and feet.

HEAD
Round and broad, with a snub nose that should have a pink nose pad.

Full neck ruff

EARS
Small and round-tipped.

EYES
Large and round. Color should be deep orange or brilliant copper.

Firm chin

FACIAL CHARACTERISTICS
Tortie Cameo Persian

Ear tufts

White undercoat

FEET
Paws are large and round with pads that should be pink.

Tortie Cameo Persian
Black, red, and cream tips combine in the Tortie Cameo to produce a stunning, luxurious coat.

Smoke Persian

As the British standard describes it, this is a beautiful "cat of contrasts." Deep tipping gives the appearance of a solid color, but when the cat moves, the pale undercoat shows through momentarily to produce a delightful shimmer. Keeping the coat in optimum condition is a time-consuming task, and preparation for a show may take weeks. Showing is generally best left for the winter months, because bright sunlight can cause the coat to fade.

Silver ear tufts

EARS
Small and round-tipped.

EYES
Large, round, and copper or orange in color.

Black nose pad

Black mask

HEAD
Round and broad, with a short nose.

FACIAL CHARACTERISTICS
Black Smoke Persian

History
Thought to have originated from chance matings between Blacks, Blues, Whites, and Chinchillas, the Smoke Persian is mentioned in the record books as early as 1860, and appeared in the first cat shows. Numbers quickly declined, however: only eighteen were registered in 1912, with the breed becoming almost extinct by the end of World War II. The 1960s saw a revival of interest, and although still uncommon, the breed's future is undoubtedly assured.

Temperament
"Smokey" has the relaxed, good-natured, and gentle character typical of most Persians.

Varieties
Only the black-tipped and blue-tipped varieties of the Smoke are recognized in both Great Britain and the US. Other varietes have tipping in tortoiseshell, chocolate, lilac, and blue-cream. All varieties have orange or copper eyes.

Tortoiseshell Smoke Persian
A female-only variety, the Tortie has a white coat tipped in patches of black, red, and cream. The face and feet should be a solid color, and a red or cream facial blaze is considered a desirable feature.

Black Smoke Persian
Only when a kitten is some months old is it possible to tell whether it will mature into as fine an example as this. Until then, solid-colored Blacks and Smokes in the same litter may be indistinguishable. One of the most attractive features of the Black Smoke is the contrast between the silver neck ruff and the dark head. If preparing for a show, it is advisable to keep the Smoke out of bright sunlight to avoid the coat becoming bleached.

BODY
A solid, cobby type, that tends, in Britain, to be slightly lighter than usual for a Persian.

COAT
The fur is silky, thick, and dense. The undercoat should be milk-white, with black tipping that is solid to the roots in Great Britain, and white at the roots in the US.

TAIL
Short and bushy.

LEGS
Short and thick. They should be solid black in color.

FEET
The paws are large and round; the paw pads should be black in color.

Bicolor Persian

W HITE PLUS ANOTHER COLOR is a classic combination and, despite the numerous bicolored street cats, this breed can be thought of as very much a "designer" cat.

History
Bicolor Persians were given their own class only in the late 1960s. The original standard stipulated that the patching should be exactly symmetrical; this proved so difficult that requirements were eased to allow any even distribution of color.

Temperament
The Bicolor Persian is a placid, affectionate charmer.

Varieties
These beautiful cats can be any solid color plus white, the most widely accepted being Black-and-White, Blue-and-White, Red-and-White, and Cream-and-White. In the US, the Persian Van Bicolor is a recognized variety whose head and tail patching resembles that of the Turkish Cat.

EARS
Small and round-tipped.

Ear tufts

EYES
Large, round, and orange or copper in color.

Pink nose pad

HEAD
Round and broad, with a snub nose. The nose pad should either be pink or match the colored patches of the coat.

Full cheeks

A white inverted "V" on the face is a desirable feature

FACIAL CHARACTERISTICS
Black-and-White Bicolor Persian

Lilac-and-White Bicolor Persian
To produce the delicate, pinkish dove-gray color of this cat, as well as even patching, takes dedicated breeding.

Black-and-White Bicolor Persian
The original form of the Bicolor, the Black-and-White was at first meant to imitate the symmetrical markings of a Dutch rabbit. The standard was eventually altered, however, when this proved virtually impossible to achieve.

Cream-and-White Bicolor Persian
As with all Bicolors, the white of this fairly new variety's coat should cover a maximum of half of the cat, and the colored patches up to two-thirds.

COAT
The fur is dense, silky, and lush; the colored patches should be solid and evenly distributed.

BODY
A solid, cobby type.

TAIL
Short and bushy.

FEET
The paws are large and round.

Pink paw pads

LEGS
Short and thick.

Tabby Persian

MUCH RARER than the corresponding shorthaired breed, the Tabby Persian is nonetheless an old-timer, making its first appearance in Europe by the end of the seventeenth century.

History
The Modern Tabby Persian emerged during the latter half of the nineteenth century.

Temperament
Some owners consider that the Tabby is more independent than is typical for a Persian, but it still has the same equable nature.

Varieties
The Classic should have a butterfly shape on the shoulders, three stripes running down the spine to the base of the tail, an oyster-shaped spiral on each flank, and narrow "necklaces" across the chest. Both the tail and the legs should be evenly ringed, the abdomen spotted, and a characteristic "M" should decorate the forehead. The Mackerel pattern is less blotchy, more striped and lacks the spirals on the flanks. A "Torbie", or Patched Tabby, is also recognized in the US. The original tabby colors of brown, red, and silver are recognized by all associations, but the newer varieties (see chart) have still to gain universal acceptance.

Varieties	Coat	Eyes
Red Tabby	Rich copper marked in red	Copper or orange
Brown Tabby	Tawny brown marked in black	Copper or orange
Silver Tabby	Silver-gray marked in black	Copper, green or hazel
Blue Tabby	Bluish-ivory marked in slate-blue	Copper
Cream Tabby	Pale cream marked in rich cream	Copper
Cameo Tabby	Off-white marked in red	Copper
Patched Tabby	Silver, brown or blue marked with extra red and/or cream patches	Copper or hazel
Chocolate Tabby	Bronze marked in chocolate	Copper or hazel
Lilac Tabby	Beige marked in lilac	Copper or hazel

COAT
The fur is dense and silky. The Classic tabby markings should be slate-blue over a bluish-ivory base color.

Brown Classic Tabby Persian
"Brownies" may be the oldest variety of the Tabby Persian, but they are still the most rare.

Ring markings on the tail are obscured by the long, fine hair

TAIL
Short and bushy.

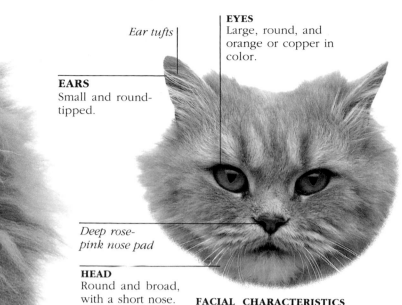

Ear tufts

EYES
Large, round, and
orange or copper in
color.

EARS
Small and round-
tipped.

*Deep rose-
pink nose pad*

HEAD
Round and broad,
with a short nose.

FACIAL CHARACTERISTICS
Blue Classic Tabby Persian

BODY
A solid, cobby,
type.

LEGS
Short and thick.

FEET
The paws are large
and round, with
pads that should be
rose-pink in color.

Silver Classic Tabby Persian
Considered by many to be the most
difficult cat to breed to the required
standard, the Silver Tabby is also one of
the most stunning.

*Side markings
should be
symmetrical*

**Blue Classic
Tabby Persian**
The deep, slate-blue markings
of this variety may, to the uninitiated,
make it hard to distinguish from a Brown
Tabby — until the fur is parted to reveal the
bluish-gray base color.

Tortoiseshell Persian

A VIRTUALLY FEMALE-ONLY breed, the Tortoiseshell is the center of some debate on how difficult it is to breed: American breeders do not regard it as especially problematic, whereas in Britain the desired mixture of red, cream, and black patches has proved more elusive, with good specimens still quite rare.

History
Longhaired cats with tortoiseshell markings were first recorded towards the end of the nineteenth century, and appeared in the early cat shows of the 1900s. They probably originated from accidental matings between longhaired black cats and shorthaired tortoiseshells.

Temperament
The Tortoiseshell Persian is affectionate, gentle, and placid, with a reputation for being a good mother to its kittens.

Varieties
Shell and Shaded Tortoiseshell Persians are grouped together within the Shaded Division in the US; in Britain they are known as Cameos.

Because it is impossible to breed like with like, the Tortoiseshell includes numerous other Persians in its pedigree. This has resulted in a cobby build that is a fine example of the Persian type.

American Tortoiseshell Persian
The US standard stipulates a black cat with unbrindled patches of red and cream. A desirable feature on both sides of the Atlantic is a red or cream blaze on the face, running from the nose to the forehead.

Full neck ruff

FEET
Paws are large and round, with pads that should be pink or black in color.

Toe tufts

LEGS
Short and thick.

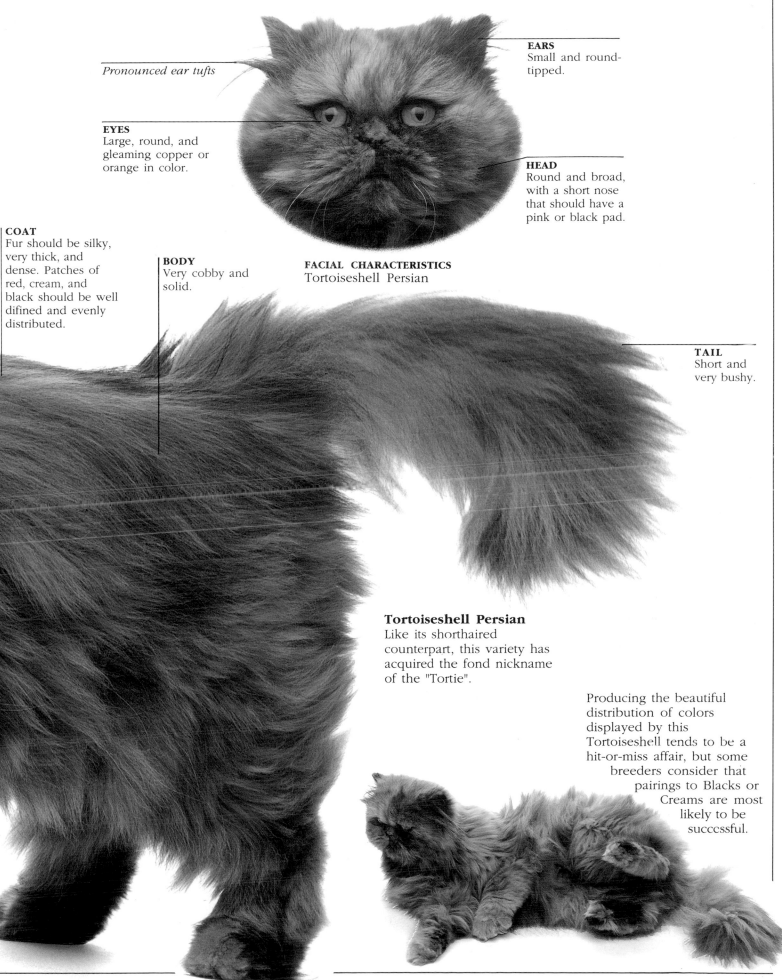

Pronounced ear tufts

EARS
Small and round-tipped.

EYES
Large, round, and gleaming copper or orange in color.

HEAD
Round and broad, with a short nose that should have a pink or black pad.

COAT
Fur should be silky, very thick, and dense. Patches of red, cream, and black should be well difined and evenly distributed.

BODY
Very cobby and solid.

FACIAL CHARACTERISTICS
Tortoiseshell Persian

TAIL
Short and very bushy.

Tortoiseshell Persian
Like its shorthaired counterpart, this variety has acquired the fond nickname of the "Tortie".

Producing the beautiful distribution of colors displayed by this Tortoiseshell tends to be a hit-or-miss affair, but some breeders consider that pairings to Blacks or Creams are most likely to be succcssful.

Calico Persian

T HE CALICO was so named because its bold splashes of color resemble the popular type of printed cotton. It is basically a Tortoiseshell cat with white patches in addition to those of black, red, and cream. Another female-only variety, the Calico Persian is not easy to produce true to type. The kittens are always appealing, however, and there is never a shortage of prospective owners.

History
Although the Calico Persian's origins are obscure, it probably developed, like the Tortoiseshell Persian, from matings between longhaired cats and non-pedigree shorthaired tortoiseshells. Known at one stage as a "Chintz" cat, it was accepted for championship in the mid-1950s. More recently, consistently good types have been bred by mating queens with Bicolor studs produced from Calicos.

Temperament
This is a calm, sweet-natured, and extremely friendly cat.

Varieties
The US standard for the Calico Persian differs from that of Great Britain, calling for a white cat with colored patches, the white to be concentrated on the underparts. The British cat, which is known simply as a Tortoiseshell-and-White, has less white in its coat and more evenly distributed patches of color. In both countries, the Dilute Calico Persian is a newly recognized variety that is seen at an increasing number of shows. The standard for this most attractive cat is the same as for the Calico, but with blue and cream patches instead of black and red.

Dilute Calico Persian
This variety frequently appears in the same litter as Calico Persians.

A cream or white blaze on the face is a desirable feature

LEGS
Short and thick.

Two views of the same Dilute Calico Persian reveal clearly the random, but still more or less even, distribution of colored patches.

The coat is particularly long and flowing

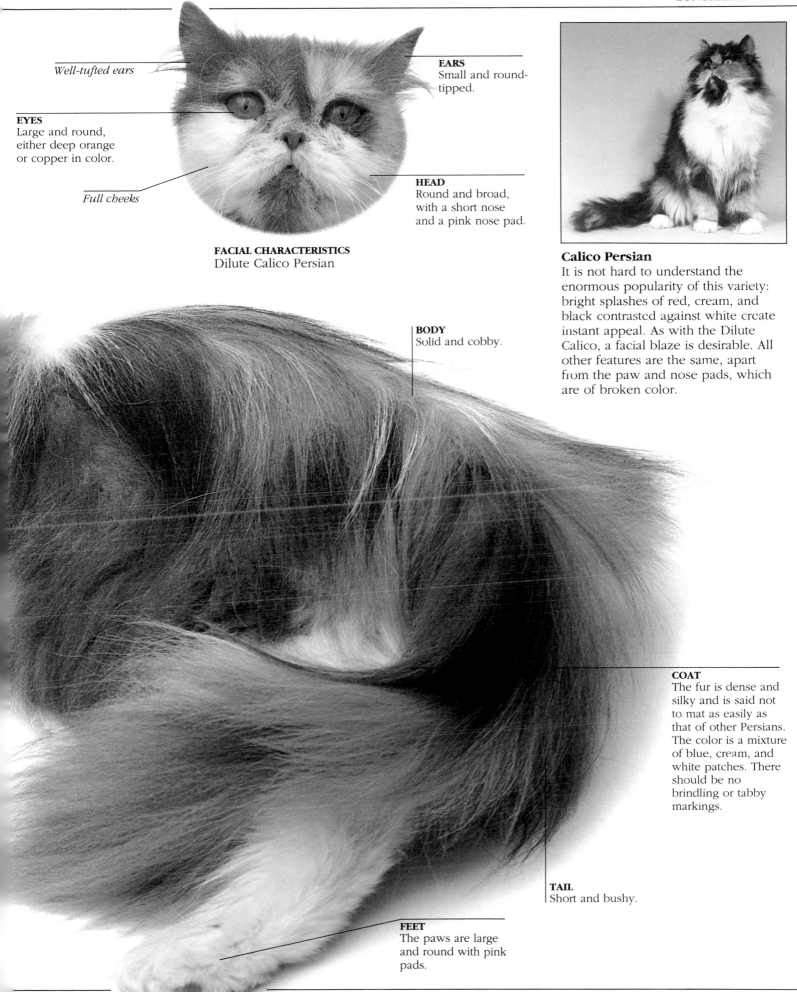

Well-tufted ears

EARS
Small and round-tipped.

EYES
Large and round, either deep orange or copper in color.

Full cheeks

HEAD
Round and broad, with a short nose and a pink nose pad.

FACIAL CHARACTERISTICS
Dilute Calico Persian

Calico Persian

It is not hard to understand the enormous popularity of this variety: bright splashes of red, cream, and black contrasted against white create instant appeal. As with the Dilute Calico, a facial blaze is desirable. All other features are the same, apart from the paw and nose pads, which are of broken color.

BODY
Solid and cobby.

COAT
The fur is dense and silky and is said not to mat as easily as that of other Persians. The color is a mixture of blue, cream, and white patches. There should be no brindling or tabby markings.

TAIL
Short and bushy.

FEET
The paws are large and round with pink pads.

Himalayan

REAL GLAMOR CATS, the Himalayans combine the luxurious sophistication of the Persian family with the poise, good looks, and markings of the shorthaired Siamese. Like the Siamese, a Himalayan invariably has bright, sapphire-blue eyes, and a mask, ears, legs, feet, and tail (the points) that are a different color to the rest of the body.

History
Experimental breeding programs in Sweden and the US during the 1920s produced the first Himalayans, but it was not until the late 1940s, after a succession of carefully planned crossbreedings between Persians and Siamese, that the modern cat finally emerged.

Temperament
To their owners, Himalayans combine the best of two worlds: they have the gentle nature of a Persian, but they can also be as spirited as a Siamese without being so demonstrative.

Varieties
All point colors are possible, giving a large number of varieties. Not all, however, are recognized. The most popular are shown in the chart.

Varieties	Coat	Markings
Seal	Warm cream	Deep seal-brown
Blue	Bluish-white	Slate-blue
Chocolate	Ivory	Warm brown
Lilac	Glacial white	Pinkish-gray
Flame	Creamy white	Orange or red
Cream	Creamy white	Buff cream
Tortie	Warm cream	Red and cream patches
Blue-Cream	Bluish or creamy white	Blue and mottled cream
Lilac-Cream	Glacial white	Pinkish-gray, patched in cream
Chocolate-Tortie	Ivory	Chocolate, patched in red and/or cream
Lynx	Ivory	Tabby points in seal, chocolate, lilac, red or blue

Seal-point Himalayan
The Seal-point was one of the first varieties of Himalayan to be developed.

BODY
A solid, cobby type.

COAT
The fur is dense, lush, and silky to the touch. The color should be warm cream with deep seal-brown points.

TAIL
Should be short and
very full.

EARS
Small and round-
tipped, with a good
width between them.

EYES
Large, round, and
bright; sapphire-blue
in color.

*Color of the nose
pad matches that of
the points*

HEAD
Round and broad,
with full cheeks and
a short nose.

FACIAL CHARACTERISTICS
Seal-point Himalayan

Blue-point Himalayan
Slate blue markings set off to
perfection the cold,
bluish-white coat of
this variety.

LEGS
Short, thick, and
strong.

FEET
Paws are large and
round with seal-
brown pads.

Long toe tufts

Seal Lynx-point Himalayan
One of the newer varieties, this cat is the
result of crossing Brown Tabby Persians
with Seal-point Himalayans.

Pewter Persian

THE COLORING of this exquisite cat resembles that of the Shaded Silver variety of Chinchilla, with which it is sometimes confused. It has a similar handsome white coat, subtly shaded with black over the head, back, flanks, legs, and tail to give the effect of a pewter mantle. Its eye color is different, however, being bright orange or brilliant copper.

History
The Pewter Persian was produced as a result of crossing Chinchillas, Blues, and Blacks.

Temperament
This is an exceptionally affectionate and even-tempered cat.

Varieties
There are no varieties.

EARS
Small, round-tipped, and tufted, with a good width between them.

Black eye rims

EYES
Very large and round, either orange or copper in color.

Brick-red nose pad

HEAD
Round and broad with a snub nose.

FACIAL CHARACTERISTICS
Pewter Persian

BODY
A chunky, cobby type.

Pewter Persian
"Pewter" describes perfectly the color of the breed's tipped mantle.

Characteristic flat profile

COAT
Silky, thick, and dense. Color is white with subtle black tipping.

New Persians are being developed all the time, among which the Pewter must rank as one of the most attractive. On first inspection it may look like a Shaded Silver Chinchilla, but orange or copper-colored eyes are a distinguishing feature that firmly identifies the breed.

LEGS
Short and thick.

Shorter hair on forelegs

Long guard hairs

When it is lying down, the Pewter's thick, luxurious, coat and full frill make it virtually impossible to discern the cat's cobby build.

TAIL
Short with a full brush.

Guard hairs of the tail are delicately tipped in black

A Pewter that is destined for the show ring ideally should have a full neck ruff that extends into a deep frill between the front legs.

FEET
The paws are large and round with brick-red pads.

Chocolate and Lilac Persians

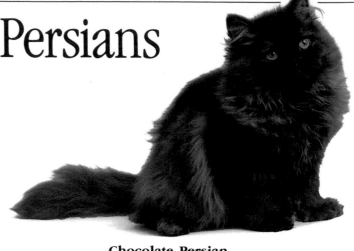

THIS STUNNING PAIR represent a triumph of selective breeding, and might be considered the ultimate "designer" cats: the warm brown tones of the Chocolate and the pinkish dove-gray coat of the Lilac would make a charming decorative addition to any interior color scheme.

History
Breeders did not seriously consider developing a chocolate-colored Persian until breeding programs for Himalayans produced solid-colored kittens in the same litter. Early examples had fur that was prone to fade and bleach, weak eye color, noses that tended to be too long, and ears that were too tall. It took several years before the color was made more stable, the type improved, and a standard was able to be laid down. If anything, the Lilac Persian, which was produced by introducing blue genes into breeding lines, proved even more elusive, and it is still relatively rare. At one stage, these cats were categorized in the US as solid-colored Himalayans or Kashmirs, but these descriptions have now been dropped by most associations.

Temperament
Having inherited some of the Siamese blood carried by their Himalayan relations, Chocolates and Lilacs tend to be more outgoing and inquisitive than is usual for Persians.

Varieties
There are no varieties of the Chocolate or the Lilac Persian.

Chocolate Persian
A bi-product of the Himalayan breeding program, this cat should have a rich, medium to dark chocolate-brown coat, brown nose and paw pads, and orange or copper-colored eyes.

Full frill

Color should be sound to the roots

FEET
The paws are large and round.

EARS
Small, round-tipped,
and set wide apart.

Ear tufts

EYES
Large and round;
color should be
orange or copper.

Pink nose pad

HEAD
Round and broad,
with a snub nose.

FACIAL CHARACTERISTICS
Lilac Persian

Although breeders
experienced early
difficulties in
achieving the desired
cobby build for the
Chocolate, once
those problems had
been overcome,
producing a Lilac of
good type, if not of
good color, was
comparatively
straightforward.

COAT
The fur should be
silky, lush, and thick;
color should be a
pinkish dove-gray or
lavender.

Lilac Persian
The Lilac is an example of a recently
developed Persian and illustrates
beautifully the aesthetic possibilities of
"man-made" varieties.

*There should be no
sign of a pale
undercoat*

TAIL
Short and bushy.

Pink paw pads

BODY
A cobby, chunky,
solid type.

LEGS
Short and thick.

New Longhaired Cats

CAT BREEDERS NEVER CEASE in their endeavors to create yet more beautiful variations on the longhaired theme. Recent developments include the Golden Persians and the Cymric.

History
The Chinchilla Golden and the Shaded Golden were bi-products of the Chinchilla breeding program. Often referred to as "Brownies", they appeared regularly in the litters of Silvers, but were mostly petted out. They have achieved show status only within the last ten years or so. The Cymric is essentially a longhaired Manx and was developed during the 1960s from mutant kittens that were born from time to time in some American Manx litters. They were first recognized in 1980.

Temperament
The new varieties of Persian usually display the gentle, affectionate, disposition typical of the type; the Cymric has the same loyal and friendly nature as the Manx.

Varieties
Other new Persians include the delightful Lilac-Cream, Chocolate Tortoiseshell, Golden Tabby, and Golden Torbie. The Cymric is bred in most Manx colors.

Chinchilla Golden Persian
As with all varieties of Chinchilla, the Golden requires a great deal of preparation if the coat is to be shown to best advantage.

COAT
The fur is silky, thick, and dense. The color should be rich cream, with seal-brown or black tipping.

BODY
A cobby, solid type.

LEGS
Short, thick, and furry.

FEET
The paws are large and round.

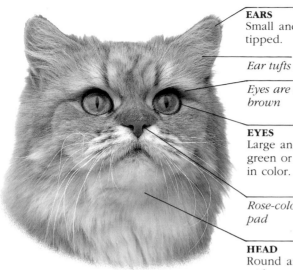

EARS
Small and round-tipped.

Ear tufts

Eyes are outlined in brown

EYES
Large and round, green or blue-green in color.

Rose-colored nose pad

HEAD
Round and broad, with a snub nose.

FACIAL CHARACTERISTICS
Chinchilla Golden Persian

Shaded Golden Persians
Long, silky, fur, and a mantle of black tipping over a warm-cream undercoat, makes for a rich combination that is bringing these cats increasingly before the public eye.

TAIL
Short and bushy.

Seal-brown paw pads

Cymric
"Cymric" is Welsh for "Welsh", although the breed has no known connection with the land of leeks and laver bread! It is exactly the same as the tailless Manx, but for a medium-long, soft, heavy coat.

Birman

THE "SACRED CAT OF BURMA", as the Birman is popularly known, has a longer body and narrower face than a typical longhaired cat, with markings reminiscent of a Siamese; giving it as oriental an aura as the legends that shroud its past.

History
Said to have originated in the temples of Burma, the Birman has a more recent history that is almost as colorful. In 1919 two of these cats were sent to Major Gordon Russell in France as a token of gratitude from the priests he had helped to escape from Tibet. The female of the pair subsequently gave birth to kittens, and may have helped found the breed in the West. Birmans were recognized for showing in France in 1925, in Britain in 1966, and in the US a year later.

Temperament
Amenable, civilized, and gentle, the Birman enjoys family life and adapts well to other animals.

Varieties
Varieties include the original, "sacred", Seal-point, and also the Blue-point, for which the UK and US standards differ.

Blue-point Birman
Tradition has its own story to tell of the development of the Birman. Before the birth of the Lord Buddha, a sacred Burmese temple containing pure white cats was attacked, during which the high priest collapsed and died. His favorite cat jumped onto the old man's head and was suddenly transformed: its coat became golden with points the color of the Burmese soil, and the eyes turned blue. Where the cat's paws touched the priest, the fur remained white — a symbol of goodness. Encouraged by the miracle, the remaining priests were able to successfully fend off the invaders. However true the tale, the development of this variety was definitely the result of modern selective breeding.

TAIL
Medium in length and bushy, but slightly longer and finer than in most longhaired cats.

LEGS
Medium in length and thick-set.

Coat is non-matting

FEET
Paws are large and round, gloved in white. The rear pair should have white gauntlets, extending into "laces" up the back legs.

Stomach fur has a tendency to curl

Seal-point Birman
A characteristic soft, golden hue to the coat, especially over the back, lends this variety a distinguished appearance.

COAT
Medium in length and silky in texture. The British standard calls for a color that is beige-gold with blue-gray points; in the US, these cats are bluish-white with deep blue points.

Blue-point and Seal-point Kittens
A more appealing group would be hard to picture.

HEAD
Fairly round and broad with full cheeks and a medium-length nose. The US standard requires that the nose is "Roman", and that the forehead is slightly convexed and backward-sloping, with a small, flat area just in front of the ears.

EARS
Should be medium in size, round-tipped and almost as wide at the base as they are tall.

EYES
Almost round, set well apart, and slightly slanted. Color should be deep blue.

Slate-gray nose pad

FACIAL CHARACTERISTICS
Blue-point Birman

BODY
Strongly built, elongated but still quite stocky; neither svelte nor cobby.

Pink paw pads

Variety	Body	Points
Seal-point	Beige-gold	Seal-brown
Chocolate-point	Ivory	Chocolate
Blue-point	Bluish-white	Deep blue
Lilac-point	Milk-white	Pink-tinged gray

Ragdoll

THE RAGDOLL is a cat of contrasts: it has the large, imposing physique of a Birman, but when picked up it relaxes all its muscles to become as weak as a kitten, and as floppy as the doll from which it takes its name. Not content with one unique feature, it is also said to have a high tolerance to pain, a characteristic that is thought to be inherited from the original Ragdolls born to a longhaired queen that had been injured in an automobile accident. However, many breeders are adamant that in their experience the Ragdoll's pain threshold is no different to that of any other breed, and that to believe otherwise may be detrimental to individual cats.

TAIL
Long and fluffy.

EYES
Large and oval, set far apart. The color should be blue.

Ears tilt forward

Dark brown nose pad

Full cheeks

Full, round chin

FACIAL CHARACTERISTICS
Seal-point Colorpoint Ragdoll

History
California in the 1960s was the birthplace of the Ragdoll, largely through the efforts of one woman. It is fairly rare outside the US, where it was recognized in 1965. It has only recently been recognized for showing in Great Britain.

Temperament
The Ragdoll is a cat that is extremely tolerant of the foibles and whims of others, and quickly becomes devoted to its owner.

Varieties
There are three recognized coat patterns for the Ragdoll: the Bicolor has a pale body, a white chest, underbelly, and legs, with a dark mask, ears, and tail; the Colorpoint has a pale body with darker points; and the Mitted has a white chest, bib, chin, and front paw "mittens," but is otherwise the same as the Colorpoint. The established colors are Seal-point, Chocolate-point, Blue-point, and Frost-point.

Heavy hindquarters

Bicolor Ragdoll Kitten
Ragdoll kittens are slow to mature, and it may be three years before the shading of the coat and the point colors are fully developed.

Color shades to pale cream on underparts

Seal-point Colorpoint Ragdoll
Despite the origins of its name, physiological tests have detected no difference between the Ragdoll and other breeds.

HEAD
Wedge-shaped with a medium-length nose.

Skull between ears is flat

Mask is dense, seal-brown, providing a distinct contrast with body color

EARS
Medium in size and round-tipped.

BODY
Similar to the Birman; a long, muscular, solid type.

COAT
Long, full, and silky. The body color should be pale fawn, with dark, seal-brown points.

Chocolate-point Mitted Ragdoll Kitten
The white "mittens" and boots are clearly visible even at this early age.

Deep chest

Fur is extra-long on chest and stomach

Coat is usually longer in warm climates, molting considerably in summer

LEGS
Medium in length.

Forelegs are slightly shorter than the hind legs

Fur mats less than is usual for longhaired cats, and breaks when the cat moves

FEET
The paws are large and round, with pads that are either dark brown or black.

Seal-point Bicolor Ragdoll
Dense, seal-brown ears, tail, and mask are contrasted against the fawn and pale cream of the rest of the coat in this variety. The inverted white "V" on the face is characteristic of Bicolors.

Balinese

WHEN THIS CAT WALKS with its tail held erect, its graceful tail plume sways from side to side in a manner not unlike that of a Balinese dancer — hence its name. The natural elegance of the Balinese stems from its Siamese origins: it has the same long, svelte body, wedge-shaped head, and entrancing blue eyes. It can, in fact, be thought of as a longhaired Siamese, although its ermine-like coat is shorter than most Persians and doesn't form a ruff.

History
Most probably, the Balinese derived from Siamese parents carrying a mutant gene for long hair. It appeared first in the US during the late 1940s or early 1950s, and was accepted for championship by all US associations by 1970. The Balinese has a keen fan club in Great Britain, where it is now being bred.

Temperament
The Balinese has the reputation for being less loud and boisterous than a Siamese, but with a tendency to be very playful with its offspring. It usually adores human company.

Varieties
All the standard Siamese colors are recognized for the Balinese. Varieties other than Seal-point, Chocolate-point, Blue-point, and Frost-point are known as Javanese by some US associations.

HEAD
A long, tapering wedge shape, with a long, straight nose.

EARS
Wide at the base, large, and pointed.

Distinct tabby markings on points

EYES
Medium in size and almond-shaped. Color should be sapphire-blue.

Lavender-pink nose pad

FACIAL CHARACTERISTICS
Frost Tabby-point Balinese

Frost Tabby-point Balinese
"Frost" is a wonderful description for this variety's delicate patina of markings.

Fur is relatively non-matting

COAT
Fur is fine and silky, with a tendency to wave where it is longest. There is no soft undercoat. The mask, ears, legs, tail, and feet should be pinkish-gray in color, contrasting with an even, milk-white body color.

Blue-point Balinese
Slate-blue paw and nose pads and blue points provide striking contrast against a blue-white body in this variety.

BODY
Medium in size and lithe, but still strong and muscular.

Body has long, tapering lines

FEET
Paws are neat, small, and oval.

Forelegs are shorter than the hind legs

LEGS
Long and slim.

Lavender-pink paw pads

TAIL
Long and thin, with a fine point. The tail fur should spread out like a plume.

Chocolate Tabby-point Balinese Kittens
A popular variety of a popular breed.

Turkish Van Cat

OFTEN REFERRED TO as the "Turkish Swimming Cat", this naturally evolved breed is said to be particularly fond of playing in water. It takes its name from the geographically isolated area around Lake Van, in south-eastern Turkey, where it has been domesticated for several hundred years. In some ways, it resembles its fellow countryman, the Angora, but it is sturdier in build and immediately recognizable for its distinctive coat pattern.

History
Two Turkish Vans were imported into Britain in the 1950s by a couple who were struck by the unusual markings of the cats they saw while on holiday in Turkey. The pair were found to breed true, and after a slow start, and the introduction of more Turkish stock, recognition was granted in 1969. The popularity of the breed has grown in recent years, especially in the US and Australia, where it is now eligible to be shown.

Temperament
Affectionate, lively, and highly intelligent, the Turkish Van makes an excellent companion.

Varieties
Apart from the original Auburn-and-White variety, Cream-and-White, Black-and-White, and Tortoiseshell-and-White Turkish Vans are now being developed.

No woolly undercoat

No other cat has markings that are quite like those of the Turkish Van Cat. The white, thumb-like, patch on the forehead is said by the Turkish people to symbolize the mark of Allah.

BODY
Medium in size, long and muscular.

COAT
The fur is silky and long, and should be chalk-white in color with Auburn markings on the face and tail.

Odd-eyed Auburn-and-White Turkish Van Cat
Usually amber-eyed, Turkish Vans with odd eyes occasionally appear in litters. They may be prone to the same problems of deafness that afflict other blue- or odd-eyed white cats.

Cream-and-White Turkish Van Cat
Still fairly uncommon, this is a new variety that will no doubt increase in numbers once its delicately shaded markings are more widely appreciated by cat fanciers.

TAIL
Long and feathery.

*Inside of ears should
be shell-pink*

EARS
Large, pointed,
and tufted.

Pink rims to eyes

EYES
Large and round;
pale amber in color.

HEAD
Short and wedge-
shaped, with a long
nose. The nose pad
should be pink.

FACIAL CHARACTERISTICS
Auburn-and-White Turkish Van Cat

Auburn-and-White Turkish Van Cat
As befits a cat that comes from a region of
Turkey that is extremely cold in winter, but hot
in summer, the Turkish Van moults
considerably during warm spells, becoming
virtually a Shorthair in look.

LEGS
Medium in length
and muscular.

FEET
The paws are small,
neat, and round, with
pads that should be
pink in color.

Toe tufts

Turkish Angora

EARS
Large, wide at the base, and pointed.

Ear tufts

EYES
Medium to large in size, almond-shaped and slanted. Eye color should be green or hazel.

Red nose pad

FACIAL CHARACTERISTICS
Chocolate Tabby Angora

Probably the first longhaired cat to be seen in Europe, the Angora hails from what is now Ankara, the capital of Turkey. Lithe, with long, silky hair and a plumed tail, it is a most attractive cat that has a venerable background.

HEAD
Small to medium in size, wedge-shaped with a long nose.

History
Turkish sultans were sending these cats as gifts to the nobles of France and England during the sixteenth century, but by the end of the nineteenth century they had fallen out of fashion, being ousted by the new longhaired cats and original Persians. Happily, the Ankara zoo came to the rescue and the Angora became something of a protected species. In the early 1960s, an American couple purchased two of the cats from the zoo, and re-established the breed in the US.

Temperament
Gentle, friendly, and intelligent, the Angora is a fun-loving cat that enjoys playing games.

Varieties
The first American Angoras were pure white (and prone to the deafness associated with the color). Now, most Persian coat colors are accepted, some of the most common of which are shown in the chart.

Chocolate Tabby Angora
A British variety. Angoras in Britain were developed "artificially" from breeding programs using Siamese blood rather than by importing Turkish stock, producing a cat that looks the same as the original and American Angoras, but that has a more querulous voice.

COAT
The fur is medium-long, very fine and silky, with a tendency to wave. There should be a well-developed, lush, ruff. The cat moults during the winter months.

Variety	Coat	Eyes
White	Pure white	Orange, blue, or odd-eyed
Black	Jet black	Orange
Blue	Blue-gray	Orange
Black Smoke	White, black tips	Orange
Blue Smoke	White, blue tips	Orange
Silver Tabby	Silver, black markings	Green or hazel
Red Tabby	Red, rich red markings	Orange
Brown Tabby	Brown, black markings	Orange
Blue Tabby	Bluish-ivory, blue markings	Orange
Calico	White, black and red patches	Orange
Bicolor	Black, blue, red, or cream with white	Orange

BODY
Medium in size, lithe and athletic.

TAIL
Long and tapering, frequently carried proudly curled.

Full tail brush

No thick woolly undercoat

LEGS
Long and slim. The forelegs are shorter than the hind legs.

Toe tufts

FEET
The paws are small, dainty, and round.

Odd-eyed White Angora

Tiffany

A CAT THAT IS ESSENTIALLY a longhaired Burmese, the Tiffany has the elegant combination of a modified Foreign or Oriental body type with a luxuriously long, silky coat.

History
Produced from crossing Burmese cats with Persians, the Tiffany is still relatively unknown — even in the US, where it was originally developed by North American breeders and cat fanciers.

Temperament
As a hybrid breed, the Tiffany displays a range of inherited characteristics: it has the gentleness typical of a Persian, but with the more outgoing and inquisitive personality associated with Shorthairs.

Varieties
Although there are a number of Burmese varieties, only one color is recognized in the US for the Tiffany: the original Brown or Sable. There is a move in Great Britain, however, toward the recognition of a greater number of varieties.

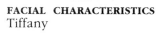

Ears tilt forward

EARS
Medium in size; they should be slightly rounded at the tips and set well apart.

EYES
Rounded to slightly slanted, set wide apart; the color should be golden.

HEAD
Rounded, with a shortish nose and firmly rounded chin.

Brown nose pad

FACIAL CHARACTERISTICS
Tiffany

Tifffany kittens are born a color that has been described as "cafe´ au lait". The darker, mature, coat develops gradually, but is usually still slightly lighter in tone than for a Burmese.

Tiffany
Apart from the length of the coat, all the other features of the breed should be the same as the Burmese.

COAT
The fur is long and silky, and should be a warm sable brown in color.

BODY
Medium in size; more muscular and rounded than a Siamese.

TAIL
Medium in length and bushy.

LEGS
Long and slim, in proportion to the body.

FEET
The paws are oval to round.

Brown paw pads

Somali

A WILD-LOOKING CAT that might, to the imagination, have just walked out of an ancient forest, the Somali is a longhaired version of the Abyssinian. The fur is lush and slightly shaggy, without any tendency to wooliness. Whereas Abyssinian coat hairs have two to three bands of color that form the ticking, the longer Somali hairs carry ten or even more, giving a very rich color density.

History

The longhaired gene may have been introduced into Abyssinian lines during the 1930s, or even before, but Somalis were not systematically developed by North American breeders until the 1960s. A breed club was founded in 1972, and by 1978 the Somali was recognized by all American governing bodies. The breed is now widely distributed throughout Europe and is particularly successful in Australia, where Somalis are bred almost to the exclusion of Abyssinians.

Temperament

Somalis are highly intelligent, good-tempered, and playful. They may be slightly more shy than Abyssinians, but are similarly unsuited to a life spent entirely indoors.

Varieties

The two most commonly seen varieties are the Usual, or Ruddy, which has a golden-brown coat, ticked with darker brown or black, and the Sorrel, or Red, which has a warm copper coat ticked with chocolate. A recent addition to the show bench is the Silver Sorrel, which, according to the preliminary standard, should have a sorrel topcoat and a pale undercoat.

Silver Sorrel Somali
A very new, and still unusual, variety, the Silver Sorrel has already attracted much attention.

Usual Somali
Also known as a Ruddy, this variety has a rich golden-brown coat ticked with black. Darker shading may form a line along the spine and tail, which ends in a black tip. The two short, vertical lines above each eye are a characteristic feature.

BODY
Medium in length and elegant; slightly larger than an Abyssinian, and not as fine-boned as a Siamese.

COAT
Fur is medium-long, dense, silky, and fine-textured. The undercoat should be pale, ticked with chocolate, to give a silvery-peach effect.

FEET
The paws are small and oval with pads that should be pink.

TAIL
Long, thick at the base, and slightly tapering.

Tail should have full brush

Ear tufts

Dark lid-skin

Hazel-colored eyes

EARS
Large, set well apart, and pointed.

EYES
Large and almond-shaped. Color can be amber, hazel, or green.

Pink nose pad

HEAD
A moderate wedge-shape with a medium-size nose.

FACIAL CHARACTERISTICS
Silver Sorrel Somali

Coat is non-matting

Sorrel Somali
The body color of the Sorrel, or Red, should be as deep as possible, with chocolate brown ticking.

Like all varieties of Somali, the Silver Sorrel's coat may take up to two years to develop its mature, ticked appearance.

Coat is longer on stomach

LEGS
Long and slender.

Chocolate ticking should extend up back legs

Toe tufts

73

Maine Coon

THE MAINE COON has the distinction of being both the oldest American breed and one of the largest. It may well have roamed free in the State of Maine during the early days of its history, drawing comparisons to the indigenous racoon, which has a similar appearance to tabby-type Maine Coons and similar hunting habits. The severe New England climate contributed to the development of the Maine Coon's thick coat, a feature that it shares with yet another cold-climate mammal, the Norwegian Forest Cat.

History

Robust American farm cats and longhaired cats brought back to Maine by traders and sailors from Europe make up the Maine Coon's probable early forebears. The breed was shown at the 1860 New York Cat Show, was registered in 1861, and won the Madison Square Garden Show of 1895. However, its popularity diminished once Persians were introduced into the US, and did not revive again until the 1950s. The Central Maine Coon Cat Club, established in 1953, contributed directly to the breed's resurgence, which was given further impetus by the setting up of the Maine Coon Breeders and Fanciers Association in 1976, the same year as the breed was given official recognition in the US.

Temperament

Two characteristics are unique to the Maine Coon: perhaps because of its humble origins, it is used to "sleeping rough" and is found curled up in the oddest positions, in the oddest places; it is also notable for the delightful, quiet chirping sound that it produces. Maine Coons make affectionate, companionable pets.

Varieties

Apart from chocolate, lilac, or Siamese-type patterns, the Maine Coon is bred in every color and combination of colors.

Brown Tabby Maine Coon
A colorful tradition holds that the Maine Coon is descended from the American racoon; the more mundane truth is that such an ancestry is a genetic impossibility.

HEAD
Fairly large, but small in proportion to the body. Should be wedge-shaped, with a medium-long nose.

Fur is shorter on shoulders and front

Moderate neck ruff

Broad chest

LEGS
Medium in length and strong.

FEET
The paws are large and round. Color of pads should match that of the coat.

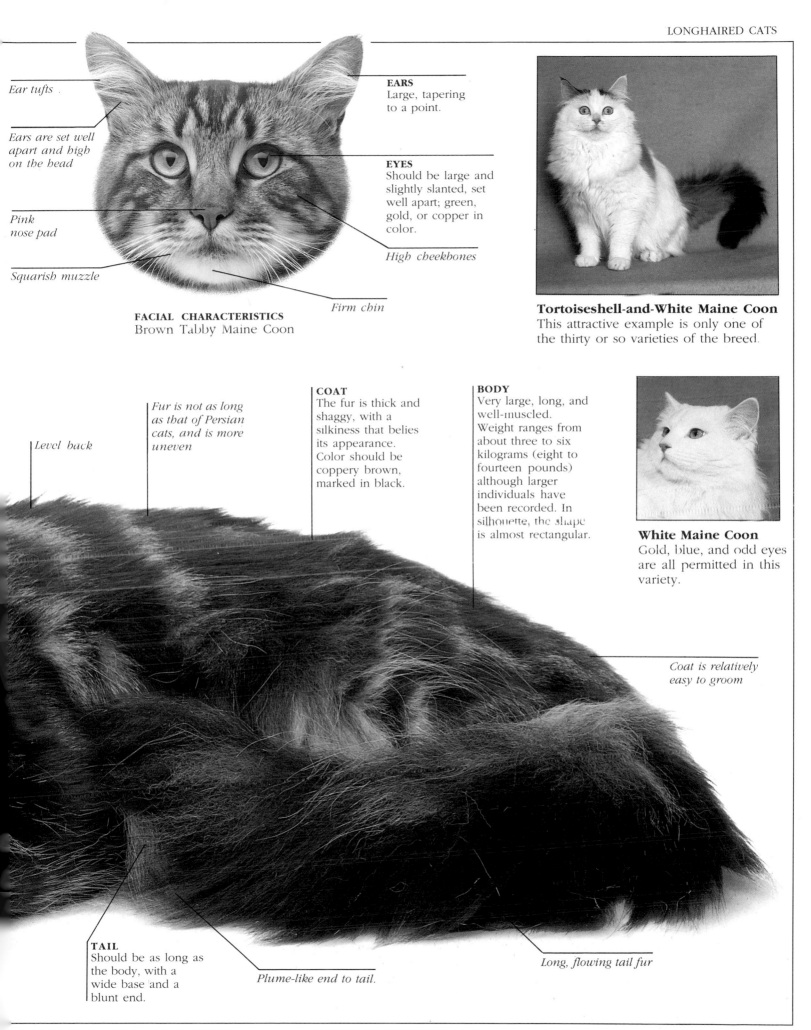

Ear tufts

Ears are set well
apart and high
on the head

Pink
nose pad

Squarish muzzle

EARS
Large, tapering
to a point.

EYES
Should be large and
slightly slanted, set
well apart; green,
gold, or copper in
color.

High cheekbones

Firm chin

FACIAL CHARACTERISTICS
Brown Tabby Maine Coon

Tortoiseshell-and-White Maine Coon
This attractive example is only one of
the thirty or so varieties of the breed.

Level back

Fur is not as long
as that of Persian
cats, and is more
uneven

COAT
The fur is thick and
shaggy, with a
silkiness that belies
its appearance.
Color should be
coppery brown,
marked in black.

BODY
Very large, long, and
well-muscled.
Weight ranges from
about three to six
kilograms (eight to
fourteen pounds)
although larger
individuals have
been recorded. In
silhouette, the shape
is almost rectangular.

White Maine Coon
Gold, blue, and odd eyes
are all permitted in this
variety.

Coat is relatively
easy to groom

TAIL
Should be as long as
the body, with a
wide base and a
blunt end.

Plume-like end to tail.

Long, flowing tail fur

Norwegian Forest Cat

Norse legend describes the Norwegian Forest Cat as a mysterious, enchanted animal, and perhaps no other breed looks quite so wild or so much like a temporary visitor to the domestic hearth. Although it is in fact no more wild than the Maine Coon, which it resembles, it is still a natural breed that is rugged, hardy, and well-adapted to the cold Scandinavian winters. Most distinctive of these adaptive features is the Norwegian Forest Cat's double coat, which keeps out the wind and the snow, keeps in the warmth, and dries in about fifteen minutes after a drenching.

Tabby Norwegian Forest Cat
Tabbies tend to have heavier coats than other varieties of the breed, but as in all Norwegian Forest Cats, the fur is surprisingly resistant to tangles.

History
All that is certain about the Norwegian Forest Cat is that it is an old breed. Its ancestors may include shorthairs brought from Great Britain by the Vikings and longhaired cats brought by the Crusaders, which then mated with farm and feral stock. Alternatively, the Norsk Skaukatt, as it is known in its native land, may be none other than the troll cat of Scandinavian fairy tales. It was recognized in Norway in 1930 and first shown in 1938. For a while, no cats were allowed to be exported and the breed was largely unknown outside its own country. In recent years, however, it has achieved a higher international profile, and pedigree breeding lines have been established.

Temperament
"Wegies" love people and can be very demanding of affection; in exchange they offer intelligent, friendly, playful company. Used to the outdoor life, where they make fine, swift hunters, they can nonetheless adapt happily to staying indoors, as long as they are given plenty of space.

Varieties
All coat colors and patterns are acceptable for the Norwegian Forest Cat, with or without white.

Profuse neck ruff is usually shed in summer

Long neck

COAT
Of double type, consisting of long, water-resistant guard hairs covering thick underfur. Color is blue with white showing through.

Smooth and oily guard hairs

Special claws allow for rock, as well as tree, climbing

FEET
Wide with heavy paws. Pads correspond in color to the coat.

LEGS
Long and powerful.

Hind legs are slightly longer than the forelegs

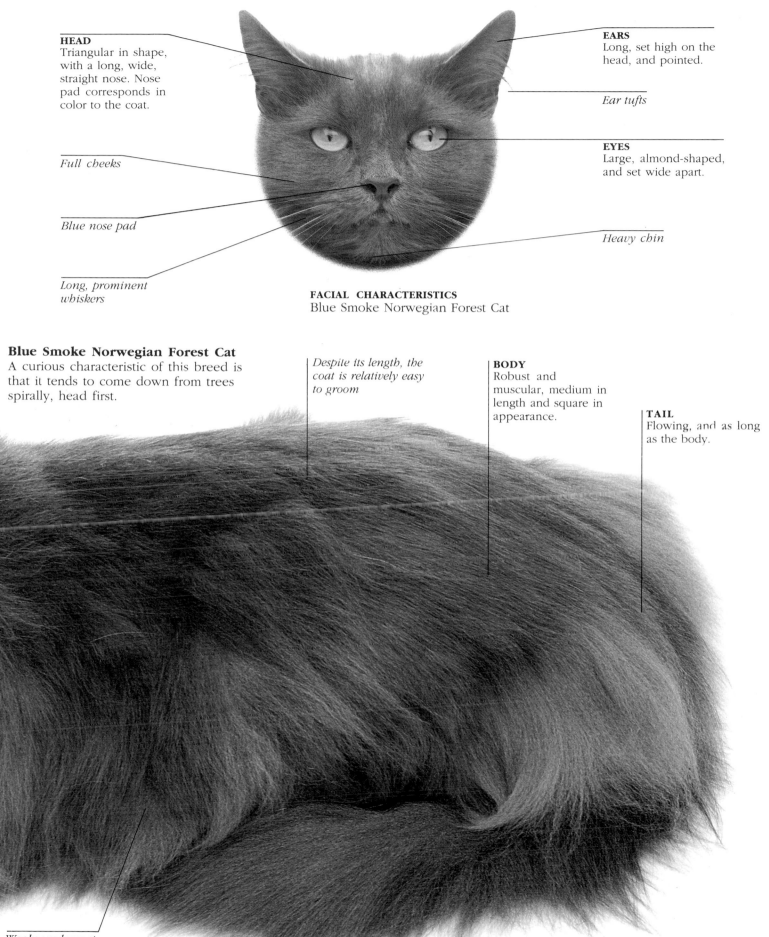

HEAD
Triangular in shape, with a long, wide, straight nose. Nose pad corresponds in color to the coat.

EARS
Long, set high on the head, and pointed.

Ear tufts

EYES
Large, almond-shaped, and set wide apart.

Full cheeks

Blue nose pad

Heavy chin

Long, prominent whiskers

FACIAL CHARACTERISTICS
Blue Smoke Norwegian Forest Cat

Blue Smoke Norwegian Forest Cat
A curious characteristic of this breed is that it tends to come down from trees spirally, head first.

Despite its length, the coat is relatively easy to groom

BODY
Robust and muscular, medium in length and square in appearance.

TAIL
Flowing, and as long as the body.

Wooly undercoat

Non-pedigree Cats

Although longhaired cats are traditionally associated with the show ring, non-pedigree longhaired cats grace many a home and hearth. Like the more common non-pedigree Shorthair, they should not be thought of as somehow "second-best" to the refined show specimen — they may not have the same illustrious parentage, but they still have the same, innate, feline appeal.

Non-pedigree Bicolored Persian

History

Longhaired cats probably arose as the result of a spontaneous mutation within an isolated, perhaps cold, region that enabled the feature to be perpetuated through interbreeding. The modern longhaired cat is mostly descended from Turkish and Persian cats brought to Britain during the late nineteenth century. Non-pedigree longhaired cats can be the result either of crossbreeding Persians or of matings between long- and shorthaired cats.

Temperament

Like all cats, the non-pedigree longhaired cat has a personality uniquely its own, formed by heredity, upbringing, and social environment, but is nonetheless likely to be more docile than its shorthaired relation.

Varieties

As you would expect, a limitless number of "varieties" are possible for the non-pedigree longhaired cat!

BODY
Strong and stocky.

Non-pedigree Tabby Persian

As with the non-pedigree Shorthair, the cross-bred Persian is more likely to have tabby markings than any other because they comprise the basic feline coat pattern. The length of the fur tends to make the markings less evident, but a Tabby is nevertheless always unmistakable.

TAIL
Medium-long and fluffy.

EARS
Medium in size and round-tipped.

Distinctive "M" on forehead

EYES
Large and round.

HEAD
Medium in size, round, with a medium-length nose.

Red nose pad

FACIAL CHARACTERISTICS
Non-pedigree Tabby Persian

COAT
Long, thick, and silky.

LEGS
Medium in length and thick.

FEET
The paws are large and round.

Non-pedigree Tabby-and-White Persian
As attractive as any pedigree version.

Non-pedigree Smoke Persian
An indefinable color, but still a most resplendent cat!

Shorthaired Cats

In both wild and domestic cats, short hair is much more common than long. The main reason for this is that the genes for short hair are dominant over the ones for long hair. Also, in the wild, whether as a leopard or a feral inner-city tom, long hair can tangle on things when stalking and ambushing, give enemies something to grab hold of, and without an attentive owner to do the grooming, become matted and likely to cause skin diseases. These are important disadvantages that natural evolution came to terms with.

Shorthaired coats, on the other hand, don't get in the way and are simple to care for — wounds can be easily tended and parasites don't find it such a good environment in which to make a home. Twice weekly grooming is sufficient and many shorthaired cats can very adequately look after their coats themselves.

Shorthaired cats fall into three main types: the British Shorthair, the American Shorthair, and Oriental or Foreign Shorthairs.

The British Shorthair is a sturdy cat with a strong, muscular body on short legs, and which sports a short, dense coat. It has a broad, rounded head, with a short, straight nose, and large, round eyes. European Shorthair breeds are identical.

American Shorthairs developed from ancestors of the British and European Shorthairs, which were taken to the US by the early settlers. It is a different strain of cat, larger and leaner than the British type, and with slightly longer legs, a more oblong head with a square muzzle, a medium-length nose, and large, round eyes.

Foreign or Oriental Shorthairs have a conformation quite different to the rounded, sturdy British and American Shorthairs. This type of cat has a wedge-shaped head with slanting eyes and large, pointed ears, a lithe, slim body with long legs, and a very fine, short coat. This category embraces the most well-known example, the Siamese, as well as the Korat and the Havana. In some countries, including the US, these cats are known simply as Oriental Shorthairs, or as Oriental in type, whereas in others, notably Britain, Australia, and New Zealand, particular colors and coat patterns are designated as being either Oriental or Foreign.

British Blue Shorthair
Probably the most popular of the British Shorthairs, the Blue has the typical round face, sturdy build, and muscular body set on short legs. The fur is particularly plush, even for its type.

Manx
A tail-less breed, the Manx has a body conformation similar to a British Shorthair, except that its hind legs are longer than its forelegs.

Oriental Shorthair
The term "Oriental" does not necessarily indicate an exotic origin (although some of these cats do indeed come from the Far East), instead it refers to a variety of breeds that have the same lithe, slim body, slanted eyes, large, pointed ears, and fine, short fur.

Abyssinian
More rugged and not as fine boned as a typical Oriental Shorthair, the Abyssinian still shares some of the same features. Where it differs markedly is in the texture and patterning of the coat, which is very thick and distinctively ticked.

Exotic Shorthair
The Exotic is perhaps the best example of a cat that has crossed the Persian/ Shorthair divide: it has the cobby build and features of a Persian, but the plush coat of an American Shorthair.

British Black Shorthair

MORE THAN ANY OTHER FELINE, shorthaired black cats have through the ages been the object of fear, superstition, and veneration — alternately persecuted as creatures of ill-omen and deified as bringers of good luck. In fact, such large numbers were executed during the Middle Ages in the belief that they were agents of the devil, and in an attempt by the Christian Church to purge Europe of the vestiges of paganism, that the black cat can indeed be thought of as a lucky animal to have managed to survive at all!

History
The British Black Shorthair was one of the first breeds to be shown at Crystal Palace in London during the late nineteenth century, and was selectively bred using the best examples of British street cats. These cats are now usually produced from like-to-like matings, although they sometimes appear in Tortoiseshell litters. They themselves are used in Tortoiseshell and Tortoiseshell-and-white breeding programs.

Temperament
Good-natured and very intelligent, the British Black Shorthair makes an ideal cat-about-the-house.

Varieties
There are no varieties of the British Black Shorthair.

British Black Shorthair
Shorthaired black cats are a common sight everywhere, but they usually have green eyes, rather than the sparkling orange or copper eyes of the pedigree version, which provide such glorious contrast against the dense, black coat.

FEET
The paws are large and round.

LEGS
Short and well-proportioned.

Black paw pads

Best known as the supposed familiar of witches, who could, it was thought, adopt the feline form at will, black cats have always attracted the attention of the superstitious and credulous.

EARS
Medium in size, and round-tipped.

EYES
Large and round; either bright orange, gold or copper in color.

HEAD
Round and broad with a short, straight nose.

Black nose pad

Well-developed chin

FACIAL CHARACTERISTICS
British Black Shorthair

Color should be sound to the roots

BODY
Strong, stocky, and muscular; usually an excellent example of the Shorthair type.

The coat of the British Black Shorthair may take on a brownish tinge if the cat spends long periods of time basking in the sun — a particularly unwelcome feature in a show specimen. Kittens may legitimately have some rustiness; this should disappear in six months or so.

COAT
The fur is short and dense and should be a perfect, jet black color, without any white hairs.

TAIL
Short and thick.

British White Shorthair

WHITE SHORTHAIRED CATS have always been much prized for the purity of their coats, and in many countries are regarded as a symbol of perfection. As in the White Longhair, the blue-eyed variety is genetically predisposed to deafness.

History
The modern breed originates from the selective breeding of street cats during the late nineteenth century.

Temperament
As one would expect from its origins, the British White Shorthair is intelligent and street-wise, as well as making a friendly companion.

Varieties
There is a trio of varieties: Blue-eyed, Orange-eyed and Odd-eyed. (Non-pedigree, shorthaired white cats usually have green eyes.)

British Orange-eyed White Shorthair
A perfect white shorthair with no hint of any other color is a relatively rare, and therefore sought-after, animal. The orange-eyed variety, which does not suffer from the problems of deafness associated with the blue-eyed types, is regarded even more highly.

EARS
Medium-sized, round-tipped, and set well apart.

EYES
Large, round, and orange-colored; each eye should be equal in depth of color.

FACIAL CHARACTERISTICS
British Orange-eyed White Shorthair

COAT
The fur is short and dense. The color should be pure, snowy white, and without any tinge of gray or yellow.

HEAD
Round and broad, with a well-developed chin, a straight nose, and a pink nose pad.

British Odd-eyed White Shorthair
The variety of British White Shorthair that has one orange eye and one blue eye is a side-effect of breeding programs designed to produce orange-eyed cats with perfect hearing. Deafness may be apparent on the blue-eyed side.

BODY
Strong, muscular, and stocky.

TAIL
Short and thick.

LEGS
Short, but well-proportioned.

FEET
The paws are large and round, with pink pads.

British Cream Shorthair

THIS LUSCIOUS CAT should look as if it has been freshly dunked in a pail of clotted cream. In practice, however, it is not easy to produce the desired pale, even, coloration, and good examples are more rare than they are for other Shorthairs. Breeding from Tortoiseshells tends to produce a coat that is too red, or "hot"; and, because the dominant tabby gene is difficult to suppress, many kittens retain tabby markings into adulthood. Even if these eventually fade, extreme hot or cold weather may cause them to reappear.

History
Cream Shorthairs originated toward the end of the nineteenth century when they started appearing in Tortoiseshell litters. For a good while, it was not known how to produce the breed except by accident. For this reason, official recognition did not come until the 1920s, by which time a breeding program had been established. Widespread interest in the breed developed even later, becoming evident only during the 1950s.

Temperament
The British Cream is extremely good natured, intelligent, and affectionate toward its owner.

Varieties
There are no varieties.

EARS
Medium in size and round-tipped.

EYES
Large and round; color should be copper, orange, or Welsh gold. Hazel-colored eyes were allowed at one stage, but no longer.

FACIAL CHARACTERISTICS
British Cream Shorthair

HEAD
Round and broad, with a short nose.

British Cream Shorthair
Blue-Cream females mated to Blue or Cream males generally produce the best examples of this breed.

Pink nose pad

COAT
Short and dense, yet fine. The color should be an even-toned cream, with as few markings as possible and no white hairs. Paler shades are preferred.

BODY
Strong, stocky, and muscular.

LEGS
Short, but well-proportioned.

TAIL
Short and thick.

Pink paw pads

British Cream Kitten
The pale coat of this kitten suggests that it may eventually be good enough to show.

FEET
The paws should be large and round.

British Blue Shorthair

AN IDEAL BODY CONFORMATION, extra-plush fur, and a heavenly blue-gray color that is set off by orange or copper eyes have given this cat a consistent number-one ranking in the Shorthair popularity stakes.

History

The British Blue Shorthair evolved during the late nineteenth century from breeding programs using the very best street cats. It made an early appearance at shows, but the scarcity of studs during World War II, and outcrosses to other breeds after the end of the war, caused the type to deteriorate. The introduction of Blue Persians into breeding lines resulted in some improvement, although the fur tended to be too long. It was not until the 1950s that very selective breeding was, finally, able to restore the original Blue Shorthair type.

Temperament

A sharp-witted and particularly affectionate cat, the British Blue Shorthair makes an excellent companion and confident that some owners report has a hankering for the quiet life.

Varieties

The Chartreux is considered by some associations to be a true variety of the British Blue, but others judge it by the same standard. It is thought to have been developed in France during the Middle Ages by the monks belonging to the monastery of La Grande Chartreuse (famous for its green liqueur), using cats imported from North Africa. It is given its own class in North America, where a sturdier cat than the British Blue is called for, with a higher proportion of gray in the coat, and a face that is less rounded.
In Great Britain, selective breeding has brought the Chartreux so close in type to the Blue Shorthair that no distinction is made between the two.

HEAD
Round and broad, with a short, straight nose.

EARS
Medium in size, and round-tipped.

EYES
Large and round; color should be copper or orange.

Blue nose pad

Well-developed chin

FACIAL CHARACTERISTICS
British Blue Shorthair

British Blue Shorthair
To preserve the breed type, occasional outcrossings to Blue Persians and Black Shorthairs are recommended in some countries.

FEET
The paws are large and round with blue paw pads.

LEGS
Short, and well-proportioned.

A perennial favorite, the British Blue Shorthair has a well-balanced, but still sometimes mischievous, disposition.

Selective breeding of the Blue Shorthair has produced a body conformation that is a perfect example of the British Shorthair type.

COAT
The fur is short and dense. At one stage, a dark slate-blue color was accepted, but now the standard requires a medium to light blue. There should be no tabby markings.

BODY
Strong, muscular, and stocky.

Chartreux
In some countries, this cat is allowed to retreat into the monastic seclusion of its own class.

TAIL
Short and thick.

British Blue Shorthair kittens are particularly irresistible and pretty. They may have faint tabby markings that should disappear within a few months.

British Blue-Cream Shorthair

A S THE NAME SUGGESTS, this cat is essentially a cross between Blue and Cream Shorthairs, although Tortoiseshells are also used for breeding. The British standard calls for a subtly toned cat with an intermingling of the two colors, whereas the American Blue-Cream has clearly defined patches. The way that color genes are linked to sex in some cats means that no male Blue-Creams have been recorded as having survived into adulthood.

An alert, curious nature has endeared the Blue-Cream to countless fond owners.

History
The British Blue-Cream is a comparatively new breed, and was not recognized in Great Britain until the late 1950s.

Temperament
This cat is as affectionate and lively as its shorthaired relatives.

Varieties
There are no varieties of the Blue-Cream Shorthair.

BODY
A strong, muscular, stocky type.

TAIL
Should be short and thick.

LEGS
Short and well-proportioned.

FEET
Paws are large and round with pads that are pink or blue or a mixture of the two colors.

EARS
Medium in size and round-tipped.

HEAD
Round and broad with a short, straight nose.

EYES
Large and round; either copper, orange or rich gold in color.

Blue nose pad

Well-developed chin

British Blue-Cream Shorthair
Litters produced by crossing Blues and Creams may contain solid-colored kittens as well as Blue-Creams.

FACIAL CHARACTERISTICS
British Blue-Cream Shorthair

The cream hairs tend to be finer than the blue in the British Blue-Cream, and the coat may therefore require regular grooming when the cat is moulting.

COAT
The fur is short and dense. The color should be a soft intermingling of blue and cream with no tabby markings.

The best examples of the British Blue-Cream have very pale coloring.

British Tabby Shorthair

THE EPITOME of cat patterning and design, the Tabby is the closest that the domestic cat comes to its pre-domestic forebears. The tabby gene is a dominant type, and the new-born kittens of other breeds often have faint, transient, tabby markings that bear witness to their original ancestry and the need for their untamed cousins to have effective camouflage in the wild. Despite the "pushiness" of the tabby gene, however, the exacting demands of the breed standard have ensured that the pedigree Tabby is no common or garden, run-of-the-mill cat!

History
Tabby cats appear on the murals of Pharaonic Egypt, and they have been depicted by artisans and artists ever since. Indeed, the name comes from Attabiya, a quarter of old Baghdad in which a striped cloth was made, known in Britain as tabbi silk. The modern, pedigree, version of this venerable cat originated from crossing the best of British street cats during the nineteenth century.

Temperament
The British Tabby Shorthair is a good-natured, affectionate, and intelligent cat that makes the best sort of friend.

Varieties
The British Tabby Shorthair is bred in two coat patterns, and in several colors. The Mackerel is the more striped cat and lacks the spirals of the Classic. Brown, Silver, and Red are recognized colors in both Britain and the US, with the latter recognizing Blue and Cream as well.

British Brown Classic Tabby Shorthair
The correct color combination of a rich or coppery brown with dense black markings is difficult to produce, making Brown Tabbies relatively uncommon.

Unbroken lines should run from the outer corners of each eye

British Red Classic Tabby Shorthair
A Classic Tabby should have a butterfly shape on the shoulders, from which three stripes run along the spine, an oyster-shaped spiral on each flank, and narrow necklace-like stripes across the chest. The abdomen is spotted and the forehead should have frown marks that form a letter "M". Both the tail and legs should be evenly ringed.

LEGS
Short but well proportioned.

Legs ringed with "bracelets"

Deep red paw pads

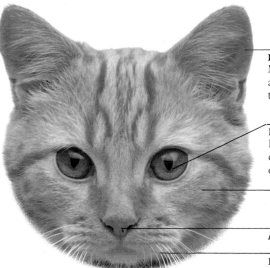

EARS
Medium in size and round-tipped.

EYES
Large and round; copper, gold or orange in color.

Tabby "pencilings" on cheeks

Brick-red nose pad

HEAD
Round and broad, with a short, straight nose and a well-developed chin.

FACIAL CHARACTERISTICS
British Red Classic Tabby Shorthair

A pedigree Red Tabby Shorthair may bear a superficial resemblance to the neighborhood ginger tom, but its rich red coat and distinctive dark red markings put it streets ahead.

COAT
The fur should be short and plush. The deep red markings should correspond to the classic tabby pattern, and be set against a rich red ground color.

BODY
A strong, muscular, stocky type.

Ground color and markings should be evenly balanced

Markings on each side of the cat should be identical

TAIL
Short and thick.

FEET
The paws are large and round.

British Silver Classic Tabby Shorthair
Probably the most popular variety of Tabby, the Silver is also said to be the most friendly. It should have sharply defined, dense, jet-black markings that stand out against the silvery-gray ground color. The nose pad is either brick-red or black and the eye color should be green or hazel in Britain and gold, orange or hazel in the US.

British Tortoiseshell Shorthair

ALTHOUGH THE COAT of the British Tortoiseshell, with its distinctive patches of black, cream, and red, makes it one of the most familiar of all the domestic cats, it is surprisingly difficult to breed. To produce the desired patterning, queens are best mated to a solid-colored black, red, or cream stud, but even then the resultant litter may contain only one kitten true to type. Because of the way the genes that determine color are inherited, almost all Tortoiseshells are female.

EYES
Large and round; color should be either deep orange or burnished copper.

Black nose pad

FACIAL CHARACTERISTICS
British Tortoiseshell Shorthair

Short, dense fur

History
Like most British Shorthairs, the Tortoiseshell was developed from the best street cats. It was one of the first to make an appearance on the show benches.

Temperament
The British Tortoiseshell is a sharp-witted, affectionate, and charming cat that has long been highly popular as a pet.

Varieties
There are two varieties. The Tortoiseshell-and-White is the same as the Tortoiseshell but for the addition of white patches. In the Blue Tortoiseshell-and-White, known as a Dilute Calico in the US, the black is replaced by blue and the red is replaced by cream.

TAIL
Short and thick.

British Tortoiseshell Shorthair
Affectionately known as the "Tortie", this breed has made a faithful fireside companion since the late nineteenth century.

EARS
Medium-sized and
round-tipped.

HEAD
Round and broad,
with a straight nose.
The nose pad should
be pink or black or a
mixture of the two.

*Bold, clearly defined
patches of black,
cream, red, and
white*

COAT
Must be evenly
patched with black,
red, and cream; a
cream or red blaze
on the head is
particularly
sought after.

BODY
Strong, muscular,
and stocky.

LEGS
Short, but well-
proportioned.

Pink-and-blue paw pads

FEET
The paws are large
and round. The pads
need to be pink or
black or a mixture of
the two.

British Tortoiseshell-and-White Shorthair
Formerly known as a Chintz or Spanish Cat, this
variety is exactly the same as the Tortie, but with
the addition of white patches. Bicolors usually
make the best sires.

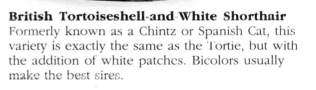

*Pink-and-blue
nose pad*

British Blue Tortoiseshell-and-White Shorthair
The black and red in the coat of the Tortoiseshell-and-
White are replaced by blue and cream in this recently
developed variety. The nose and paw pads are pink or
blue or a mixture of the two colors.

British Spotted Shorthair

IF YOU OWN a British Spotted Shorthair, look out for cat thieves! Its gorgeous coat is an eye-catcher that never fails to turn heads. Reminiscent of some of its smaller wild cousins, "Spottie", as it is affectionately known, is basically a Mackerel Tabby with the markings broken up into spots.

History
A cat very similar to the British Spotted was known in Ancient Egypt, where it was revered in mythology as the killer of the serpent of evil. Like most British Shorthairs, the modern breed was selectively bred from street cats and made an early appearance at the cat shows held during the 1880s. It fell out of favor at the beginning of this century, but regained popularity by the mid-1960s.

Temperament
Spottie is good-natured, affable and affectionate.

Varieties
Any tabby-type color combination is permissible for the British Spotted, as long as the spots match the coat color. The most common varieties are the Brown, Silver, and Red. The British standard is more specific about the distribution of markings than that of the US.

British Silver Spotted Shorthair
The markings on the British Spotted need to be as numerous and distinct as possible. The spots can be round, oval, or rosette-shaped.

Broken rings on tail

TAIL
Short and thick.

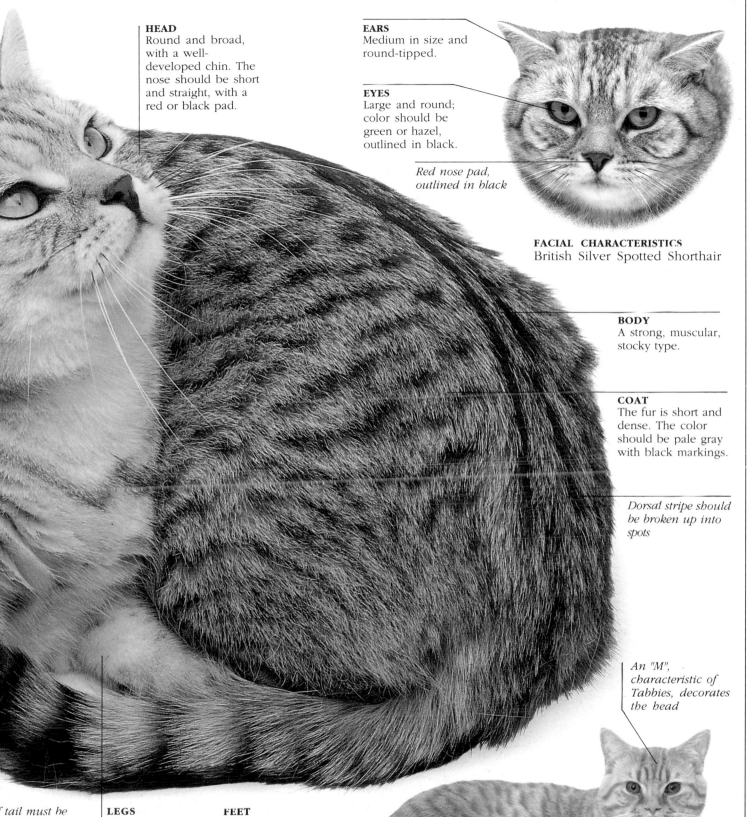

HEAD
Round and broad, with a well-developed chin. The nose should be short and straight, with a red or black pad.

EARS
Medium in size and round-tipped.

EYES
Large and round; color should be green or hazel, outlined in black.

Red nose pad, outlined in black

FACIAL CHARACTERISTICS
British Silver Spotted Shorthair

BODY
A strong, muscular, stocky type.

COAT
The fur is short and dense. The color should be pale gray with black markings.

Dorsal stripe should be broken up into spots

An "M", characteristic of Tabbies, decorates the head

Tip of tail must be same color as markings

LEGS
Short, but well-proportioned.

FEET
The paws are large and round, with black or red pads.

British Red Spotted Shorthair
For this variety, the standard calls for a light red coat, spotted in rich red, coupled with deep orange or copper eyes.

British Bicolor Shorthair

BICOLORED CATS, white cats patched with another color, are plentiful in every neighborhood, but the uppercrust, pedigree, version is much more rarely seen because of the difficulty of meeting the breed standard. The white should cover no more than half the coat, and the second color no less than half and no more than two-thirds. Ideally, the patching should be symmetrical, but in practice this is rarely possible to achieve.

History
Perhaps surprisingly, in view of the large numbers of non-pedigree bicolored cats that have existed for as long as the domestic cat itself, the British Bicolor has only recently been recognized for showing.

Temperament
This is an eminently even-tempered, friendly, and intelligent cat.

Varieties
There are four varieties: Black-and-White (known as the "Magpie"), Blue-and-White, Red-and-White, and Cream-and-White.

British Blue-and-White Bicolor Shorthair
Before pedigree lines were introduced, the most well-known bicolored cat was one owned by the Earl of Southampton, a friend of Shakespeare. A contemporary painting shows them doing "time" together in the Tower of London.

TAIL
Short and thick.

There should be no white hairs visible in colored patches

British Blue-and-White and Cream-and-White Bicolor Shorthair Kittens
Undeniably pretty as adults, the kittens of the breed are truly irresistible. The Cream-and-White is the most uncommon of the varieties, all of which tend to mature early.

LEGS
Short, but well-proportioned.

British Red-and-White Bicolor Shorthair
Although very appealing in its own right, this cat's tabby markings rule out a career on the show bench.

From a back view of the Blue and-White Bicolor, only one small, white spot mars the symmetry of the patching.

BODY
A strong, muscular, stocky type.

COAT
The fur is short and dense. Color should be white, evenly patched with blue.

HEAD
Round and broad with a short, straight nose that should have a nose pad that is either pink or that matches the color of the patches.

Face should be patched

EARS
Medium in size and round tipped.

FEET
The paws are large and round with pads that are either pink or that match the color of the patches.

EYES
Large, round, and copper or orange in color. Green rims are a fault.

A white facial blaze is a desirable feature

FACIAL CHARACTERISTICS
British Blue-and-White Bicolor Shorthair

British Smoke Shorthair

EARS
Medium in size and round-tipped.

EYES
Large and round; should be copper, orange or deep gold in color.

Black nose pad

FACIAL CHARACTERISTICS
British Black Smoke Shorthair

THE MAGICAL, "now you see it, now you don't" quality of the British Smoke comes from its unusual fur. This is composed of a one-colored topcoat over a white undercoat. When the cat is in repose it looks solid-colored, but when it moves the white can be seen flickering through to beautiful effect.

History
The British Smoke can count Silver Tabbies and solid-colored British Shorthairs in its ancestry, which extends back to the late nineteenth century. These days, Smokes are usually either mated to other Smokes or, to improve the breed type, to Blue Shorthairs.

Temperament
This is a pleasant-natured, affectionate and intelligent cat.

Varieties
Only two varieties of British Smoke are recognized in both Great Britain and the US: the Black Smoke and the Blue Smoke.

British Black Smoke Shorthair
The appearance of the Smoke's coat is determined by two genes: one inhibits pigmentation of the undercoat and the other enhances the tipping of the cat's topcoat.

COAT
The fur should be short and dense. The undercoat is white, or pale silver, covered by a topcoat that is tipped with black.

HEAD
Round and broad, with a short, straight nose.

BODY
Strong and muscular.

Undercoat

Pink paw pads

British Tortoiseshell Smoke Shorthair
A variety that is not yet fully recognized in the US, the Tortie Smoke's coat markings produce a wonderful, hazy effect.

Topcoat

Deep tipping is almost indistinguishable from a solid color

TAIL
Short and thick.

FEET
The paws are large and round with black pads.

LEGS
Short, but well-proportioned.

British Tipped Shorthair

HEAD
Round and broad
with a straight nose.

EARS
Medium in size and
round-tipped.

EYES
Large and round;
color should be
bright green.

Pink nose pad

Well-developed chin

L IKE THE LONGHAIRED Chinchilla and Cameo, this breed has a white undercoat and a tipped topcoat, a beguiling combination that produces a distinct sparkle when the cat moves. The tipping should be evenly distributed and largely confined to the upper part of the body.

History
A complex breeding program that incorporated cats with silver genes, Blues, and Smokes produced the cat that we know today. Known originally as a Chinchilla Shorthair, it was recognized under its present name in 1978.

Temperament
Good-humored and intelligent, the British Tipped makes an affectionate companion.

Varieties
The tips of this much-admired breed can be any British color, with the addition of chocolate and lilac.

BODY
A strong,
muscular,
stocky type.

FACIAL CHARACTERISTICS
Black-tipped British Shorthair

Cream-tipped British Shorthair
"Cream on white" — the tipping is barely noticeable, but still visible enough to give this variety a soft, refined appearance.

Black-tipped British Shorthair
Green eyes, outlined in black, make this variety stand out from the crowd; all other varieties have orange or copper-colored eyes.

COAT
The fur is short and dense. Color should be white with black tipping on the back, flanks, head, ears, and top of the tail.

The white of the undercoat should be as pure as possible

Legs may be marked with faint "ghost" rings

TAIL
Short and thick.

LEGS
Short, but well-proportioned.

FEET
The paws are large and round with pads that are pink or that match the color of the tipping.

99

Manx

A CAT WITHOUT A TAIL may seem like a contradiction in terms, but the Manx has long been established as a breed. Resembling a British Shorthair in some respects, a "true", or "Rumpy", Manx should have only a small hollow where a tail would have been, although cats with residual tails are also born — these are known as "Risers", "Stumpies" or "Stubbies", and "Longies", depending on the tail length. The lack of a tail is not simply a quaint anomaly; the mutant gene responsible has been implicated in skeletal defects, and like-to-like matings of completely tail-less Manx usually results in the kittens dying before, or shortly after, birth.

History
Legend relates how this unfortunate cat lost its tail when Noah closed the door to the Ark a little too hastily; its more modern history is no less intriguing. One school of thought holds that tail-less cats swam ashore to the Isle of Man, off the west coast of England, in 1588 from galleons of the shattered Spanish Armada; another that the cats arrived on merchant ships traveling from the Far East. Either way, the isolation of the island allowed the tail-less trait to be perpetuated.

Temperament
The Manx is good natured and friendly — very much a family cat.

Varieties
Most recognized colors, coat patterns, and color combinations are permitted for the Manx.

TAIL
Non-existent. It should be possible to detect a hollow at the end of the backbone.

Red Tabby Stumpy Manx
A variety with a residual tail.

Rump should be rounded and higher than the shoulders

FEET
The paws are large and round; the color of the pads should correspond to that of the coat.

Clearly defined patches of red, cream, black, and white

EARS
Medium in size, with slightly rounded tips.

Nose pad patched in pink and black

Copper-colored eyes

EYES
Large, round, and set at a slight angle toward the nose. The color should conform to that of the coat.

HEAD
Round and broad, with a short to medium-length nose that is straight in Britain and more curved in the US. The color of the nose pad should conform to that of the coat.

Rounded whisker pads

Well-developed chin

FACIAL CHARACTERISTICS
Tortoiseshell-and-White Rumpy Manx

Blue Stumpy Manx
Although "Stumpies" may be thought to resemble Japanese Bobtails, the two breeds are genetically very different: the tail-lessness of the former is caused by a dominant gene, whereas in the latter it is a recessive genetic condition.

BODY
A strong, muscular, stocky type.

Tortoiseshell-and-White Rumpy Manx
Although Manx cats are still very much associated with the Isle of Man, where they are depicted on tourist souvenirs, coins, and stamps, examples of the breed, including the ever-popular Tortie-and-White, are now more widely distributed around the world.

COAT
A double type, comprising of a short, very thick, undercoat that has been described as having a "cottony" feel, and a slightly longer topcoat. The appearance is glossy.

LEGS
The forelegs are short and set well apart; the hind legs are longer with heavy, muscular, thighs that give the cat a characteristic "bunny-rabbit" gait, although this is considered a fault in the US.

Red Tabby Stumpy Manx
A very rounded side-view when sitting is a characteristic of the breed, caused by forelegs that are considerably shorter than the hind legs.

American Shorthair

As the standard describes it, the American Shorthair is eminently adapted to the ethos of a country forged by frontiersmen and women: "lithe enough to stalk its prey but powerful enough to make the kill easily" with legs "long enough to cope with any terrain and heavy and muscular enough for high leaps". It is a very athletic cat, with a larger and more powerfully built body than its British relation, harder fur, and a more oblong face.

History
The American Shorthair undoubtedly sprang from the tough, hardworking cats that accompanied the Pilgrim Fathers and later settlers to the New World. The first feline colonists thrived in the American environment, adapting to the climate, landscape, and lifestyle, and developing their own unique characteristics. Selective breeding to perpetuate the best of these features began early this century.

Temperament
Courageous, intelligent, energetic, and hardy, the American Shorthair does its country proud!

Varieties
The American Shorthair is bred in any number of colors and coat patterns, of which the more popular are shown in the chart.

HEAD
Large, with full cheeks, almost oblong in shape; the nose is medium in length and should have a pad that matches the coat color.

Blue eyes

EARS
Medium in size and round-tipped.

EYES
Large and wide with an upper lid shaped like half an almond, and the lower lid shaped in a fully rounded curve. The color should match that of the coat.

Pink nose pad

Well-developed chin

FACIAL CHARACTERISTICS
Van Pattern Tabby American Shorthair

Van Pattern Tabby American Shorthair
This example shows off the best features of its type: a robust, muscular build, an open, appealing face, and general hardy disposition — a cat equally at home on the range or in the parlor.

BODY
Large to medium in size; powerful, strongly built and well balanced, with well developed shoulders, chest, and hindquarters.

COAT
The fur is thick, dense, and hard; a soft or silky coat would be a fault. The color is white with red tabby markings on the face, legs, and tail.

FEET
The paws are heavy and rounded with pads that match the color of the coat.

LEGS
Medium in length, although slightly longer than the British Shorthair, and heavily muscled.

Pink paw pads

Silver Tabby American Shorthair
A Classic variety of Tabby

Shaded Silver American Shorthair
Exactly like its British counterpart in color, but larger in build.

Broad, level, back

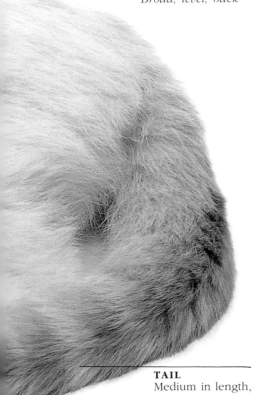

TAIL
Medium in length, tapering to a rounded tip.

Varieties	Coat	Markings	Eyes
White	Pure white	None	Deep blue, brilliant gold, or odd-eyed
Black	Coal black	None	Brilliant gold
Blue	Pale blue-gray	None	Brilliant gold
Red	Deep, rich red	None	Brilliant gold
Cream	Buff-cream	None	Brilliant gold
Bicolor	White	Black, red, blue, or cream patches	Brilliant gold
Shaded Silver	White undercoat	Mantle of black tipping, shading towards white	Green or blue-green
Chinchilla Silver	Pure white undercoat	Black tipping on back, flanks, head, and tail	Emerald-green or blue-green
Shell Cameo	White undercoat	Red tipping on back, flanks, head, and tail	Brilliant gold
Shaded Cameo	White undercoat	Like Shell, longer tips	Brilliant gold
Cameo Smoke (Red Smoke)	White undercoat	Very deep red tipping	Brilliant gold
Black Smoke	White undercoat	Tipped with black	Brilliant gold
Blue Smoke	White undercoat	Very deep blue tipping	Brilliant gold
Blue-Cream	Blue	Clear patches of cream	Gold
Tortoiseshell	Black	Red and cream patches	Gold
Tortoiseshell Smoke	White undercoat	Black, red, and cream tips in tortie pattern	Brilliant gold
Van Pattern	White	Auburn with patching similar to Turkish Cat	Brilliant gold
Calico	White	Black and red patches	Brilliant gold
Dilute Calico	White	Blue and Cream	Brilliant gold
Brown Tabby	Coppery brown	Black Classic or Mackerel pattern	Brilliant gold
Red Tabby	Rich red	Deep, rich red Classic or Mackerel pattern	Brilliant gold
Silver Tabby	Pale, clear silver	Black Classic or Mackerel pattern	Green or hazel
Blue Tabby	Pale, bluish-ivory	Very deep blue Classic or Mackerel pattern	Brilliant gold
Cream Tabby	Very pale cream	Buff or cream Classic or Mackerel pattern	Brilliant gold
Cameo Tabby	Off-white	Red Classic or Mackerel pattern tips	Brilliant gold
Patched Tabby (Tortie-Tabby, or Torbie)	Silver, brown, or blue	Black or dark gray Classic/Mackerel; red/cream patches	Brilliant gold or (Silver only) green or hazel

American Wirehair

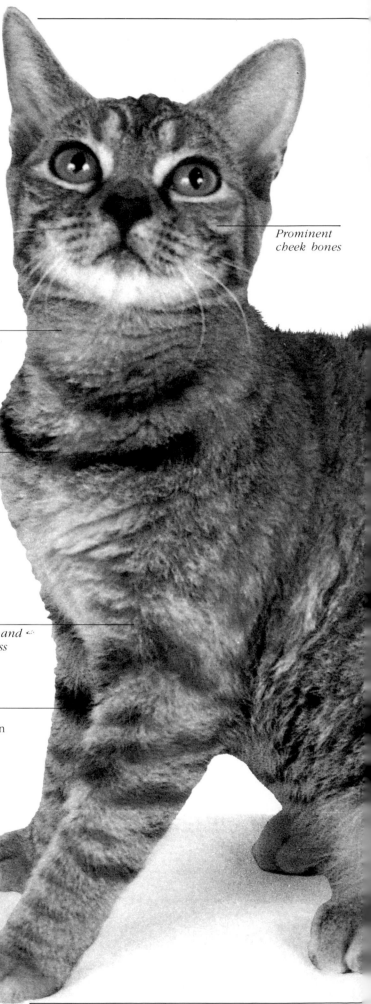

PERHAPS THE "PUNK" of the feline world, the American Wirehair is a most distinct, and still quite uncommon, cat. The fur is unusual in that each of the guard hairs — the long, thick hairs of a cat's coat which are raised when the fur "stands on end" — is crimped along its length and hooked at the end. The fur is therefore frizzy and wirey, and to the touch is not unlike the wool on a lamb's back.

History
There are records of similar cats being sighted on London bomb sites after the end of World War II, but the cat as we know it today is descended from a Shorthair queen living in the state of New York, who, in 1966, gave birth to a remarkable mutant red-and-white male that had a wavy coat. The kitten was subsequently used to develop the breed, which is still rare outside the US — although a few American Wirehairs have recently been exported to Canada and Germany, where new breeding lines are now being established.

Temperament
The American Wirehair takes a keen interest in its surroundings, and is considered to have an even-tempered and affectionate nature.

Varieties
All the colors and coat patterns of the American Shorthair are recognized for the Wirehair.

Prominent cheek bones

Thick, muscular, neck

COAT
The fur is of medium length, and should be tightly crimped, thick, springy, resilient, and coarse. The color should be brown with black markings and patches of red and/or cream.

Fur on chest and stomach is less coarse

LEGS
Medium in length, in proportion to the body, and well muscled.

FEET
The paws are oval and compact; the color of the pads should harmonize with that of the coat.

Calico American Wirehair
A variety that is white, with patches of black and red.

Red Tabby American Wirehair
The Wirehair's springy coat creates the illusion that the tabby markings are somehow "ridged" or raised.

EARS
Medium in size and round-tipped.

Ears are set well apart

EYES
Large and round, set well apart, with a slight upward tilt at the outer edge. The color should be brilliant gold.

Whiskers are crimped

HEAD
Round in shape, with a well-developed muzzle and chin. The nose is of medium-length; the color of the pad should harmonize with that of the coat.

FACIAL CHARACTERISTICS
Brown Patched Tabby American Wirehair

Brown Patched Tabby American Wirehair
Outcrosses to American Shorthairs have produced a large array of Wirehair varieties, of which the Patched Tabby is one of the more unusual. Such matings generally produce litters of fifty per cent Wirehairs.

BODY
Medium to large in size, and well muscled.

TAIL
Medium in length, tapering to a rounded tip.

Silver Tabby-and-White Wirehair
The combination of tabby markings with pure white is always attractive, and kittens are usually much in demand.

Brown Tabby-and-White American Wirehair
A delightful example.

Exotic Shorthair

A COMPOSITE CAT! The Exotic can be said to have it all: the cobby build and irresistible snub-nose and round face of a Persian, coupled with a shorter, plush, coat that is a boon for those people who do not have the time nor the inclination for regular grooming sessions.

History
The Exotic arrived on the American scene in the late 1960s, the result of interbreeding Persians, American Shorthairs, and Burmese. As a hybrid breed, it is an extremely healthy and robust cat.

Temperament
As might be expected, the Exotic combines characteristics inherited from its forebears. It is as gentle and affectionate as a Persian, but has the playful, alert intelligence of an American Shorthair.

Varieties
All the coat colors and patterns found in Persians and in American Shorthairs are permitted for the Exotic — giving over fifty varieties from which to choose. The color of the eyes and the nose and paw pads depends on the variety, but should always conform to the coat color.

Colorpoint Exotic Shorthair
Siamese-type markings, with the points a darker color than the rest of the body, make this variety instantly recognizable.

Rounded tip to tail

BODY
Medium to large in size; a solid, chunky, cobby type.

TAIL
Short, bushy, and normally carried uncurled at a level below that of the back.

LEGS
Short, thick, and sturdy.

Blue Tabby Exotic Shorthair
One reason for the Exotic's consistent appeal is the affecting, sweet expression created by the round face and snub nose inherited from its Persian background.

Like all varieties of the Exotic, the Blue Tabby has a docile nature and habits that are less destructive than many Shorthairs, making it a classic indoor cat.

HEAD
Round and broad, with a snub nose that should have a distinct "break".

EARS
Small and round-tipped; they are set wide apart and tilt forward slightly.

EYES
Large and round, set wide apart; gold in color.

Rose nose pad

Well-developed chin

FACIAL CHARACTERISTICS
Blue Tabby Exotic Shorthair

Short, thick neck

Full cheeks

COAT
The fur is medium in length, slightly longer than other Shorthairs, but not long enough to flow. It should be soft, plush, and sufficiently dense to stand out from the body. There are no ear or toe tufts, and no feathery hairs on the tail.

Deep chest

FEET
Paws are large and round with rose-colored pads.

Blue Exotic Shorthair
The distinctive hallmarks of the Exotic, the beautiful, plush fur and cobby build, are shown off to perfection by this example of the breed. Although the popularity of the Exotic is mostly still confined to the US, these cats are rapidly gaining fans world-wide. They are said to be especially adaptable to the show ring.

Siamese

IMPERIOUS, IMPORTUNING, impertinent, arrogant, aloof, loud, vulgar, subtle, beguiling — a Siamese is all of these and more. With its svelte, "Oriental" build, its gorgeous pointed coat pattern and sapphire-blue eyes, this is a cat that demands attention on every level.

History
In Bangkok, the National Library possesses a collection of manuscripts, the *Cat Book Poems*, dating from possibly the fourteenth century, in which a Siamese-type called the "vichien mas" is depicted, and it is thought that similar cats lived in what is now Thailand for hundreds of years. Siamese were first imported into the US in the 1880s.

Temperament
The Siamese is the most extrovert of all domestic cats, with a loud "voice" that is impossible to ignore.

Varieties
There are four classic varieties: the Seal-point (pale fawn to cream coat with seal-brown markings), Blue-point (bluish-white coat with deep blue markings), Chocolate-point (ivory coat with milk-chocolate markings), and Lilac-point (glacial white coat with frosty-gray markings). Newer varieties, developed by mating Siamese with other breeds, are called Colorpoint Shorthairs by the main governing body in the US, but in Britain they are not shown separately.

Seal Lynx-point Colorpoint Shorthair Kitten
Siamese kittens are born all-white, without points.

BODY
Medium in size, long, lithe, and svelte, with a refined appearance.

LEGS
Long and slim, in proportion to the body.

FEET
The paws are dainty, small, and oval.

Lilac-point Siamese
The first Siamese to be imported into England are believed to have been a gift to the British Consul from the court of Siam. Today, the breed looks very different from those nineteenth-century examples, having a less round face and a paler coat. The Lilac was the last of the four classic varieties to be recognized.

Seal-point Siamese
The first variety to be recognized, the Seal-point is genetically a black cat where the pigment has been watered down and restricted to the extremities of the body.

Chocolate Lynx-point Colorpoint
A variety with an ivory-colored body and points broken up by chocolate-brown bars separated by a lighter background color.

EYES
Medium in size, almond-shaped, slanted, and sapphire-blue in color. Crossed eyes, which were once commonly seen in Siamese are regarded as a fault.

EARS
Large and pointed.

HEAD
Wedge-shaped, long and narrow, with a long nose.

Lavender-pink nose pad

FACIAL CHARACTERISTICS
Lilac-point Siamese

COAT
The fur should be short, fine-textured and glossy. The color should be glacial white with frosty-gray shading on the "points" — the mask, ears, legs and tail.

TAIL
Long, thin, and tapering.

Fur should be close-lying

Tail should be free of kinks

Hind legs are slightly longer than the forelegs

Lavender-pink paw pads

Colorpoint Varieties	Coat	Markings
Red	Clear white shading to apricot	Reddish gold
Cream	White shading to pale cream	Warm cream
Lynx	White	Tabby
Seal Tortie	Pale fawn	Seal-brown patched in red and/or cream
Blue Tortie	Bluish-white	Blue patched in cream
Chocolate Tortie	Ivory	Chocolate-brown patched in red and/or cream
Lilac Tortie	Glacial white	Pinkish-gray patched in cream

Russian Blue

THE DISTINGUISHING feature of the Russian Blue is its double coat, which has a plushness that is unrivaled by any other cat. Probably the most famous, and certainly the most cosseted, example of the breed is Vashka, who was owned by Tsar Nicholas I of Russia — where these cats are considered a welcome omen of good luck.

History

The variety of names that the Russian Blue has had bears witness to the confusion surrounding its origins. The evidence is strong for its being a natural Russian breed, evidence that is supported by the large numbers that have long been found in Sweden; but its subsequent history is much less certain. It was known at first as the Archangel Cat because examples were brought back to Britain from the Russian port of Archangelsk by Elizabethan sailors. Later, it was known as both the Spanish Cat and the Maltese Cat, the latter name persisting in the US until the beginning of this century. The breed declined during World War II, and attempts to revitalize it by using British Blue and Siamese outcrosses led instead to its virtual disappearance: the cat became a blue Siamese in type and almost lost its distinctive double coat. The late 1960s saw a return to the original type after concerted efforts by breeders on both sides of the Atlantic.

Temperament

The Russian Blue is obliging, rather shy, and quiet. In fact, Blues are so quiet that it may be difficult to tell when a queen is calling.

Varieties

Experimental all-white and all-black Russians have been produced, but they have not attracted much interest outside New Zealand.

Almond-shaped eyes

Russian Blue
Only a strict breeding program has enabled this breed to survive in its original form.

Thick fur makes face broad across the eyes

Blue nose pad

LEGS
Long and fine-boned. In Britain the forelegs are shorter than the hind legs.

FEET
The paws are small and oval in Britain, with blue pads. In the US they are more rounded, with pads either pink or mauve in color.

EARS
Large and slightly pointed. The skin is thin and only lightly covered with very fine fur, making the ears almost transparent.

EYES
Should be vivid green in color, set wide apart. They are almond-shaped in Britain and more rounded in the US.

HEAD
Should be neither short nor long. It is wedge-shaped, with a medium-long nose. The nose pad is colored blue in Britain and slate-gray in the US.

Strong chin

FACIAL CHARACTERISTICS
Russian Blue

The long, slender, neck of the Russian Blue is seen most clearly when it is stretched; usually the cat's thick fur makes it appear shorter.

BODY
Long, slender, and elegant.

Fine-boned, but still muscular, the Russian Blue is an athletic-looking cat.

COAT
The short, plush coat has a seal-like texture. It is a double type, standing out from the cat's body because of its density. The color should be an even blue, with a distinct sheen produced by silver-tipped guard hairs.

TAIL
Long, tapering from a moderately thick base.

Abyssinian

WHO COULD FAIL to be enchanted by this wild-looking creature? Certainly not the Ancient Egyptians, who, if popular theory is to be believed, worshipped the Abyssinian's antecedants as incarnations of the goddess Bast.

History

As befits its arcane aura, the Abyssinian's origins have become largely hidden with time. The breed is arguably natural, possibly old, and probably descended in modern times from a cat called Zula who was imported into Britain from Ethiopia in 1868. Because Zula, of whom we have a photograph, didn't look anything like today's Abyssinians, there are those who believe that the cat is either a product of chance matings between ordinary tabbies, or is the result of early breeders trying to produce an "Egyptian-like" cat. Other Abyssinian fanciers point out that the Romans are known to have imported cats from Egypt into Britain, and may therefore have introduced the gene for the "Egyptian look" into the native feline population.

Temperament

The Abyssinian's alert expression is reflected in its delightful personality. It is sweet-tempered, intelligent, and described by some as obedient.

Varieties

There are a number of varieties (see chart), although some are still shown in assessment classes.

EARS
Large, set wide apart, and pointed.

Ear tufts

EYES
Large, almond-shaped and amber, hazel or green in color.

Eyes are rimmed in black or dark brown, encircled by a paler area

Brick-red nose pad

HEAD
Round and gently wedge-shaped, with a medium-size nose.

FACIAL CHARACTERISTICS
Ruddy Abyssinian

In profile, this Ruddy Abyssinian's proud, Sphinx-like, bearing inevitably prompts comparison with the cats portrayed on the murals of Ancient Egypt — giving credence to the belief that this was the cat so revered by the Pharoahs.

Ruddy Abyssinian

The original variety, the Ruddy was at one time known as a Rabbit or Hare Cat — a reference to the similarly ticked coat, which, as in all varieties of Abyssinian, is characterized by a distinctive agouti (a form of tabby) fur that has two to three darker-colored bands along each hair.

TAIL
Thick at the base, fairly long and tapering.

Tail tipped with black

Variety	Base Color	Ticking Color
Ruddy	Ruddy brown	Black or dark brown
Red	Copper-red	Chocolate
Blue	Warm blue-gray	Steel blue
Fawn	Medium fawn	Deep fawn
Lilac	Light pinkish gray	Darker pinkish gray
Silver	Silver	Black
Silver Sorrel	Silvery peach	Chocolate
Silver Blue	Silvery blue-gray	Deep steel blue

Silver Sorrel Abyssinian
Chocolate ticking over a silver-peach base color gives this recently developed variety a soft, graceful, charm.

COAT
Glossy and soft, but also dense and resilient to the touch. The fur is short, but still long enough to accommodate two to three bands of black or dark brown ticking over a ruddy brown base color.

Blue Abyssinian
Unusually, the ticking of this naturally occurring variety is blue, over a blue-gray base color, rather than the black that might be expected.

Elegant arched neck

Ruddy Abyssinian Kitten
Abyssinian litters are usually small and mostly male. The kittens mature early (although it may be eighteen months or so before the coat develops fully) and are particularly lively and friendly.

LEGS
Long, slender, and fine-boned, giving the impression of being on tip-toe when standing.

BODY
Medium in length, lithe and graceful, but with a muscular appearance.

FEET
The paws are small and oval-shaped.

Black paw pads

Korat

ONE OF THE OLDEST natural breeds, the Korat is said to have been named after the Thai province where the cat originated by King Rama V. In its native land it is known as "Si-Sawat", which refers to the good fortune that its possession is believed to bring. With its beautiful silver-blue coat and heart-shaped head, the modern cat is not much changed from its ancient ancestor.

History
The first Korat to be officially exhibited in Europe was entered in a British cat club show in 1896 — as a blue Siamese. A male and female pair were imported to the US in 1959, where recognition was granted in 1966. Recognition in Great Britain did not come until 1975.

Temperament
Intelligent and very sweet-natured, the Korat makes a loving companion, particularly for children.

Varieties
There are no varieties.

Korat
"The hairs are smooth, with tips like clouds and roots like silver; the eyes shine like dewdrops on a lotus leaf." A wonderfully evocative description of the Korat, taken from the *Cat-Book Poems*, written between 1350 and 1767, and held in the Bangkok National Library.

Large, flat forehead

EARS
Large and round-tipped, set high on the head.

EYES
Prominent, round, and luminous green. Kittens and adolescents may have yellow or amber-green eyes that change hue by the time they mature.

FACIAL CHARACTERISTICS
Korat

HEAD
Heart-shaped. The nose should have a lion-like downward curve just above the nose-pad, which is dark blue or lavender in color.

COAT
The fur should be short, flat, silky, and fine, with a distinct sheen to its silver-blue color.

BODY
Semi-cobby, lithe, and muscular.

A characteristic feature of the coat is the way the fur breaks when the back is bent

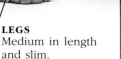

Forelegs are slightly shorter than the hind legs

LEGS
Medium in length and slim.

FEET
Small, oval paws with pads that should be dark blue to pinkish-lavender in color.

TAIL
Medium in length, and round-tipped.

Havana

THE HAVANA lives up to its name not only because its rich, brown coat resembles the color of the expensive cigar tobacco, but also because it has the elegance, refined manners, and distinctive history that reeks of exclusivity.

History

During the 1950s in Great Britain a Seal-point Siamese crossed to a black shorthaired cat of Siamese ancestry formed the foundation of the breed, which was recognized in 1958. The British breeding program continued to use Siamese outcrosses, but American breeders decided to prohibit the use of Siamese, preferring to produce a cat that maintained the look of the original imports, was less Oriental in type, and which they called the Havana Brown.

Temperament

The Havana is an active, affectionate, and highly intelligent cat.

Varieties

There is one color variety, the Frost, which is exclusive to the US, where also the breed is judged by a different standard to the British. The American Havana Brown is a more sturdy cat, with a medium-length torso, a rounder face, oval eyes, round-tipped ears, and longer fur.

EARS
Large, with slightly pointed tips.

EYES
Almond-shaped, slanted, and pale to mid-green in color.

HEAD
Long and wedge-shaped, with a short, straight nose that should have a brown or rosy-pink pad.

FACIAL CHARACTERISTICS
Havana

COAT
The fur is very short and glossy; the color should be an even, rich, chestnut-brown.

Long, slender neck

BODY
Long, svelte, and muscular.

Forelegs are shorter than the hind legs

TAIL
Long and elegant.

LEGS
Long and slim.

FEET
The paws are small and oval with pads that should be either brown or rosy-pink in color.

Havana Brown
The American Havana tends to be more quiet than its British cousin.

Havana
The Havana's original name of Chestnut Brown Foreign Shorthair perhaps more accurately describes its origins.

115

Burmese

UNLIKE THE BALINESE, the Burmese can claim a connection with the country after which it is named. Known as "Rajahs", brown cats similar to today's Burmese were recorded as dwelling in Buddhist temples in Burma as far back as the fifteenth century.

History

The modern breed was founded by "Wong Mau", a cat imported into the US from Burma in 1930 who was crossed with a Siamese tom. There may have been subsequent imports of cats from Burma, but certainly by 1936 the cats were breeding true enough to be granted recognition in the US. However, the large amount of Siamese blood that had been introduced caused the original type to be overwhelmed and the registration was temporarily dissolved during the 1940s. Despite their Siamese content, they were given British recognition in 1952. A year later, with the American breed once more conforming to type, it was again recognized in the US.

Temperament

The breed is famous for its affectionate, intelligent personality: these cats love people.

Varieties

Not only do the number of Burmese varieties differ on each side of the Atlantic, but also the American and British standard. The American Burmese (see chart) has a rounder body, head, eyes, and feet than the British cat.

Platinum Burmese
A popular British variety whose color ranges from bluish lilac to creamy fawn.

Blue Tortoiseshell Burmese
Tortie Burmese are produced by mating Reds and Creams with Sables, Blues, Champagnes, and Platinums, and are bred primarily to preserve the breed type, rather than for the coat color. However, to meet the standard, this variety should have clearly defined patches of blue and cream without any barring.

Distinct nose break

High cheek-bones

COAT
The fur is gloriously glossy, short, with a satin finish.

BODY
Medium in size; more muscular and rounded than a Siamese.

LEGS
Long and slim.

FEET
The paws are small and oval with pads that should conform to the color of the coat.

Ears tilt forward slightly

EARS
Medium in size, slightly rounded at the tips, and set well apart.

EYES
Lower lids are rounder than upper lids, giving a slanted appearance. The color should be yellow to gold.

AD
medium
dge-shape,
h a shortish
e. The
or of the
e pad should
form to that
he coat.

Pink-and-blue nose pad

FACIAL CHARACTERISTICS
Blue Tortoiseshell Burmese

TAIL
Medium in length, straight and tapering only very close to the rounded tip.

Hind legs are slightly shorter than forelegs

Pink-and-blue paw pads

Sable Burmese
The original and, to some, the ideal.

Red Burmese
A relative newcomer to the British scene.

American Sable Burmese
A breed history that diverged during the mid- to late 1940s has produced two distinct types of Burmese: the British cat is more Oriental; the American Burmese is more sturdy and cobby.

Varieties	Coat	Markings
Sable	Warm sable-brown	Lighter shading on underside
Champagne	Warm honey-beige	Pale gold shading; tan on underside
Blue	Medium blue	Warm fawn undertones; lighter on underside
Platinum	Pale silvery-gray	Pale fawn undertones; lighter on underside

Japanese Bobtail

IDIOSYNCRATIC, unlike other shorthaired breeds, and with a decided Oriental expression, the Japanese Bobtail was so named both for its country of origin and its "powder-puff", bunny-rabbit-type tail.

History
Although the breed has roots in the Far East that can be traced back to the seventh century, the Japanese showed little interest in its show qualities until fairly recently. It was left to the Americans in the late 1960s to bring the cat into the limelight and set the pedigree standard.

Temperament
The friendly Japanese Bobtail is a cat brim-full of personality.

Varieties
Traditional varieties in Japan are the tricolored cats (black, red, and white, and tortoiseshell and white) which are known as *Mi-ke*, meaning "lucky". All other colors and patterns, apart from Abyssinian- and Siamese-types are also recognized.

Coat is not prone to shedding

EARS
Large, round-tipped, set well apart and at right angles to the head, giving the impression that they tilt forward.

EYES
The eyes are large and oval, with a less rounded cornea than other breeds. The color should harmonize with that of the coat.

FACIAL CHARACTERISTICS
Red-and-White Japanese Bobtail

Red-and-White and Black-and-White Japanese Bobtails
When sitting, Bobtails often raise one paw, a gesture that is believed to bring good luck. Called *Maneki-neko*, or "beckoning cats" they are often represented in prints and models and displayed in Japanese homes and shop doorways to welcome visitors. One temple in Tokyo, the Gotokuji, has a façade decorated with these cats, all with one paw lifted to greet supplicants.

Black-and-White Japanese Bobtail
Mi-ke models are in the background.

HEAD
Should form almost a perfect triangle. The nose is long with a pad that should match the coat color.

COAT
The fur should be soft, silky and medium in length. Color should be red and white or black and white.

Eyes appear slanted when they are seen from the side

Black-and-White Japanese Bobtail
A variety popular with all.

Fur is longer and thicker on the tail, disguising its true size

BODY
Medium-sized, lean and elegant.

TAIL
Very short and curled.

LEGS
Long and slender. Hind legs are longer than the forelegs.

FEET
The paws are medium in size and oval. The pads match the coat color.

Singapura

SINGAPURA is the Malaysian name for the island of Singapore, from where these cats originated. Like the Abyssinian, the Singapura has a ticked coat, but which has a different, smoother feel — almost as if a piece of satin had been draped over the cat.

History
Imported into the US in 1975, the Singapura was first shown only a year later and rapidly gained acceptance by most associations. It is still a fairly unusual breed in the US, and is rare in the West.

Temperament
Because in its native land the Singapura appears to seek shelter and a place to nap in drains, it was once known as the "Drain Cat" — a perhaps unfortunate sobriquet suggesting a lowly feline, and one that has now been dropped. Although it is reserved and somewhat shy, the Singapura is nonetheless a social cat that loves being around people.

Varieties
There are no recognized varieties of the Singapura.

Blunt tip to tail

Singapura Queen and Kittens
The first Singapura to be imported into Great Britain, in 1989, gave birth while still in quarantine, where this photograph was taken. Singapura queens are renowned for being particularly maternal towards their kittens.

EARS
Large and slightly pointed.

EYES
Large, almond-shaped and slanted. Color should be hazel, green or yellow.

Salmon-colored nose pad

HEAD
Rounded, with a short nose.

Well-developed chin

FACIAL CHARACTERISTICS
Singapura

Singapura
Cats similar to the Singapura are numerous not only in Singapore, but also throughout Asia. Since its introduction into the US, however, the breed has been developed and the standard revised, with the result that it is one of the more rare pedigree cats.

BODY
Small to medium in size; a muscular, moderately stocky type.

Eyes are outlined

Nose pad is outlined

TAIL
Fairly short and slender.

COAT
The fur is very short, silky and close-lying. The color should be that of old ivory with bands of dark bronze and warm-cream ticking, giving a refined, delicate appearance.

LEGS
Medium in length and muscular.

FEET
The paws are small and oval, with pads that should be rosy brown in color.

Tonkinese

ORIENTAL IN NAME, but American by design, the Tonkinese is the result of crossing Siamese and Burmese, and is said to combine the best qualities of each.

History
"Tonks" were developed on a small scale in North America during the 1930s. These early Hybrids, known as "Golden Siamese", were largely ignored, and it was not until the late 1960s, when the breed made its debut as the "Tonkinese", that they started attracting their fair share of attention. Full recognition in the US came by the 1980s, but this has still to happen elsewhere.

Temperament
Ultra-affectionate, the Tonkinese is one of the most people-oriented of Shorthair breeds.

Varieties
Only five varieties of Tonkinese are recognized in the US (see chart), but in Britain the one association that accepts the breed has introduced a new standard that allows for all recognized Burmese colors.

BODY
Medium in size, lithe and muscular; mid in type between a svelte Siamese and the more compact Burmese.

Red-point Tonkinese
A new, and uniquely British variety, the Red-point corresponds in color to the Red Burmese, but with Siamese-type points of a darker shade.

COAT
The fur should be medium-short, soft, and close-lying like mink, with a natural sheen. Color should be solid, shading to a slightly lighter tone on the underparts, with points that are clearly defined although less distinct than a Siamese.

All Tonkinese, not just the Red-point, have inquisitive, outgoing personalities.

FEET
The paws are dainty, and more oval than round. The color of the pads should harmonize with that of the coat.

Pink paw pads

Variety	Coat	Markings
Natural Mink	Warm brown	Dark chocolate
Blue Mink	Bluish-gray	Slate-blue
Honey Mink	Ruddy brown	Chocolate
Champagne Mink	Warm beige	Pale brown
Platinum Mink	Soft silver	Pewter-gray

Natural Mink Tonkinese
"Mink" refers not only to the soft coloring of the coat, but also to the texture of the fur. The Natural Mink is considered by many to be the breed "prototype".

HEAD
A modified wedge shape, with a square muzzle and a long nose; the color of the nose pad should harmonize with that of the coat.

EARS
Medium in size, broad at the base, with oval tips.

EYES
Medium in size, almond-shaped and set wide apart. Color should be blue-green.

Pink nose pad

FACIAL CHARACTERISTICS
Red-point Tonkinese

Hind legs are slightly longer than the forelegs

TAIL
Long, in proportion to the body, and tapered.

LEGS
Long, slim, and elegant.

Medium-long neck

Not all British associations recognize the Tonkinese because it does not breed truc (only fifty per cent of the kittens produced from like-to-like matings will be Tonkinese); but the subtly-toned Red-point will surely be an ambassador for wider acceptance.

Platinum Mink Tonkinese
A glorious example of the breed. The coat usually takes up to sixteen months to develop fully, and some breeders believe that the sheen of the coat continues to deepen and improve thereafter. Others are of the opinion that the best time to show a Tonkinese is at two years of age.

Bombay

Blacker than black, this cat is possessed of a truly remarkable coat that is often described as having the sheen of patent leather. It is named for the city of Bombay because of its resemblance to the Indian black leopard.

History
The breed was created in the US in the 1950s by crossing a Burmese and an American Black Shorthair. It has not yet achieved recognition in Great Britain.

Temperament
The Bombay rarely stops purring, craves human companionship, and dislikes being left alone. It is quite happy to spend its entire life indoors.

Varieties
There are no varieties.

Ears are set far apart and should tilt forward slightly

EARS
Should be medium-sized, broad at the base with gently rounded tips.

EYES
Round, set far apart, and should range in color from gold to vivid copper.

Black nose pad

HEAD
Rounded, with a full face that should taper to a short, well-developed muzzle.

FACIAL CHARACTERISTICS
Bombay

TAIL
Should be medium in length.

BODY
A medium-sized, muscular type.

COAT
Color should be a gleaming jet black and the fur short and close-lying.

LEGS
Medium in length, in proportion to the body.

Bombay
Still relatively rare outside the US, this cat's elegant good looks should ensure it a wider popularity in the near future.

FEET
The paws should be small and oval with black pads.

Snowshoe

ANOTHER RECENT American breed, the Snowshoe was developed with the aim of combining Siamese-type points with the white feet of a Birman — the latter feature earning it the nickname of "Silver Laces." It has a modified Oriental body type, usually being larger and heavier with less extreme features, not unlike Siamese of thirty to forty years ago.

History
Three kittens of Siamese parentage that were born with white feet formed the foundation for the breed. Once a selective breeding program was established American Bicolored Shorthairs were used to develop Snowshoes.

Temperament
The Snowshoe has been described as having a sparkling, "bomb-proof" personality, ideal for showing.

Varieties
There are two standard varieties of Snowshoe: the Seal-point has a warm fawn body, pale fawn stomach and chest, and seal-brown points; the Blue-point has a bluish-white body, a paler chest and stomach, and points that are a deep gray-blue.

Ears tilt forward slightly

EARS
Large and pointed, set wide apart.

EYES
Large, slanting, and oval, similar in shape to a walnut. The color should be bright blue.

High cheekbones

HEAD
A rounded, triangular shape, with a medium-length nose that is straight in profile.

Gray nose pad

FACIAL CHARACTERISTICS
Blue-point Snowshoe

Blue-point Snowshoe
Still relatively rare, the Snowshoe has only two varieties, the Blue and the Seal, that are recognized by American associations. Other Siamese point colors will undoubtedly be accepted in the future.

TAIL
Medium in length and gently tapering.

BODY
A medium to large, lithe, well-muscled type.

COAT
The fur is short, glossy, and medium-coarse in texture. The mask, ears, legs, and tail should be a much darker shade of the body color, whereas the chest and stomach are paler. The feet should be white.

FEET
The paws are medium in size and oval.

LEGS
Medium in length.

Pink-and-gray paw pads

Seal-point Snowshoe
The inverted facial "V" is a desirable feature.

Oriental Shorthairs

CHIC CATS that have the build of a Siamese and which are bred in a myriad colors and patterns, Oriental and Foreign Shorthairs are among the most distingished-looking in the feline repertoire.

EARS
Large and pointed.

Green-colored eyes

EYES
Medium in size, almond-shaped and slanted.

HEAD
A Siamese wedge-shape with a long nose.

Lavender-colored nose pad

FACIAL CHARACTERISTICS
Lilac Oriental Shorthair

History
In both the US and Britain Siamese were bred to other Shorthairs to produce an elegant Oriental-type cat without point markings. Recognition was granted towards the late 1970s.

Temperament
These cats have the same energetic and inquisitive nature as the Siamese. They are highly intelligent and make loving companions.

Varieties
Varieties include Ebony, White, Blue, Lilac, Red, Cream, Silver, Cameo, Chocolate, Cinnamon, Caramel, Black Smoke, Chocolate Smoke, Cameo Smoke, Tabby, and Tortoiseshell. Eye color is green in most cases, but can be blue-colored in the American White, and must be blue in British Whites. Colors from copper to green are legitimate in the Cream and Red. In Britain, solid-colored types are known as Foreign Shorthairs, whereas Tabby, Ticked, and Spotted cats are called Oriental Shorthairs. There is a move, however, towards a redefinition of terms and a regrouping of varieties.

Blue Oriental Shorthair
A cat that deserves a high profile.

COAT
The fur is short, fine-textured, and close-lying. The color should be pinkish-gray, with a frosty-gray tone.

BODY
Medium in size; a long, svelte, lithe, type.

Hind legs are higher than the forelegs

Ebony Oriental Shorthair
Quintessential feline elegance.

TAIL
Long, thin at the base, tapering to a fine point.

Ticked Tabby Oriental Shorthair
Each hair has bands of dark shading.

EARS
Large and pointed.

Eyes rimmed with chestnut

EYES
Medium in size, almond-shaped and slanted.

Green-colored eyes

Pink nose pad, rimmed with chestnut

HEAD
A Siamese wedge-shape with a long nose.

FACIAL CHARACTERISTICS
Chocolate Tabby Oriental Shorthair

Lilac Oriental Shorthair
The Havana breeding program in Britain during the 1950s gave rise to the development of this variety. If two Havanas produced from crossing Russian Blues and Seal-point Siamese are mated together, the litter will contain Foreign Lilacs.

Chocolate Tabby Oriental Shorthair

Tabby Oriental Shorthairs
Oriental Tabbies were produced originally by mating non-pedigree tabbies with Siamese. Later on, however, Tabby-point Siamese were used in the breeding program. All colors and tabby patterns are now accepted.

Long, slender neck

LEGS
Long, slim, and elegant.

FEET
The paws are dainty, small and oval.

Lavender-colored paw pads

Blue Tabby Oriental Shorthair

Burmilla

As the name suggests, the Burmilla is the product of crossing a Burmese with a Chinchilla. It possesses the body conformation of a Burmese, but with a softer, tipped, or shaded coat. The development of the Burmilla can be said to have filled a need in the cat world: that of a tipped, silver Shorthair of Foreign type.

History
During 1981 in Great Britain an accidental mating between a Lilac Burmese queen and a Chinchilla stud, both owned by Baroness Miranda von Kirchberg, produced four kittens that were to become the Burmilla's founder-members. The possibility of establishing a new, true breed was quickly realized, and with that aim the Burmilla Cat Club came into being in 1984. The Burmilla has still to achieve recognition in Britain, and is only just about to be introduced in the US, but it is seen at an increasing number of shows and has already won numerous friends and admirers.

Temperament
This cat is renowned for its excellent, even-tempered disposition.

Varieties
The Burmilla is bred with a silver or golden ground color tipped in black, or any of the Burmese or other standard colors.

Eyes are outlined in black

Black outline to lips

LEGS
Medium length and slim. The forelegs are slightly shorter than the hind legs.

Black-tipped Burmilla
The Burmilla is rapidly becoming one of the most popular of the new shorthaired breeds.

FEET
The paws are a neat, oval shape with black pads.

Traces of tabby markings and a distinct "M" decorate the forehead

Eyes are outlined in brown

Brown outline to lips

EARS
Medium to large, set moderately apart. They are broad at the base, have rounded tips and tilt forward slightly.

EYES
Large, set well apart, with a round lower lid and straight upper lid. All shades of green are accepted.

HEAD
Gently rounded, with a medium width between the ears. The nose is short with a terracotta nose pad outlined in black.

FACIAL CHARACTERISTICS
Black-tipped Burmilla

Slight ringing on upper legs

Tail is ringed and tipped in brown

Brown-tipped Burmilla
The pads of the Brown-tipped Burmilla and the penciling around the eyes and lips correspond in color to the tipping.

BODY
Medium in length, lithe but muscular.

Fur has a rough feel at the tips

COAT
The fur is short, but longer than the Burmese, and dense and soft in texture.

Black-tipped Burmilla
Gentle shading that contrasts against a silver undercoat, and delicate tabby markings visible on the points lend this variety a quiet air of distinction.

Tail is ringed in the same color as the tipping

TAIL
Medium to long, it should taper to a round tip.

127

Rex

LOOKING AS IF it has just returned from the hairdressing salon with a rather old-fashioned permanent wave, the Rex cat is named after the Rex rabbit, which also has a curly coat.

History
Although crinkly-coated kittens are recorded to have appeared in both Europe and the US after World War II, the breed was not taken seriously until 1950, when a litter of farm kittens in Cornwall, England, included a lovely cream male with wavy fur that was mated back to its mother and found to breed true. In 1966 another, similar, kitten appeared in Devon, which, when crossed with the Cornish type produced cats with straight fur — proving that the Cornish and Devon coats were caused by different genes and that the two cats should be developed separately. Rex cats were recognized in Britain in 1967, and are now accepted for showing all over the world.

Temperament
Both the Cornish and Devon Rex are affectionate and playful.

Varieties
All coat colors and patterns, apart from bicolored in Britain, are recognized for the Rex. Those cats with Siamese-type points are known as Si-Rex.

HEAD
Wedge-shaped with a long nose. The color of the nose pad should harmonize with that of the coat.

EARS
Large and slightly rounded, set high on the head.

EYES
Medium in size and oval-shaped. The color of the eyes should harmonize with that of the coat.

Curly whiskers

Brown nose pad

FACIAL CHARACTERISTICS
Chocolate Tortoiseshell Cornish Rex

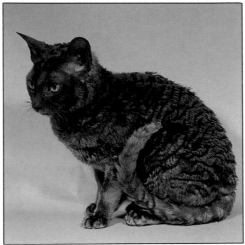

Blue Cornish Rex
The Blue's coat has a distinct sheen.

COAT
The curly fur is silky, short, and close-lying, with no guard hairs. The color should be a mixture of chocolate, red, and cream patches.

BODY
Long and slender with a naturally arched back.

TAIL
Long and slender, tapering toward the end and extremely flexible.

Fur should be particularly curly on the back and tail

Chocolate Tortoiseshell Cornish Rex
The Cornish is characterized by curly, very short, fine fur that is less coarse than the Devon. It has few, if any, guard hairs, so that its coat usually consists solely of down and awn hairs.

LEGS
Very long, straight, and slender.

Cat stands high on its legs

FEET
The paws are dainty and slightly oval. The color of the pads should harmonize with that of the coat.

Brown paw pads

HEAD
A modified wedge in shape, with full cheeks and a short nose, contributing to the cat's elfin appearance.

EARS
Very large, set low on the head, with rounded tips. They may be tufted.

EYES
Large, oval-shaped, and set wide apart. The color should harmonize with that of the coat.

Pronounced cheek bones

Pink nose pad

Curly whiskers tend to be brittle

FACIAL CHARACTERISTICS
White Devon Rex

Silver Tabby Devon Rex
Tabby markings accentuate the waves of the coat.

COAT
The fur is very short, fine, wavy, and soft, although slightly coarser than the Cornish. The color should be pure white, without any markings.

BODY
Medium in size, slender, hard and muscular.

TAIL
Long, fine, and tapering, well covered with fur.

Slender neck

White Devon Rex
The Devon has a unique "pixie" face that differentiates it from the Cornish. Its fur is also different in feel, containing all three types of hair that make up the coats of other cats. The Devon's habit of apparently wagging its tail when particularly happy has earned it the nickname "poodle cat".

Broad chest

LEGS
Long and slim.

FEET
The paws are small and oval. The color of the pads should harmonize with that of the coat.

Brown paw pads

Egyptian Mau

MAU OR MIW was the Ancient Egyptian name for the divine household cat, and of all domestic felines the Egyptian Mau is probably the most august.

EARS
Medium to large in size, set well apart, and moderately pointed.

Ear tufts

Scarab mark on forehead

EYES
Almond-shaped and pale green in color.

HEAD
A slightly rounded wedge in shape, with a short nose.

FACIAL CHARACTERISTICS
Pewter Egyptian Mau

History
Cats similar to the Egyptian Mau go far back into history, particularly in the Middle East, and it is believed that the Mau is a natural breed originating in the area of Cairo. The Mau first appeared in Europe at a cat show held in Rome in the mid-1950s, and from there was exported to the US in 1953, with initial recognition coming fifteen years later. It is not recognized in Great Britain, where Siamese-derived spotted cats formally called Maus are now known as Oriental Spotted Shorthairs.

Temperament
The Egyptian Mau is loving and playful, and is said to be good at learning tricks. It is one of the few breeds that enjoys walking on a lead.

Varieties
There are five varieties: the Silver has a silver body with black markings; the Bronze has a light brown body with dark brown markings; the Pewter has a rose-gray body with black or brown markings; the Smoke has a pale silver body with black markings; and the Black has the same coloring as the Smoke, but without the white undercoat.

Smoke Egyptian Mau
The Smoke's coat may attract thieves, so owners should be wary.

Pewter Egyptian Mau
A popular belief is that the Mau may be descended from the cat symbolized by the Ancient Egyptian gods of Ra and Bast, a theory that is given credence by the pattern on its brow that resembles the sacred scarab beetle, which is often found on the foreheads of cats depicted on Egyptian murals.

BODY
Medium in length, graceful, and muscular.

Legs are barred

COAT
The fur is fine and silky, but dense and resilient to the touch. It is medium in length and composed of hairs that bear two or more even bands of ticking. The color should be rose-gray with brown markings.

LEGS
Medium in length, in proportion to the body.

Hind legs are longer than the forelegs

FEET
The paws are small, dainty, and slightly oval.

Heavily banded tail

TAIL
Medium in length, tapering slightly.

Sphynx

A BIRTHDAY SUIT CAT! The virtually hairless Sphynx, a cat without its traditional covering of fur, is not to everyone's taste, but is an undoubted attention-grabber.

History
Hairless cats are said to have been bred by the Aztecs, and there are references to the "Mexican Hairless" in books from the turn of the century, but the modern cat was developed only after 1966 from a mutant kitten born in Ontario, Canada. It is rare outside North America.

Temperament
Contrary to popular belief, the sphynx is an affectionate cat that enjoys being cuddled.

Varieties
The Sphynx can have any recognized coat color or pattern. Eye color should harmonize with the coat.

EYES
Deep set, lemon-shaped and slanted; the color should complement the coat.

EARS
Very large and round-tipped.

HEAD
Neither round nor wedge-shaped, but slightly longer than it is wide; the nose should be short with the pad a color that conforms to the coat.

Prominent cheek bones

Absence of whiskers

FACIAL CHARACTERISTICS
Black-and-White Sphynx

Blue-and-White Sphynx
Despite the lack of fur, the Sphynx has a higher skin temperature than other breeds, and is warm and soft to the touch — earning the description of a "suede hot-water bottle" Unusually, the Sphynx is a cat that sweats, and needs to be sponged regularly to remove the dander that forms.

Black-and-White Sphynx
The modern Sphynx originated from a spontaneous mutation in the late 1960s. Similar hairless kittens have been recorded in the past, particularly during the 1930s, but were largely ignored.

LEGS
Long and slim, with a bow-legged stance caused by the barrel-shaped chest.

FEET
The paws are neat and oval-shaped, with long toes. The color of the pads should conform to that of the coat.

BODY
Medium in size, fine-boned but muscular, with a barrel chest.

COAT
Hairless, apart from a fine down on the face, ears, feet, and tail. The skin is wrinkled on parts of the head, body, and legs, but should be taut elsewhere.

TAIL
Long, hard, and tapering.

New Shorthairs

EVEN MORE SO than for longhaired cats, new Shorthairs are remarkable for what breeders have been able to achieve. They include the American Curl, which has ears that curve away from the face, the American Bobtail, which has a tail rather like a powder-puff, the California Spangled, which is spotted, and the cats featured here — the Bengal, Ocicat, and Scottish Fold.

History
Cat fanciers have always tried to push back the genetic frontiers of feline breeds, but they have probably never been so ingenious as in recent years — a trend that will no doubt continue, with the creation of ever more new cats.

Temperament
The temperaments of new Shorthairs are as diverse as their origins.

Varieties
With each new breed that comes into being, the challenge to develop new varieties is usually rapidly taken up.

EARS
Small to medium in size.

EYES
Large and round.

HEAD
Should be large in size, with a short nose.

FACIAL CHARACTERISTICS
Bengal

Bengal
An extremely expensive cat of which there are up to two hundred in the US, where it originated. It was developed by crossing the Asian leopard cat with a Tabby, in the express aim of creating a wild-looking cat that had the gentle temperament of a domestic Shorthair. The result is one of the most beguiling felines around, and must rank high on the list of breeding successes.

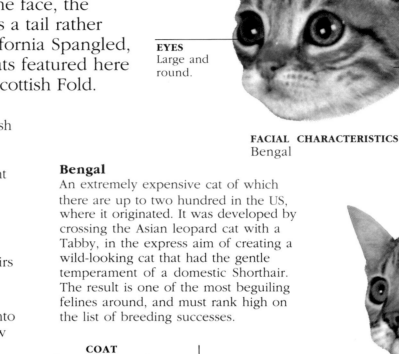

COAT
The fur is short to medium in length, silky, soft, and thick. The color should consist of dark, random or horizontally aligned, spots on a rufus ground color. "Rosettes", light spots within a darker outer circle, are accepted.

BODY
Long, sleek, and muscular.

Bengal Kitten
Although Bengal kittens are born spotted, their initially rough fur disguises the patterning for three to four months.

TAIL
Long and muscular.

LEGS
Relatively short. Hind legs are shorter than fore legs, giving a "stalking" appearance.

FEET
The paws are very large and round.

Ocicat

This American cat was the unexpected result of an attempt to produce an Aby-pointed Siamese. Its spotted coat, tabby face and resemblance to a small ocelot won instant admiration, and breeding lines were quickly established. American Shorthairs were subsequently added to the foundation breeds of the Abyssinian and Siamese to increase the number of color varieties. The Ocicat achieved championship status in 1987, and is renowned for the dog-like devotion that it forms toward its owners.

HEAD
A modified wedge in shape, with a broad muzzle and a short nose.

EARS
Moderately large in size.

EYES
Large, almond-shaped, and slightly slanted.

FACIAL CHARACTERISTICS
Ocicat

BODY
Large, well-muscled, graceful, and lithe.

TAIL
Fairly long and slim, with a slight taper.

LEGS
Medium-long, powerful, and in proportion to the body.

FEET
The paws are compact and oval, with five toes on the front paws, and four on the back.

COAT
The fur is short, glossy, fine, close-lying, and ticked with several bands of color. The dark spots should be clearly defined against the lighter background.

EARS
Should be small and neat, rounded at the tips, and set wide apart. The front of the ear should fold over to completely cover the ear opening.

EYES
Large, round, and set well apart.

FACIAL CHARACTERISTICS
Scottish Fold

Scottish Fold

If records are correct, the gene for folded ears has been present in the domestic feline population for one hundred and fifty years or so, but the modern cat arose from a mutant kitten that appeared in 1966 in Scotland, from where it was exported to the US in the early 1970s.

HEAD
Well rounded, with full cheeks, and a short, straight nose.

COAT
The fur should be short, dense, and resilient. Amost all colors and coat patterns are accepted.

LEGS
Medium in length, and fairly muscular.

FEET
The paws are neat and round.

BODY
Medium in size, rounded, and well padded.

TAIL
Medium in length, and flexible.

133

Non-pedigree Shorthairs

ALL CATS, pedigree or non-pedigree, are aristocrats, with blood lines that run back to the sacred cats of the Pharoahs — the humble mixed-breed no less than the most dignified of Grand Champions. All have their own individuality, but share the same charm, elegance, and feline mystique.

American Non-pedigree Silver Shorthair
The American domestic cat has its own, unique, attraction.

History
Shorthaired cats have graced human society for thousands of years, and were differentiated from pedigree types only in the late nineteenth century, when the best examples of British and American street cats were selectively bred for showing.

Temperament
Mixed-breed cats are the original fireside companions, chosen not for their venerable parentage, but because they are appealing and lovable in their own right. In a receptive household, all make firm and lasting friendships.

Varieties
"Varieties" are dependent only on the ingenuity and resourcefulness of mother nature.

Faint tabby markings

BODY
Strong and muscular.

Although the patching is uneven, and there are obvious tabby markings, the contented dignity of this Ginger-and-White quells any notion of its being a poor relation to its pedigree counterpart.

LEGS
Short and well-proportioned.

FEET
The paws are large and round.

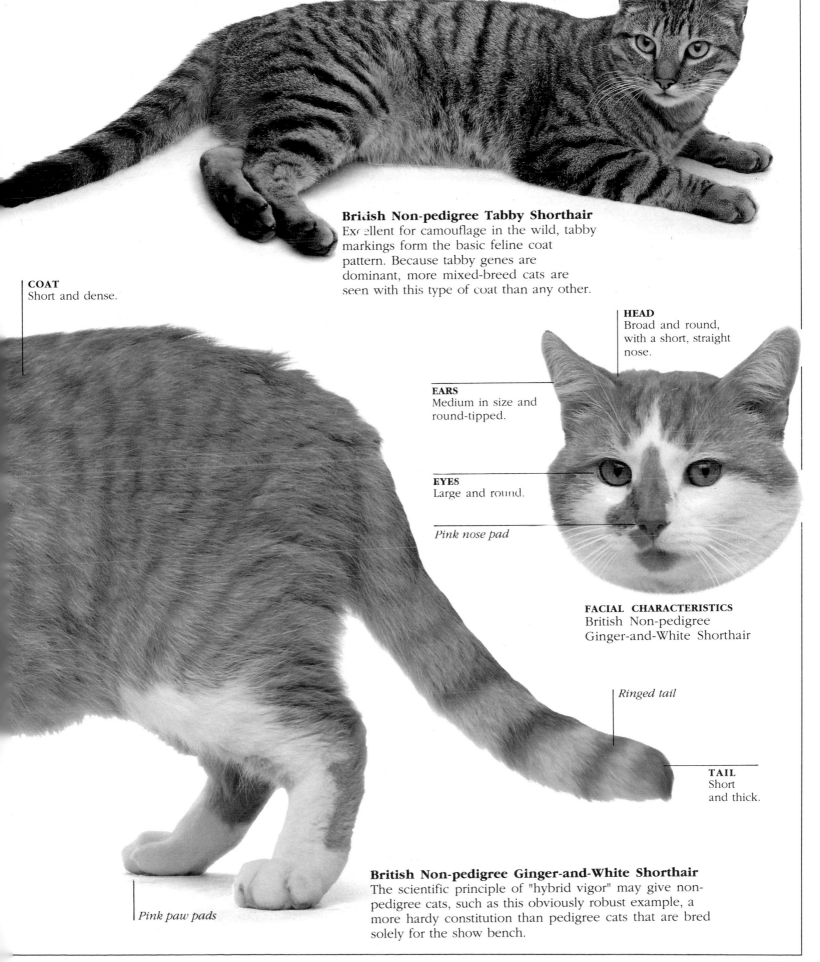

British Non-pedigree Tabby Shorthair
Excellent for camouflage in the wild, tabby markings form the basic feline coat pattern. Because tabby genes are dominant, more mixed-breed cats are seen with this type of coat than any other.

COAT
Short and dense.

HEAD
Broad and round, with a short, straight nose.

EARS
Medium in size and round-tipped.

EYES
Large and round.

Pink nose pad

FACIAL CHARACTERISTICS
British Non-pedigree Ginger-and-White Shorthair

Ringed tail

TAIL
Short and thick.

Pink paw pads

British Non-pedigree Ginger-and-White Shorthair
The scientific principle of "hybrid vigor" may give non-pedigree cats, such as this obviously robust example, a more hardy constitution than pedigree cats that are bred solely for the show bench.

Keeping a Cat

It may happen that a cat chooses to come and live with you. That is how it has been for me on a number of occasions. It begins with trial visits in the style of a good food guide inspector; your establishment, the cat's possible future home, is given the once-over — more than once usually! And, in the manner of a food inspector, close attention is paid by Mister or Ms Felix (without, of course, announcing its identity) to the quality and ready availability of meals, but also, and very importantly, to the warmth of the reception given and the comfort of the place. If you are "picked" in this way by a cat, and are not one of that bizarre minority of folk who inexplicably count themselves to be ailurophobes, without a scrap of feeling for felines in their souls, you've got your cat, or rather your cat's got you.

People decide for a variety of reasons that they want to acquire a cat. It may be for companionship, (almost never for rodent control), or, most often, because cats are great to have around. What other domestic animal combines sophistication with friendship, while being able to warm your lap, deter mice, grace any room and give early warning of impending earthquakes? All provided at a highly economical running cost.

Your New Cat

There's more to deciding to share your home with a cat than simply looking up the local breeders in the telephone book. Are you fit to be a cat companion?.

Questions to ask include: what other animals live in the house and how might they interact with a new arrival? Will the cat have to be permanently confined indoors because you live in a one-room high-rise apartment? If the cat is to be allowed outdoors, can arrangements be made to have a cat-flap fitted to a door or window? Have you the time and patience to give certain kinds of cat the grooming they regularly require? What arrangements can you make for the pet's welfare during your vacations? Can you afford the basic equipment needed, daily supplies of high-quality cat food and the cost of both preventive medicine and any unexpected course of medical treatment?

What kind of cat?
Careful thought and preparation must precede the acquisition of a cat. You must first decide what kind of cat would be mutually suitable. If you are planning to show and/or breed cats, obviously only a pedigree animal will fit the bill. But if you simply want a cat friend, a cat-about-the-house, there are the humane society clinics and reception centers stuffed with abandoned, unwanted cats — most of them on Death Row with dates of execution set if they are not given a good home by that time. Should you be new to cats, don't get the idea that there's such a thing as a "best" cat. All cats are individuals. All are aristocrats.

Now, more decisions to be made. Do you prefer a kitten or an adult cat? Kittens, like kids, have their problem periods as they grow up. Are you able and prepared to cope? Tom or queen? Entire toms *can* make marvelous companions, but they remain essentially a mixture of Arnold Schwarzenegger and Don Juan — regularly off to war or obsessed with the latest amorous encounter. And some toms do leave their strong characteristic odors around, marking your house as their territory or attracting rival males to leave droplets of smelly urine on the doorstep. Queens, of course, tend to bring forth kittens with monotonous regularity, and crossbred kittens are not easy to find homes for. Again, are you prepared for all this?

Happiness to three kittens is a paper basket.

1 When choosing a kitten you must check it thoroughly to ensure it is in good condition. Part the hair to look for signs of parasites, particularly the fine "coal dust" that indicates the presence of fleas.

2 You should also inspect the ears carefully. Ensure that there are no discharges and that the ears do not contain dirt that may indicate infection or parasites.

3 The eyes should be bright, clear, and free from discharges.

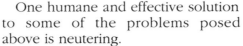

One humane and effective solution to some of the problems posed above is neutering.

Choices must also be carefully made, and not purely on grounds of esthetics if you want a pedigree cat. Persians need regular grooming and will take far more of your time than do shorthaired breeds. Russian Blues or Persians generally make better indoor cats than most shorthaired breeds. By contrast, Abyssinians and Somalis adore their freedom and aren't suited to life in an apartment. Some, like the Siamese, demand lots of attention and fuss. A few, such as the Sphynx, need special care and handling. All pedigree cats, particularly the more glamorous breeds, can attract the attention of cat thieves.

Buying a cat

When choosing your cat, pedigree or crossbred, it is best to avoid pet stores. Deal instead with a recommended breeder, a humane society, a friend or neighbor. How do you pick the right cat or kitten? Some folk believe that the cat of your life might be found in the stars. If you know the date of a particular animal's birth, there are astrologers willing to draw up its personal horoscope. By matching it up with your own, they say, you can increase the chances of a perfect relationship. For example Virgo cats (24th August to 23rd September) are predicted to be excellent, conscientious, dedicated, down-to-earth cats especially suited to Capricorn and Taurus owners.

For most of us, more mundane considerations must influence our selection. In essence the difficulties about choosing one's cat are similar to those involved in buying a second-hand car. How do you spot the faults? Is it really in good running order? Although it is unlikely to be an expensive mistake if you acquire a

4 It is important to look at the mouth for evidence of plaque build-up, sore, inflamed gums and abnormal teeth. Hold the kitten's head from behind as shown here and gently prise open the mouth.

5 Beneath the tail should be clean and dry; free from evidence of diarrhea or urine scalding.

6 The cat should be alert and interested, show no evidence of pain when handled and react amicably when picked up. Remember to be gentle when picking up a young kitten as its ribcage is delicate and can be easily hurt.

crossbred cat with, metaphorically speaking, its gear-box full of sawdust or its mileage clock wound back, if you are buying pedigree stock you *must* get expert advice before parting with large sums of money for potential show champions.

For all cats, pedigree or not, the following list of points should be checked by the prospective owner. Just as if you were buying a gleaming new car, do not meekly accept the salesman's word, but look at the cat's condition and state of health carefully and critically. Any responsible vendor will not object to your making a thorough examination of a prospective new pet. If all is well, buy the cat – if possible on approval – and then have the animal overhauled by the veterinarian as soon as possible. *Never* buy a cat from a back-street pet store or from a "cat farm", as young cats are very susceptible to disease and infection, and these can spread easily. It is *never* sensible to buy a kitten younger than ten weeks old.

A cat should:

• Be alert and interested in its surroundings.

• Move around readily with its head held straight.

• Spring to the ground easily from table height.

• Have clear, bright eyes without any white film (the "haw") showing.

• Have clean ears, mouth, and nose without discharges.

• Have clean white teeth without accumulations of tartar, and salmon-pink gums and tongue.

• Have a smooth, clean skin, with sleek fur composed of a full bushy undercoat and a glossy topcoat.

A cat should not:

• Suffer from diarrhea.

• Sneeze, cough or wheeze.

• Appear to be in pain when touched or handled.

• Show any trace of blood.

• Have any holes, breaks, or blemishes in its coat.

Choosing a pedigree animal demands more than just fitness checks. The quality, points, and prize-winning potential of any individual can only be gauged by an expert eye. You should therefore take along somebody who is knowledgeable about the breed you want to buy, and who knows what you are hoping for in the cat.

Pedigrees are expensive but, if you can't quite afford the full price, you may be able to obtain a "bargain" by buying a pet-quality cat, or by making a breeding agreement. "Pet-quality" cats are ones that do not reach the standards required for showing, but that nevertheless make perfectly good pets. Under a breeding agreement, you buy a show-quality cat, and return it to the breeder at pre-arranged times for breeding. You must agree who will own any subsequent kittens, and put whatever is agreed in writing.

All pedigree animals should be registered under an individual name, with details of their color and parentage, when they are about five weeks old. Unless this is done, they won't be permitted to enter a cat show in a pedigree class.

When selecting a cat always look for one that is playful, alert, and willing to be handled. With kittens, go for the bolder, quick-to-come-forward individual, rather than the most retiring one, as it may be a weaker or more sickly specimen.

Check that a kitten has been vaccinated against Feline Enteritis and Feline Influenza at least one week

After a few moments of uncertainty a firm friendship is in the making. Such introductions will almost always be successful but require careful "refereeing" by the owner.

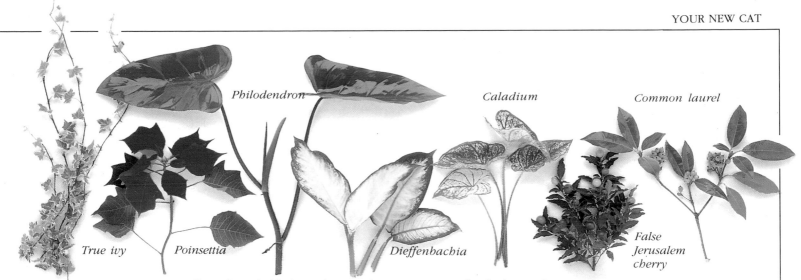

Philodendron

Caladium

Common laurel

True ivy

Poinsettia

Dieffenbachia

False Jerusalem cherry

Some household plants that are dangerous to cats (and other pets).

before purchase, and that adults were vaccinated as youngsters and regularly boosted thereafter. Vaccination certificates signed by a veterinarian should be provided as proof. If you have other cats and are anxious to keep them free from Feline Leukemia, ask a vet to carry out a simple blood test on the new animal and to provide a certificate stating that the test result was negative.

The new arrival

Only when you have prepared yourself, by obtaining all the basic equipment, should you bring a new cat to your home. Transport your cat in a proper carrying container. These come in various designs and materials – stout cardboard ones can be purchased cheaply from pet stores, humane societies, and veterinarians.

If you are obtaining an adult cat from a friend, try to bring with it some familiar piece of cat furniture such as its bed or litter tray. Once at your house, allow the cat to explore thoroughly on its own, introducing it to one room at a time without interference from children or other pets. Keep other animals away until the new arrival has had a chance to roam around the place. Then, allow the "resident" animals into a room where you are holding the latest addition to the family. Supervise the initial encounters carefully and give both sides equal amounts of affection and attention. There is bound to be some antipathy between the animals as cats are so territorial; this may last hours or weeks, but it will gradually fade to become a reasonable

Hazards

The average house is full of potential hazards for cats and you should think carefully about the risks before the pet's arrival.

House plants should be of non-poisonous varieties. Don't allow access to the following species, particularly if your cat is prone to nibble plants:

Tree lovers
(*Philodendron* spp.)

Dumb canes
(*Dieffenbachia* spp.)

True ivies
(*Hedera* spp.)

Elephant's ears
(*Caladium* spp.)

Poinsettia
(*Euphorbia pulcherrima*)

False Jerusalem cherry
(*Solanum capiscastrum*)

Oleander spp.

Rhododendrons and Azaleas
(*Rhododendron* spp.)

Common or cherry laurel
(*Prunus laurocerasus*)

Misteltoe

- Keep cats away from hot ovens, boiling liquids, and fires. Use a safety guard around an open fire.
- Keep washing machine, refrigerator, freezer, and oven doors shut.
- Ensure that garbage cans are inaccessible to cats.
- Don't let your cat chew electric cables and disconnect power when not in use.
- Place valued objects such as fragile ornaments out of the cat's reach – remember how they love exploring shelving.
- Don't leave sharp kitchen utensils out.
- Don't leave toxic household products in accessible places; beware of antifreeze-contaminated puddles of water in the garage.
- Don't leave plastic bags out; if a cat climbs inside it may suffocate.
- Don't leave small objects where your cat may chew and swallow them.
- Don't put a hot electrical iron where a cat could knock it over.
- Don't allow cats onto a high balcony or windowsill.

accommodation on both sides and generally a good friendship. Kittens are accepted more readily than adult cats by other pets.

The first week

Spoil and fuss over the cat during its first week with you, and be ready to play with it. Find out from the previous owner what its feeding routine and particular dietary fancies are and try to oblige them. Keep it indoors for about one week, and make sure you accompany the animal when you allow it to make its first outdoor exploration. *Never* allow a newly arrived cat, even if it is an adult, to stay out at night.

Basic Equipment

Cats are not expensive to house, but they must be provided with certain items of basic equipment, such as somewhere to sleep, a litter tray, feeding and drinking bowls, a collar, a carrying box and basic grooming equipment. Useful, but not essential, extras are items such as a scratching pad or post, a cat flap (if your cat is able to go outside), a playpen and some toys.

Cat flap and playpen
A cat flap should be fitted no higher than 6cm (two or three inches) from the base of the door or windowsill. All flaps should be lockable. Some have magnetic strips along the sides which help avoid drafts, by creating a tight seal.

A playpen is useful for kittens until they are acclimatized to their new home.

Toys
You can buy these from pet stores, or simply supply things like empty thread reels which give endless enjoyment. Avoid soft rubber toys; they can cause choking and other problems.

Litter tray
Cats are clean animals and toilet training is relatively simple.

Grooming equipment
As well as a brush and combs, such as those shown here, you will need nail clippers (see page 153).

Collar and walking lead
Cats should at all times wear collars with address tags and an elasticated insert which stops the cat choking if it is snagged. If your cat is willing to walk on a lead, an adjustable harness is preferable to a collar. Choose a lightweight lead.

Scratching pad or post
These are particularly useful for indoor cats.

Feeding and water bowl

Each cat should have its own dishes. They must always be kept clean and separate from the household crockery.

Carrying basket or box

Cat bed

Beds can be purchased in a wide variety of designs, from traditional wicker baskets, to bean-bag types, to cat igloos made out of plastic, to the good old cardboard box lined with newspaper.

Diet

The cat is a creature built to eat meat. This is not to say that cats do not like or need some vegetable matter in their diet. Among wild species, the flat-headed cat of Malaysia and Indonesia has a particular love of fruit and sweet potatoes.

Although proteins play important roles in a cat's diet, particularly at certain times of life, a purely protein diet for a cat would be unnecessarily expensive and wasteful. There are also health aspects. Proteins produce many waste products after digestion, and these have to be eliminated by the kidneys, organs which may be under great pressure in older animals. A luxurious menu consisting of nothing but raw *filet de boeuf,* contains far too little calcium and vitamins for healthy feline living.

Variety, then, is the watchword for your familiar's diet,

is freshness. Do not give him stale food or food you bought because it was cheap but which may have been on the store shelf so long that it has lost its nutritional value.

Proteins

As mentioned above, protein is one of the essential parts of a cat's diet and should form at least 25 per cent of the diet of an adult cat, or 35 to 40 per cent of a kitten's. The daily requirement of an adult cat is 3 grams (1/8 ounce) of protein per 450 grams (1 pound) bodyweight, and for a kitten this should be increased to 8.5

found in the protein foods mentioned above, but can be specially augmented by adding one teaspoonful of fat to the food of older animals which no longer absorb nutrients very well, and have lost their layers of insulating fat. The best sources of high-quality fat are soft animal fat (chicken fat or bacon grease), butter, and lard.

Filler foods

Cats also often get their energy in the form of filler foods such as carbohydrates, bulk and fiber. These are not essential but can be included to make up to half of the ration if desired. Filler foods include fruit and vegetables, and starchy foods such as bread, pasta, and cereals.

Minerals and vitamins

Minerals of all kinds are essential for a cat's growth and the maintenance of its vital functions. If you feed your cat a well-balanced, varied diet, mineral deficiencies are most unlikely to occur. The same is true with regard to the vitamins, and special vitamin supplements are not normally necessary for the healthy cat unless recommended by the veterinarian. The cat does not have the same need as a human of vitamins B12, C, and K in its diet.

Accustom your kitten to a varied diet.

and will enable a cat to balance its diet instinctively. Accustom a kitten to a broad selection of foods. Even if you inherit an old animal that is set in its ways and seems determined to fast until death unless fed on nothing but shrimp or caviar, there is a fair chance that a bit of culinary effort will succeed in enticing him out of his monotonous diet.

When acting as chef to a newly arrived puss, introduce your carefully considered diet gradually. Change him from the old menu to the new bit by bit over a period of a couple of weeks or so.

Besides variety, the other important factor in feeding your cat

grams (1/4 ounce). Protein foods include the pre-packed special cat foods you can buy, and fresh foods such as meat, poultry, fish, eggs, milk, and cheese.

Fats

In addition to proteins, your cat needs fats as an important source of calories, particularly as the animal gets older. Fats should form 15 to 40 per cent of the ration, and they have the advantage that they do not load the kidneys with waste products. It is essential to avoid feeding fats that are old or rancid, as although a hungry cat may accept such foods, they can make it ill. Fats are usually

Water

As long as fresh, clean water is always available, worry not about how much of the stuff your feline friend is drinking, unless you have settled for the lazy man's diet of nothing but food pellets. It is well known that animals can survive perfectly well on a diet of fish and beef without ever drinking water. A meat diet has a high water content, and the cat's kidney is capable of concentrating the urine and thereby saving water; about two-and-a-half times more

A double feeding bowl for water and food. Cats should always have water available.

than the human kidney. Of course, outdoor cats may be tippling at a favorite puddle.

If your cat really does seem to do without H$_2$O, there is no cause for concern — it is quite a common phenomenon. As well as the water in the food itself, all creatures get a large proportion of their daily water requirements by chemical action — the fats and carbohydrates in their food are "burned" within their bodies, producing water molecules. Cleverly, cats also lose very little water through panting or sweating, and only an insignificant quantity evaporates during breathing. Even big wild cats like lions have been

known to go without a drink for up to ten days. Nevertheless, a supply of fresh, clean water must be made available at all times for your cat.

We should perhaps pause at this point to doff our hats in memory of one Jack, a black tom living in Brooklyn, which in 1937 at the age of three, gave up water-drinking for milk laced with Pernod. As he grew older he demanded stiffer and stiffer saucers of "milk", until it was a question of lacing the Pernod lightly with milk. Jack gave up the ghost in the bar where he lived when he was eight years old. At the post-mortem his liver was found to be in a distinctly sad state.

Seasoning and supplements

Most cats are discerning and prefer intelligent seasoning of their food. I have had cats who adored curried chicken and spaghetti with clam sauce — very civilized and utterly beneficial. If you are cooking some of your pet's meals, season with iodized salt to taste (your taste). Enough iodine, which is a trace element, can be assured in this way.

yeast tablets

mineral/vitamin powder

cat "candies" containing vitamins

fortified milk-food powder

Extra vitamins and minerals may be given to your cat.

It is particularly important in pregnant queens where iodine is needed to prevent resorption of the fetuses within the womb. Bouillon cubes make a gravy containing all essential salts.

If you are using proprietary dry or soft-moist food, remember that these products tend to be low in fat content. Add eight teaspoonfuls of fat, butter, or lard per 500 grams (1 pound).

MYTHS AND FALLACIES

Eating grass

Having labored like Escoffier over your friend, do not be alarmed if he or she still insists on chewing grass and weeds at the first opportunity. Grass is good for cats. It contains certain vitamins and also acts as an efficient emetic, helping the animal regurgitate unwanted matter such as fur balls. If you and your cat share a high-rise apartment without ready access to a garden, grow him some grass from seed in a window box. Chewing grass is not a sign that the cat feels ill.

Mousing

Cats hunt mice, birds, insects, and so on for sport, not as a food source. True, they may on occasion eat part or all of their prey, but

Contrary to popular myth, eating grass is a normal occurrence.

basically they are in it for the fun of the game. So you need not think that by underfeeding, or indeed not feeding your cat, he will be encouraged to clear your premises of small rodents. The opposite is true. Well-fed cats are the best mousers. They have the stamina, energy, and quick reactions required for the sport.

Flies

"Cats that catch flies and eat them go thin" is a very common saying. Although there is the possibility that a cat eating a blue-bottle might also take in disease bacteria, the problem is a minute one. Occasionally worm eggs might be carried by flies from one cat to another, but other than this slight risk, fly-eating cats rarely come to much harm.

How much to feed

Scientists have calculated that the daily requirements of a cat on a diet containing 25 per cent protein is 1/2 ounce (15 grams) of food per 1 pound (450 grams) of bodyweight, but this is a theoretical guide only. In practice, like their human companions, cats vary widely in appetite. The ancient Greeks believed that cats put on weight as the moon waxed and lost weight as it waned. In my opinion, obesity does not generally lead to the health problems for cats that it does for dogs. Show cats may need to have their outlines watched, but the fireside feline is a different case and my advice is to feed him up.

The following is a rough guide to daily food quantities for kittens and cats of different ages:

Planning your cat's meals

Age	Meals per day	Amount in ounces
Weaning to 3 months	4-6	2-3
4 to 5 months	4-6	10
6 to 7 months	3-4	13
7-8 months	3	13
9 months and over	2-3	14
Pregnant Queens	3-5	15-16
Senior citizens	3-6	11-13

Fresh food and water are a must for cats, whose noses are as sensitive as that of a good food inspector. Cats will stalk away from the first hint of staleness. Giving fresh food frequently is the best way to avoid waste and the risk of tummy upsets.

Under abnormal circumstances, cats can go without food for weeks and lose 40 per cent of their bodyweight without dying, although if they lose 10 to 15 per cent of the total water in their bodies that is usually fatal.

THE MAJOR FOODS

So many different foods are available that the suitable combinations are numberless. I shall therefore deal only with the main kinds.

Canned food

These products consist of meat and/or fish, salts, jelling agents, vitamins, coloring chemicals, preservatives, sugar, water, and sometimes cereals. The advantages of canned food are that it is very nutritious. Its disadvantage is that it is relatively expensive.

Canned food is popular and nourishing. It is also practical, stores well and is sterile. The brands available today cater to finicky cats — and their owners.

To all cats, water is both an essential and fascinating element.

A well-thought-out diet is welcomed.

You are buying a fair quantity of water, particularly where the "jelly" is much in evidence. Also, the canning and storage time may result in a drastic reduction of the vitamin level, particularly heat-unstable vitamins such as vitamin B.

Soft-moist products

These look good, taste not quite so good and contain meat, soya bean, fats, vitamins, preservatives, coloring chemicals and often thickening agents and sugar.
Advantages: Like canned foods, they are usually very nutritious and can make up a large proportion of the diet; you are buying less hidden water than is often the case with canned food, and they can be stored reasonably well.
Disadvantages: They are expensive, do not store as well as canned or dry foods, and are generally too low in fat

Soft-moist products are nutritious but low in fat.

Dry food

These mini-biscuits contain cereals, fish, meat, yeast, vitamins, fats, and coloring agents. *Advantages:* Many kinds are fairly well balanced, they are cheaper and contain less water than canned or soft-moist food, store well and are pleasant to handle. They combat tartar. *Disadvantages:* They are frequently much too low in fat content for cats and if fed as the only food have been suspected of causing bladder problems and difficulty in passing urine. Their low water content, with the salt analysis of some brands, may produce "sludge" in the cat's urine, which can block up the animal's

Most cats like these mini-biscuits.

Fresh food, a little and often, is best.

waterworks. Where much dry food is fed, adequate fresh water must be available at all times and, best of all, the pellets may be moistened with gravy, milk, or water. Use dry foods sparingly if at all for cats with a history of urinary troubles. Probably the best rule is to give some dry food to all cats but as part of a varied menu.

Meat

This may be beef, lamb, or pig. Except for pork, which *must* be cooked, it is good to give ground raw meat occasionally. Get it from the butchers, not from the meat yard where it is likely to be cheap but teeming with bacteria. Cooked meats should be baked or broiled rather than boiled, to retain nutrients and tasty juices. If meat is boiled, however, the water should be seasoned and used as a gravy on some drier foods. Variety meats (lungs, tripe, udder, etc.) should always be cooked. All cooked meat should be cut into small cubes.

Poultry

Scraps of cooked birds left over from the family table provide good pickings for puss. Few humans pick a chicken clean of such parts as the kidneys or parson's nose, which are greatly prized by cats. Most bird bones are very splintery and should on no account be fed to your pet.

The same holds true for rabbit as for poultry.

Eggs

Eggs are a good source of protein, but are better fed cooked and chopped rather than raw. Egg white should never be fed raw, since it contains a chemical which neutralizes an essential B vitamin. A total of two eggs per week is the maximum for a cat. Separated egg yolks can be given more often if you wish.

Milk

Not all cats like milk. If yours does not drink milk, why worry? Water is always necessary for cats, but milk is not. Some cats cannot digest the milk sugar (lactose) in cow's milk and get diarrhea after drinking it.

Cheese

This is an excellent source of protein, either raw, in which case it should be grated or cubed, or cooked with some other item.

Fish

Fresh fish, chopped and boned if from a species larger than a herring, is admirable up to once or twice a week. In Britain fish is often fed raw, but in America it is generally cooked. Cooked fish is better steamed or baked rather than boiled, again to retain maximum nutrients. Canned fish such as sardines can be given whether in oil or tomato sauce. The oil has a beneficial effect on the bowels and helps to dispel stomach fur balls that sometimes accumulate particularly in longhaired cats. Diets composed of nothing but fish are unbalanced and tend eventually to produce problems as the cat grows older. However, it is not true to say, as some books do and as folklore sometimes has it, that too much fish releases poisons or causes the disease named "fish eczema."

Vegetables

Boiled potato can be added to meat or fish, forming up to about one-third of a meal. Start a cat early on such things as cooked greens, boiled young spinach, scraped raw carrot, peas, etc.

Starchy foods

Crumbled, toasted bread can be used like potato and mixed with gravy or fish stock, as can pasta such as macaroni, spaghetti, or noodles. Cereals can also be fed to cats. Cornflakes, wheat flakes, porridge or baby cereal can all be used with milk, particularly for the first meal of the day and for kittens.

Fruit

If your cat fancies the occasional segment of tangerine or slice of apple (and it is surprising how many do — particularly Siamese), good for it! It is thought, incidentally, that seventy-five per cent of all cats are partial to the odd sweet grape.

Every cat should have its own dish.

A Cat in the House

Handling your cat

While it is a good thing to handle your pet, remember always to support the full body. Don't just let it dangle from its "armpits" as the cat will resent this, and may possibly struggle or even bite.

The beginning of a beautiful life-long friendship. It is important that children learn the proper handling of family pets as early as possible.

Pick an adult cat up by putting one hand under the chest just behind the front paws, and the other under the "bottom", tucking the tail in. Once up, let it sit in the crook of your arm with its forepaws on your shoulder or held in your other hand.

Kittens should be handled especially carefully, as their rib cages are very soft and they can easily bruise internally if roughly treated.

Although queens pick up and carry kittens by the scruff of their necks, you should avoid doing this except for brief periods when grabbing cats that may be uncooperative or agitated. Scruffing a cat by taking firm hold of the loose skin at the back of the neck doesn't hurt the animal, but it is a rather undignified procedure. Where a cat has had an injury to its body, particularly a fracture, "scruffing" is allowable.

Kittens quickly learn how to use their litter trays. Have them in place by the time the kittens reach three or four weeks of age.

House training

Cats are neat and nimble, and housing them indoors doesn't present the problems associated with dogs. They can, where necessary, be kept permanently indoors and will happily adopt as their territory even the smallest apartment. Some breeds are particularly suited to this cloistered life. Earlier I mentioned the basic equipment needed to keep a cat healthy and happy. Sanitation arrangements and coping with scratching are the two principal items that need to be given further special attention.

It is important to spend some time, particularly with younger cats, in teaching them how to behave. The earlier your begin, the better. When kittens first start to eat solid food at three to four weeks of age, toilet training should be introduced. Place the litter tray in a convenient, easily reached, but quiet spot and, as soon as the animal looks like urinating or defecating (easily spotted as they crouch, tail raised and with a certain faraway look in their eyes), pop them on it. Never rub a kitten's nose in any "mess" that it makes.

Felines are clean and train quickly. Very old cats may become forgetful or lose control on occasion. Bear with them.

A litter tray should be made of metal or plastic and be large enough for the cat to stand in. It should be lined with newspaper and then covered with a 1 1/2 inch (4 centimeters) deep layer of peat moss or proprietary cat litter. Ashes can be used, though they are rather dusty. Sawdust is messy when dry and quickly becomes soggy and smelly when wet. Remove the soiled litter

daily and clean and disinfect the tray weekly, using any household disinfectant except those containing phenol, carbolic acid or any coal-tar chemicals; these can poison cats by absorption through the skin. Rinse a disinfected tray thoroughly.

Cat flaps

To train a cat to use a flap, begin by fastening the flap open and allowing the cat to familiarize itself with the hole. Then, use bits of food to entice your pet through the flap, helping to push it open. It will learn quickly.

Cat flaps are easily fitted to doors and the intelligent cat soon learns the knack of using its "private door".

Obedience

All cats should be taught to recognize their own name. Use it regularly, particularly at feeding times. Make a point of having regular set times for feeding, grooming, etc. Cats can be trained to do little tricks like begging for food but this can only be achieved by kindness and reward in the form of tidbits of favorite food, and always depends on the animal being in the right mood. You can't force cats to do anything against their wills. Nevertheless, it is possible to dissuade them from undesirable habits like biting or jumping on people. From the earliest age, firmly but gently pick up the cat, place it on the floor and say "No." Some anti-social behavior will be reduced if the cat can be allowed out of doors or given a scratching pad.

Scratching

Scratching is, in more ways than one, a very touchy subject, particularly if your cat has no eye for interior decoration and takes it out on your Louis Quinze escritoire or the sofa that was your mother-in-law's wedding present. The answer is to provide a substitute scratching object of the right texture to give the cat the most satisfactory "feel." A log complete with bark, a vertical post on a stand wrapped in coarse sacking, or one of the compressed blocks of corrugated paper sold in pet shops will do. Cats have to be trained to use these devices. At the first sign of Puss contemplating the furniture, grab him and take him to the official scratching point. With a little patience he will get the message.

Surgical removal of a cat's claws under anesthetic by a veterinarian is

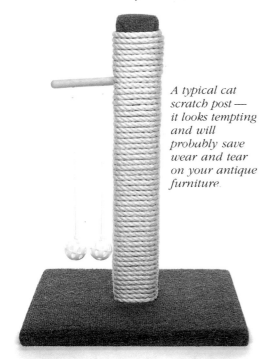

A typical cat scratch post — it looks tempting and will probably save wear and tear on your antique furniture.

possible, but such mutilations for furniture's sake are indefensible and illegal in countries such as Britain.

Sleeping arrangements

A special bed in a box or basket can be provided if you wish, but it is not absolutely essential. Most cats pick their sleeping places around the house quite independently. Young kittens should, however, be given a box (a simple cardboard one will do) in which they can sleep snug, draft-free and out of harm's way. A lining of newspaper covered by a piece of blanket that is changed regularly should be placed inside. To avoid contamination, never feed a kitten in its sleeping box.

Why don't I believe in having my cats sleeping with me? Cats, like any animals that live close to the ground, sniff each others' backsides, investigate drains and can be too intimate with germ carrying rodents. They are more likely to transmit infections to humans if draped across the pillow eight hours out of every twenty-four. There may be a risk of suffocation of a very small baby if a cat is allowed into the room in which the infant is sleeping.

Leaving your cat

A cat can be left alone in a house or apartment for as long as twenty-four hours provided that adequate food, water and litter are left. If you are likely to be away from your home for longer than a day, arrange for a neighbor to call in regularly (once every twenty-four hours at least) to replenish food and water and empty the tray. Neighbors are preferable to catteries — there is less risk of your pet picking up disease, and the animal is not wrenched away from familiar surroundings.

Exercise

Luckily for some of us, cats don't need active exercising by their owners, although it seems likely exercise is beneficial to the health.

Kittens exercise themselves in play

and will get endless pleasure and activity out of a ping-pong ball to chase around or a cardboard box to jump in and out of. For the permanently house-bound adult cat, a climbing frame and scratching post should be provided. As I pointed out earlier, if you live in a high-rise apartment or near heavy traffic, your cat is best kept indoors at all times. Restless breeds that need to spend more time outside (Rex, Somali, Abyssinian) should be avoided for such dwellings. Although even adult indoor cats usually keep themselves fit by stretching and playing by themselves, it is a good idea, and fun, to play with your cat.

Taking cats for walks on leads isn't as easy as taking dogs. Some cats object and they must never be forced to walk farther than they choose. Training a cat to a lead should begin early with a newly weaned kitten. Walks should at first be in the house, later in the garden and then, if things go well there, finally on the sidewalk. A long, thin, leather or, better, cord lead should be used for cats. Breeds that are more amenable to lead-training than others are Siamese, Burmese, Russian Blue, Foreign White, Foreign Black, Foreign Blue and Foreign Smoke.

Only some cats are amenable to being taken for walks on a lead.

The Traveling Cat

Moving

Moving does not normally trouble the family cat. It usually retains its well-loved human companions and usually many items of furniture that it knows well. After arriving at the new dwelling, the cat quickly sets about establishing its territory and leaves its calling cards with the feline patriarchs of the area.

Occasionally, longing for some old flame left behind, or preferring the surroundings in which it grew up, a cat may decide to trek back to its old haunts. The longest recorded journey is nine hundred and fifty miles from Boston to Chicago! Cats cannot find people if they up and move leaving the animal behind, but they do have the ability to locate places. It seems that, during the months or years that a cat lives in its old home, its brains automatically register the position of the house in terms of angles of the sun at certain times of day. Cats, like man and many other animals, are fitted with internal biological "clocks." If the cat is uprooted to a new home where the sun's angle at a particular hour is slightly different, and it wants to put it "right," it works by trial and error, moving in one direction and then the other in order to "improve" the angle. All of this computation is done subconsciously. Even when the sun is obscured by cloud, the cat can probably locate it by means of rays of polarized light. There may also be, as in birds, a biological compass built into the feline skull, which helps it to navigate. All of which means that cats have an uncanny sense of direction.

Two designs of cat carriers for routine journeys. Although cosier, the wicker basket is not as easy to clean and disinfect as the plastic-covered wire model.

When the cat reaches the vicinity of its old house, it completes its journey by noting familiar sites, sounds and smells.

Carriers

Every cat owner should have a cat carrier. For short journeys, to visit the vet for example, one of the disposable cardboard carriers that you can buy from veterinarians, humane societies or pet stores, is suitable. For longer journeys a more substantial container is necessary. This must be escape-proof, well ventilated and easy to clean. Although the wicker basket form is very popular, it is not always secure enough and is difficult to clean and disinfect thoroughly. A vinyl, polyethylene or fiberglass carrier is preferable. In cold weather the carrier should be lined with a blanket or a special fur fabric insulator. A thin blanket is sufficient for warm weather. In hot conditions a damp towel should be placed over the carrier (without obstructing the ventilation holes) to keep the temperature inside from rising.

When first introducing your cat to its carrier, do so in a closed room. Cats don't generally like carriers and the journeys associated with them, and some protest vigorously at being boxed up. Make sure that the cat uses its litter tray before being placed in the carrier.

Unless your cat is one of the very few that are accustomed to car travel and will lie peacefully on the back seat, take no chances and confine it to a carrier when going anywhere. If the journey lasts more than half-an-hour, stop regularly to allow your cat to use its litter tray and have food and drink. Do all this inside the car with doors and windows closed to avoid an escape.

In hot weather you should not leave a cat (or any other animal) for long periods in a closed car. Hyperthermia (over-heating), which may end fatally, can occur remarkably rapidly, particularly in an excited and apprehensive animal, which most are when enclosed.

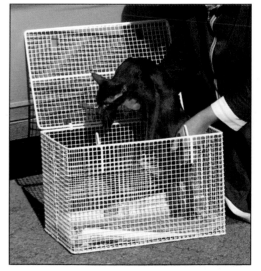

Before taking your cat on a journey, it is a good idea to let it try out its carrier.

This is an average cattery. The indoor accommodation is snug and dry and is provided with an individual run. The general design with plenty of fresh air is better than totally enclosed layouts, but the spread of diseases could still occur easily. I prefer a double gate with secure locking devices to prevent accidental escapes when people enter and leave the cats' quarters. Two cats from the same home can usually share accommodation. Always visit and inspect any cattery before booking your pet in for a stay.

You should always make sure a window is partially open if a cat is left in a car on a summer's day for even the shortest period of time.

Tranquilizers or sedatives can be given to cats that are upset by traveling, as can other drugs for those affected by motion sickness, though try to avoid using them. Seek the advice of your veterinarian if you have a cat that absolutely hates transportation.

Air travel
Taking a cat to another country needs careful planning. The most important factors are the regulations governing importation of animals that are in force in the country of destination. Check with your travel agent, shipping agent (if involved), airline freight company and, most important of all, the consulate of the country you are going to, regarding any quarantine, health certificate rules and transportation conditions.

Air travel is the most common form of animal transport on international journeys, and its speed makes it ideal for long distances. You must use a cat container that is approved by the International Air Transport Association (IATA). There are rules to ensure that cat carriers are strong enough, and properly ventilated and marked, etc. Most airlines won't accept animals unless the IATA regulations are met and some have their own rules in addition, so check the full details with the airline well before the flight.

Before taking your cat to the airport you should:

• Give the animal a light meal and a drink two hours before dispatch.

• If your vet has recommended a tranquilizer, give it as directed or just before you hand the cat over.

Railway and sea travel
In general the recommendations for containers for air travel should apply here also. Some railway companies will allow you to keep your pet with you provided it is in a carrier; others insist that the cat, in its carrier, travels in the baggage car.

Sea travel for cats takes longer than flying and there is no veterinary care. Unless the owner is also on board, daily attendance must be provided by one of the crew. Sea-sickness is, however, rare in cats.

Two excellent designs of cat carriers approved for air, sea and land transport. These are airy, strong and secure models which can be firmly locked and are constructed of materials which are easy to clean and disinfect.

Grooming

More fastidious than dogs in keeping up appearances, cats will groom themselves regularly and often. Rows of hooked, horny and backward-pointing scales (*papillae*) on the tongue form an efficient comb for raking the skin and fur.

As well as keeping the coat clean, neat and glossy, grooming serves to remove dead hair and skin cells and to tone up the superficial blood circulation and underlying muscles.

Domestic cats, and particularly Persians, do need extra grooming beyond the cleaning which they give themselves or one another, and it has to be provided by the owner. Longhaired cats moult all the year round and need daily grooming.

In good weather, groom outdoors. If you have to groom indoors, choose the bathroom or porch, and stand the cat on a sheet of plastic or newspaper.

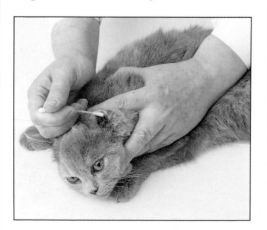

These three pictures show various classic stages in a cat's self-grooming routine. Sometimes the fussy self-cleaning of cats anxious to remove foreign substances from their coat can lead them to swallow toxic things. If you see your cat spending an unusually long time grooming itself, you should investigate to make sure it hasn't got anything nasty stuck to its coat and that it isn't suffering from any skin problems.

Grooming preliminaries

Particular attention should be paid to the cat's head when grooming. Begin with the ears, eyes and teeth.

1 Look inside each ear for any signs of dirt or the accumulation of dark-colored wax. Clean out the ears using one or two twists of cotton lightly moistened with olive oil.

2 Check the eyes. If there is any overflow of tears, caused particularly in Persians by a blocked tear duct, there will be dark staining of the face below the innermost angle of the eyelids. In the corner of the eye, crusts of dried mucus may have accumulated. Clean the area gently with a warm, weak solution of salt in water. Persistent "tear-staining" or marked eye discharge requires veterinary attention.

3 Inspect the teeth for encrustations of tartar. Is the breath sweet? Ideally get your cat accustomed to having its teeth cleaned once a week with a soft toothbrush (its own!), salt and water, or by using one of the special pet toothpastes now available. Once formed into a chalky deposit on the teeth, tartar will need to be removed by the veterinarian using de-scaling instruments or an ultra-sound machine.

GROOMING A SHORTHAIR

Shorthaired cats possess less exuberant upholstery than Persians, and are better at self-cleaning, so they need grooming only twice a week.

Q-tips

soft cloth

soft bristle brush

rubber brush

fine-toothed comb

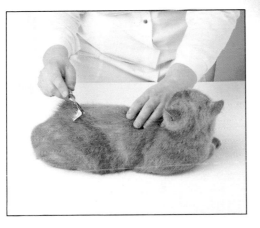

1 With a fine-toothed metal comb, work down the cat from its head to its tail. As you comb, look for black, shiny specks — a sign of fleas.

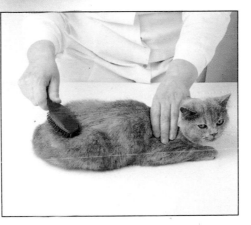

2 Use a rubber brush to brush along the lie of the hair. If your cat is Rex-coated, this brush is essential as it won't scratch the skin.

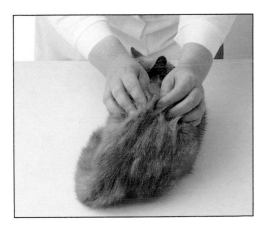

3 After brushing and combing, rub in some bay rum conditioner. This removes grease from the coat and brings out the brilliance of its color.

4 Finally, to bring up the glossy quality of a shorthaired cat's coat, "polish" it with a piece of silk or velvet, or a chamois leather cloth.

Care of the claws

If in any doubt as to how to trim the claws, let the veterinarian show you how, or let him clip them himself.

Use either very sharp scissors, human toe-nail clippers or veterinary "guillotine-type" claw clippers. Hold the animal firmly in your lap and press the pad of its paw with your fingers to make the claws extend. Examine the claw carefully. The main part includes the pinkish-colored quick which contains the nerves and blood vessels. You must *not* cut this. The white tips are dead tissue and can be cut, but not closer than 1/10 inch (2 mm) to the quick.

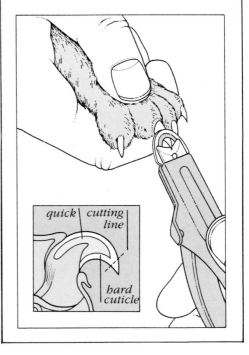

quick *cutting line*

hard cuticle

GROOMING A PERSIAN

Daily grooming really is essential for Persians. Without it, balls of matted hair can form in the coat which gradually build up in size until the only solution is for the veterinarian to remove them. Two grooming sessions a day, of fifteen to thirty minutes each, should suffice.

If, despite your best efforts, you do come across badly matted hair, hold the fur with one hand and try to tease out the mat with the other. Never cut it off with scissors — it is all too easy to "tent" the cat's pliable skin and cut it. If you can't free the knot easily, consult a vet.

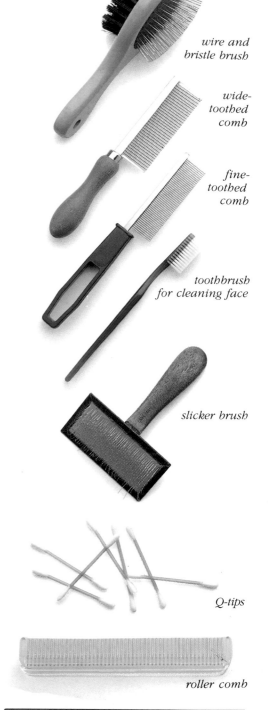

wire and bristle brush

wide-toothed comb

fine-toothed comb

toothbrush for cleaning face

slicker brush

Q-tips

roller comb

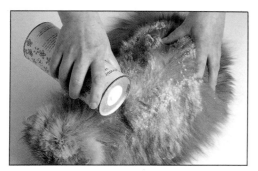

1 Once a week, as a preliminary step, powder the entire coat in sections, using either a proprietary grooming powder or a mixture of corn starch and talcum powder. This adds body and separates the coat hairs.

2 Using your hands, distribute the powder evenly into the coat, making sure that no section is more heavily powdered than another. Most cats love what they perceive as an unsolicited, all-over body massage!

3 With a pure bristle brush (which doesn't cause static or break hairs) use a "brushing up" action to lift the fur and to begin the process of removing debris and dead hair.

4 When you are satisfied that all the fur has been thoroughly lifted, change actions and brush down and up, all over the body, including the tail and the cat's underside.

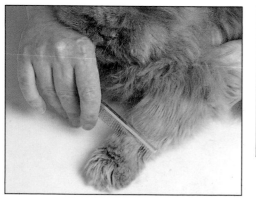

5 Change to a fine-toothed comb to tease out any snarls and tangles.

6 Depending on your preference, you may consider gently plucking out the hair growing at the tips of the ears to give them a more rounded appearance, but this is not essential.

7 As a tidy finishing touch, use a toothbrush to make the ruff stand out and to brush around the face, down the front and down the legs. Be careful not to go too close to the eyes.

WASHING

If your cat's coat gets very dirty you should give it a wet or a dry bath.

If your cat violently objects to water, give it a dry bran bath. Use this method only on shorthaired cats which are not too dirty. First heat one to two pounds (half to one kilogram) of bran in an oven at 300°F (150°C) for twenty minutes. Then stand your cat on a newspaper and massage the warm bran into its coat. When you have covered all the fur with bran, comb it out.

Washing by the wet method is shown in these photographs. You will be lucky if your cat behaves as calmly as this one!

1 Use a bowl, sink, or bath. Close all windows and doors. Put a rubber mat in the bath to stop the cat slipping. Pour on water at blood heat (test the temperature with your elbow).

2 Pour on some non-irritant baby or cat shampoo while holding the cat firmly with your other hand.

3 Work up a lather in the coat by massaging gently with your fingers. Take particular care with the head, and avoid getting water or lather in the ears and eyes.

4 Rinse thoroughly with warm water — a spray attachment is useful for this.

5 Wrap the cat in a large, warm towel.

6 Now wash the face with a cotton ball or a soft cloth dipped in warm water.

7 Keep the cat in a warm place until completely dry. A hair-dryer, if it doesn't upset the cat can be used — check the heat with your hand. Then comb the dry fur out.

Health Care

CHOOSING A VET

Before your cat is ill, you should find a veterinarian in your locality who will give your newly arrived feline a thorough check, provide all the necessary vaccinations, and tell you about any preventive medicine or special care that your cat may require. He should also provide a twenty-four hour service that can deal with genuine emergencies.

Obviously it is best to find a veterinary practice that works extensively with small animals. Other owners of cats, breeders, and humane society clinics in your vicinity will point you in the right direction. It is almost always possible to visit your cat doctor by prior arrangement in order to see all the facilities available.

A veterinarian undergoes many years of training in animal medicine and surgery, including the particular problems of *Felidae,* so that if trouble strikes, or if you have questions about breeding, nutrition, or any other aspect of management, be guided by him or her. Don't try to

Some veterinarians specialize in cat diseases or in problems of a particular part of the body.

lecture the vet after having read this book or spoken to the dogmatic breeder who supplied your cat. The veterinarian is in the best position to provide you with unbiased advice.

If you are not satisfied with the veterinary care of your cat, you are always free to obtain a second opinion — something which all veterinarians are ethically bound to agree to.

COMMON AILMENTS

Cats may have nine lives but they are, like humans and other creatures, occasionally out of sorts and sometimes downright ill. The study of feline diseases and their treatment by medicine and surgery are important areas of veterinary science, and much research is currently being done – recently a virus (FIV) has been identified as immune deficiency syndrome, which is similar in some respects to the Aids virus affecting humans but not transmittable to humans. No matter how skilled your veterinarian may be, it is the cat owner's responsibility to have some working knowledge of the common feline ailments. The owner is normally the first to spot that all is not well with an animal, and must know when to seek professional attention and how to assist the patient's return to health.

This section of the book describes the symptoms of the commoner diseases of cats, and explains what you should do about them and what treatment is available from the vet. Simple, useful first-aid techniques are included, but the emphasis is on seeking veterinary help for all but the mildest and briefest of conditions.

The mouth

Symptoms associated with mouth problems are salivating (slavering), pawing at the mouth, exaggerated chewing motions, and tentative chewing as if dealing with a hot potato.

The mouth should be inspected from time to time to see that all is in order. If tartar, a brown, cement-like substance, accumulates to any extent, it does not produce holes in the teeth; instead it damages the gum edges, lets bacteria in to infect the teeth sockets and thus loosens the teeth. (There is always some gum inflammation with tartar.) To prevent the build-up of tartar, brush your cat's teeth once a week with a soft toothbrush or cotton dipped in salt water, and take it to the vet once a

year for descaling treatment.

Check that there are no foreign bodies stuck between the teeth. Pieces of bone often become wedged between the teeth and against the roof of the mouth. Fishbone pieces sometimes lodge between two adjacent molars at the back of the mouth. You can probably flick a foreign body out with a teaspoon handle or similar instrument. If there is no foreign body, look for smooth, red, ulcerated areas on the tongue. These can be caused by licking an irritant substance, but are more commonly caused by the virus of *Ulcerative glossitis*, a member of the Feline Influenza group. Ulcers of this type are associated with profuse slavering, unwillingness to eat, and dullness. Get veterinary help, since a course of antibiotic injections may be needed to prevent secondary infection.

Make sure that none of your cat's teeth are loose or diseased by touching each tooth gently with your finger or a pencil. If any teeth wobble, or the cat gives a sign of pain, take it to the vet. Don't give aspirin to relieve toothache because it is poisonous to cats.

Don't worry if many teeth have to

To apply ophthalmic ointment, hold the nozzle parallel with the eye and squeeze the ointment onto the surface of the eyeball.

Protruding "third eyelids" always indicate some form of illness.

be removed from an elderly cat. Food such as ground cooked liver, fish, and cereals with milk are easily taken, even by toothless cats. Having no teeth at all is better than having septic gums and rotten teeth that create misery, and that can also poison the whole system.

The eyes

Signs that all is not well with a cat's eyes are when they are sore, runny, or watery, or when there is a blue or white film over the eye. The protrusion of a white skin (the "haw", "third eyelid", or nictitating membrane) over some or most of one or both eyes from the inner corner is another common eye symptom.

If the eye is obviously sore and inflamed, if the eyeball has a blue or white area on it, or if the lids are swollen, then it is probably either infected or wounded, or irritated by foreign matter such as grass seeds. Such eye conditions always need professional attention because, if they are left untreated, the eye may be progressively damaged, resulting eventually in loss of sight.

Bluish or whitish films that appear on the normally transparent front of the eye (cornea) are not cataracts. The latter are opacities of the lens behind the pupil and also produce a blue or white effect, but deeper in the eye. In dim light, when the pupil is dilated, more of the opaque lens will show and the cataract will apparently enlarge. The opposite happens in bright light.

Some old cats may seem to have bluish lenses, but these are not necessarily cataracts. Many are caused by changes (similar to those that occur in middle-aged humans) in the refractive properties of the lenses, which remain clear and transparent. Such cats are not going blind.

The partial covering of the eye by the "third eyelid" is a common and curious phenomenon. It is not a sign that the cat is going blind, and often happens in otherwise apparently healthy cats. It can be a result of weight loss, when the eye sinks back as the fat padding within the eye socket is reduced. It may be an early symptom of Feline Influenza. If it occurs, keep a careful watch on the creature and, should other symptoms develop, see the vet. If this condition persists without other signs, try boosting the food intake and give 50 micro-grams of vitamin B12 daily in the food, or as a pill.

The vet has a number of ways of dealing with the varieties of eye disease. He can use local anesthetic drops to numb the eye for the removal of irritant objects, and can apply drugs not just by ointment and drops but also by injection under the conjunctiva, the pink membrane around the eye. He can also examine deep into the eye with the ophthalmoscope, and can identify infecting bacteria by taking swabs of the cat's tears. Eye conditions such as squints, blocked tear ducts, and cataractous lenses can be dealt with by surgery.

The nose

The main problems associated with the cat's nose are running, watery nostrils, snuffling, and sneezing. The appearance of symptoms like those of the common cold in humans generally means an outbreak of Feline Influenza, which needs veterinary attention. After recovery from "Cat Flu", many cats remain snuffly and catarrhal for months, or even years.

If your cat has snuffles, bathe the delicate nose tip with warm water, soften and remove caked mucus, and annoint a little petroleum jelly into the nose.

The ears

Ear problems can be suspected if your cat starts shaking its head, scratching its ear, or tilting its head to one side, which is sometimes associated with loss of balance and a staggering gait. (In rare cases, the latter symptoms can be due to diseases of the brain in which the ear itself is not involved.) Other symptoms include the sudden "ballooning" of an ear flap, the presence of tiny white "insects" moving slowly around inside the ear,

Apply drops into the ear, fold the outer ear over, and massage gently for a moment.

and a bad-smelling, chocolate-colored or purulent discharge.

If ear trouble flares up suddenly, pour liberal quantities of mineral oil (liquid paraffin) warmed to body heat into the affected ear. Do it in the garage rather than the lounge so that Puss does not fleck excess oil all over your chintz curtains.

Head-tilting and loss of balance may indicate middle-ear disease. This is an inflammation of the middle ear, which lies behind the ear-drum. Infection usually enters this area via a channel (the Eustachian tube) that runs from the throat, so it often follows throat and respiratory infections. It needs immediate veterinary treatment, since the modern drugs used by the vet can

Repeated scratching of the ears requires investigation.

reach the inflammation in the middle ear and in almost all cases prevent permanent damage to the balancing organs and the spread of the infection to the brain.

The sudden ballooning of the ear flap of a cat is due to bleeding within the flap and the formation of a big blood blister, or hematoma, usually caused by the cat scratching its own ear vigorously, but sometimes caused by a blow or bite from another animal. It annoys the cat because the ear feels strangely heavy, and it will shake its head to try to dislodge the "weight;" but it is not painful like an abscess unless secondarily infected, which is uncommon. The condition is identical to that seen in human boxers who are repeatedly cuffed around the ears. Left untreated, the blood inside the hematoma clots and shrinks into a gnarled scar, causing the ear to crumple and resemble a cauliflower.

The vet can avoid Puss taking on the appearance of a prize-fighter by giving a general anesthetic, draining off the blood, usually through an incision, and then stitching the ear in a special way that may involve attaching steel buttons for a week or so. It is not a serious condition and the success rate following surgery is very high. Nevertheless, the cause of the original scratching (mites, canker, or whatever), must be treated to avoid a recurrence.

If your cat is simply an ear-flicker

and the ears seem dry but contain the "insects" – actually otodectic mange mites – referred to already, give some ear mange drops (available from the pet store). Any discharge means that the cat has canker and may need antibiotic treatment by the vet.

The chest

Cats can suffer from bronchitis, pneumonia, pleurisy, and other chest conditions. Common signs of chest ailments are coughing, gasping, and labored breathing.

Coughing and sneezing — all the miserable signs of a head cold — may be symptoms of Feline Influenza, which is also caused by a virus. It may be mild or severe, and is sometimes fatal. In such cases, the damage may be done by secondary bacterial infections of the lung. It is not a cold, wet-weather disease particularly; many major outbreaks occur in summer and it is often found in epidemic form in catteries during the hot holiday months. Protect your cat against Feline Influenza by ensuring that it is vaccinated and boosted regularly. Incidently, there is no connection between human and cat forms of flu.

Labored breathing without "cold" symptoms may be a sign of pleurisy or of heart disease in older cats.

Keep a cat with chest trouble warm and dry. Do not let it exert

This poor little kitten shows the typical face of a Feline Influenza patient.

itself, and give it nutritious food, either finely ground or in liquid form. The odd drop of brandy or whisky can be spooned in. Keep the nostrils unblocked as far as possible by sponging the nose and greasing it with a little petroleum jelly. In mild cases where the cat continues to eat, and its breathing is not too distressed, a quarter of a teaspoonful of Benylin syrup (obtainable from the druggist) may be given every two or three hours as a cough mixture.

More serious cases will be treated by the vet using antibiotics, drugs to loosen mucus in the lungs and, where the heart is involved, special cardiac medicines. Where fluid accumulates in the chest in pleurisy cases, the vet may tap this off under sedation. Very many cats with dicky hearts can live happy, long lives once their problem has been diagnosed and maintenance treatment prescribed.

The stomach and intestines

Signs of stomach or intestinal disorders are vomiting, diarrhea, constipation, and blood in the droppings. There are numerous causes for any of these symptoms and sometimes more than one symptom will be observed at the same time. Here the most common causes have been dealt with and no attempt has been made to describe all the diseases that involve the abdominal organs.

Vomiting may be simple and transient, due to a mild infection (gastritis) of the stomach or the presence of a furball. However, if it is severe, persistent, or accompanied by other major signs, it can indicate the presence of serious conditions such as Feline Infectious Enteritis, tumors, or obstruction of the intestine.

Diarrhea may be mild, when it is probably caused by feeding too much liver or by a bowel infection, or it may be serious, as in some cases of Feline Infectious Enteritis.

Constipation may be a result of age

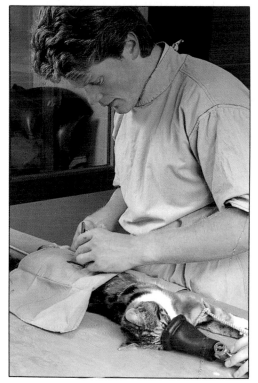

This queen is being spayed while under gas anesthetic.

and faulty diet, or an indication of an obstruction. Blood in the stools may be caused by the scratching of the intestinal lining by gobbled bone splinters, or be a side-effect of an acute attack of food-poisoning.

Use your common sense and, if any of these symptoms persist for more than a few hours or are accompanied by profound malaise and weakness on the part of the cat, you need skilled help. In mild cases, or until the vet arrives, remember that water and salt loss through vomiting or diarrhea can have serious consequences. To combat dehydration and weakness, spoon small quantities of glucose and water, seasoned to your taste with table salt, into the cat as frequently as possible. Where vomiting is the prime symptom, do not give solid food but concentrate on giving the liquid replacement. Half a teaspoonful of Maalox or baby gripe water can be given, but don't give milk or brandy.

Where diarrhea is the main symptom, concentrate on fluid administration. It is safe to introduce about a third of a cupful of strong, sweetened coffee cooled to body temperature via the rectum through a human enema syringe. It must be done slowly and gently. A teaspoonful of Kaopectate mixture can be given by mouth, but do not administer human kaolin and morphine diarrhea mixtures.

In the early stages of constipation you can try spooning two or three teaspoonsful of mineral oil into the cat. The tiny, ready-to-use, disposable enemas available at the chemist are excellent and very effective. Use a half to one tube as directed for humans on the accompanying instructions. Where constipation is a chronic problem, bulk should be added to the diet in some form (see p.162).

Severe or persistent cases of constipation will need veterinary attention. The vet can examine the alimentary tract with his fingers, by X-ray, possibly by barium meals, by gastroscope, and sometimes by exploratory operation.

Feline Infectious Enteritis, one of the major virus diseases of cats, does not only attack the intestines; it also attacks the liver and white cells of the blood. It can be fatal in a matter of hours and the symptoms are variable. Diarrhea is not always present.

Although the vet cannot kill the virus, he may use antibiotics against secondary bacterial infection. He will certainly be concerned to protect the cat from dehydrating through fluid loss, and this may mean giving transfusions of saline under the skin. The best cure for Feline Infectious Enteritis, a terrible scourge, is prevention. Have your cat vaccinated and boosted regularly.

The urinary system

Problems in this system are marked by difficulty passing urine, blood in the urine, loss of weight, and thirst.

When a cat strains to pass urine, the owner may think it is suffering from constipation, but it may have "gravel" in the urine. Cats on mainly dry-food diets, cats taking insufficient water, and tom cats castrated very early are more prone to "gravel", which is a deposit of salt crystals in the bladder that can eventually block up the water pipe (urethra) of male animals. When the bladder is over-full and tight as a drum, the cat is in considerable pain, will resent being handled, and may actually turn to look at its hind quarters and spit angrily. Take your cat to the vet for treatment, and don't try squeezing the cat's swollen bladder yourself because it is very easily ruptured.

Blood in the urine generally indicates bladder infection (cystitis). This complaint is more common in female cats and also requires veterinary treatment.

Loss of weight and thirst, particularly in old cats, can be due to kidney disease, although other diseases including diabetes can also cause these symptoms.

Preventive measures against urinary problems include making sure that your cat always eats a good proportion of moist food and has plenty of fresh water available. Do not have a tom castrated too early.

The vet can deal with urinary problems by using special urine-active antiseptics and antibiotics. He can catheterize a cat's bladder painlessly to free blockages and take urine samples for analysis. The kidneys can be X-rayed by contrast radiography and, if necessary, the bladder and urethra can be operated upon quite safely.

Genitalia

In female cats the most common symptom of a genital infection is a purulent discharge – which may be white, pink, yellow, or chocolate-colored – from the vagina. Cats that are known to be pregnant should be taken to the vet immediately. In non-pregnant queens it can be a sign of womb infection (usually following kittening), or the onset of the hormonal disease pyometra. This is commonest in queens that have

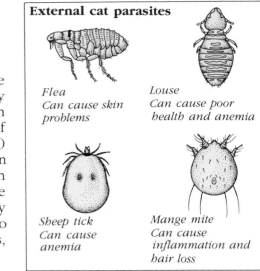
never had kittens or have had just one litter. It looks like a septic infection and can make the animal very ill through absorption of the pus-like fluid that distends the womb, although in many cases the pus is sterile. It is not an infectious disease although secondary bacterial invasions are a danger.

If you are not planning on breeding, have a female spayed when young. If discharges are seen, clean the vulval area with warm water and weak antiseptic and take the little lady along to the vet.

The vet may prescribe hormone treatment together with drugs to reduce the amount of fluid in the womb and antibiotics to tackle any opportunist bugs. His main weapon is normally surgical: the removal of the diseased womb (hysterectomy) through a side or mid-line incision under general anesthetic. If Puss is in a weak and toxic state because of the diseased womb, the vet may delay operating for some time in order to try to strengthen her with vitamins, antitoxic drugs, and antibiotics.

The skin

There are many kinds of skin disease in cats. Tell-tale signs include thin or bald patches in the fur, scratching, and wet or dry sores.

Itchy thinning of the hair over the trunk with points of oozing red scabs is one of the commonest skin diseases. Often named "Fish Eczema" this complaint has nothing to do with eating fish but is glandular in origin.

Skin parasites – fleas, lice, ticks, and mites – are most numerous in hot weather. Fleas and, less commonly, lice and ticks can cause damage to the coat. The presence of just one single flea on a cat — terribly hard to track down — may set up widespread itchy skin irritation as an allergic reaction to the flea's saliva, injected when the little devil sucks. In late summer, orange specks in the fur of the head and ears or between the toes reveal the presence of harvest mites. Irritating mange caused by an invisible mite can cause dry, motheaten-looking areas around the head and ears.

If you see or suspect the presence of any of the skin parasites, obtain one of the anti-parasitic aerosoles or powders for cats from the pet store or druggist.

If necessary, have the cause of your pet's tatty upholstery investigated by the vet. He can prescribe different drugs for the various types of disease, but may need to do sample-analysis to diagnose some conditions. To detect ringworm, for example, which takes a very subtle form in cats compared to that in humans or cattle, it may be necessary to do an ultra-violet light examination of fungus culture from a hair specimen. Ringworm can now be treated by

1 If you look closely, you will see a flea in this cat's coat.

2 To treat skin parasites, sprinkle a proprietary powder (or use an aerosol) onto the coat. Avoid eyes, nose, and mouth.

3 If using powder, gently stroke it into the coat "against the grain."

4 Comb excess powder out of the coat.

An advanced case of ringworm that has had to be rather drastically shaved for treatment. Most cases are far less dramatic.

drugs given orally and mange can be treated externally by baths, creams, and aerosols, or by tablets which work via the bloodstream. "Fish Eczema" is treated by hormone tablets.

Roundworms
These can cause bowel upsets, particularly in kittens. They can spread to humans and occasionally damage babies severely.

Rid your cat of round worms by giving one of the modern worming drugs at regular three-month intervals throughout its life.

Tapeworms
These worms do not often cause the cat much trouble but they can occasionally spread to humans.

To prevent infestation, keep your cat free of fleas because they act as host to tapeworm larvae. If you see tapeworm segments (they look like grains of boiled rice) in the stools, or stuck to the hair around the anus, give the cat a dose of one of the modern tapeworm drugs such as bunamidine or niclosamide. The very safe worming drug, mebendazole, eradicates both roundworms and tapeworms in the cat and should be used regularly.

Bites and other wounds
Cats do fight and often get bitten, particularly unneutered toms that frequent low company. Bites tend to go septic and they can prove troublesome. They may produce abscesses, which on the torso take the form of soft, low swellings covering a wide area. Hidden by the fur, and not always easy to detect by probing with the fingers, the only clue to their presence may be if the cat shows signs of pain when handled. On the limbs or tail, where the bone lies close to the surface, it is common for bacteria to reach the surface of the bone when an attacker's canine teeth pierce the skin. If not treated quickly, bites to the tail can become gangrenous. Septic wounds of the feet can show themselves as dramatically enlarged "club paws."

As soon as you detect a bite wound, clip the hair around it down to the skin with scissors. Apply a strong solution of Epsom salts (magnesium sulphate crystals) dissolved in warm water to the wound as frequently as possible. Antiseptic ointments are of little value as the bacteria have been "injected" by the biter's teeth. A single long-acting shot of penicillin from the vet is a prudent measure.

Where the animal is found to have an abscess, swollen limb, or septic tail, professional treatment is always essential.

Other types of wounds where the skin is torn, should be bathed in weak antiseptic and warm water, dried and then sprinkled with an antiseptic powder.

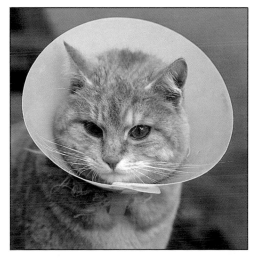

To stop a cat interfering with surgical wounds, inflamed ears or other conditions of the head, a home-made collar is effective.

Veterinary treatment will be needed for wounds that are of a size to need stitching. Small wounds, if contaminated with soil, etc., and particularly old or puncture wounds, will benefit greatly from antibiotic therapy.

Humans bitten or scratched by cats should regard their wounds as potentially dangerous. There is the possibility of infection with the germs of "cat-scratch fever", or with the bacterium often found in cats' mouths, *Pasteurella septica.*

Lumps and bumps
You may find a "growth," thickening, or swelling somewhere on your cat's body, perhaps on a leg, eyelid, or on the tummy. In the majority of cases, these are unlikely to be tumors, benign or otherwise. Blood blisters (*hematoma*), inflammation, or balls of matted hair are much commoner causes.

Tumors do occasionally arise in cats, and a small percentage of these may be malignant (cancerous). If they are caught early when they are small, it is easier for the veterinarian to remove them. Tumors tend to develop slowly while inflammatory conditions such as abcesses generally appear quickly.

OLD AGE
Inevitably, time catches up with cats. Should your pet survive beyond seventeen years, it is doing very well indeed. Very few reach one score, although the longest record at present stands at thirty-four years achieved by a tabby queen from England. Certainly cats tend to live longer than dogs – the oldest recorded dog reached twenty-seven years and the majority do not pass sixteen years.

Old cats need special attention and understanding. After years of faithful companionship, it would be a churlish owner who did not give a thought to coping with feline geriatrics.

Venerable cats change physically

A venerable seventeen-year-old cat still in excellent condition.

and frequently become rather thin. This may be accompanied by a change in appetite, with an increased or decreased demand for food. They may become more thirsty. Certainly some of these changes are the result of a failing liver and kidneys, conditions which, in the absence of other symptoms, are difficult for the vet to deal with.

If your cat's appetite increases, give more food at each meal or, better still, more meals daily. High-quality protein food (fish, meat, and poultry) and a variety of vegetables and fruit are essential for the pussy pensioner. Give more water or milk if it is wanted, as denying the increased thirst would be dangerous.

Age may bring fussiness, and increased amounts of high-quality protein may produce bowel sluggishness and constipation, as happens in some old people. Although oily fish like canned sardines help the free movement of the bowel, the basic fault generally is that, in providing rich and tasty morsels to the old-timer, owners do not give enough bulky roughage, the stuff that gives healthy exercise to the intestines. A little mineral oil (paraffin oil) mixed with the food can be used occasionally as a laxative (say two teaspoonsful once or twice weekly), but the regular daily use of mineral oil is bad, as it cuts down absorption in the stomach of the essential vitamins A, D, and E.

If Puss will not take fiber in its food in the form of bran or crumbled toasted wholewheat bread,

the daily use of a bulk-acting granular laxative is the answer. An ideal one is made from certain plant seed husks. When mixed with meat or fish, laxatives of this type are usually accepted by cats. Once swallowed, the seed husks absorb liquid and swell, becoming bulky enough to stimulate contraction of the lazy intestine-wall muscles.

In old age a special watch should be kept on the mouth. Clean the cat's teeth once or twice weekly, (see p. 156). Regular servicing by the vet throughout life should have stopped the build-up of tartar, but a fondness for soft snacks in Pussy's dotage may encourage rapid tartar formation with secondary gum damage, inflammation of the tooth sockets, and loose teeth. Catch these things early because septic areas in the mouth and bad teeth can only contribute to kidney and liver degeneration. General anesthesia for major mouth surgery (multiple extractions, etc.) can be risky in old age, so do not neglect mouth hygiene in earlier years.

There is a tendency for cats to lose personal pride when past their prime. Puss either forgets or cannot be bothered to groom itself. Groom daily with comb and brush and, with longhaired cats, watch out for knots building up in the coat.

Some old warriors lose control of their bowels or waterworks on the odd occasion. This may be forgetfulness, or it may be that the nerve control of the valves involved is weakening. If accidents becomes troublesome, let your vet check the animal. Cystitis can be a cause of involuntary "leaking" and should be treated. Lazy bowels may simply need more of the bulk content already mentioned.

Deafness or failing eyesight usually arise gradually, if at all, and the owner should be able to compensate for the loss of these senses. For example, remember that a deaf cat cannot hear if you are moving furniture, vacuuming the carpet, or bringing a

strange dog into the room — all potential dangers in the immediate vicinity from which a cat with good hearing will quickly remove itself. If you have a blind cat, keep its food dishes in the same place and protect it from open fires and similar dangers; also, try to avoid re-arranging family furniture.

Although there is no elixir of life available yet for man or his pets, there are some drugs, which the veterinarian may prescribe, that can counteract some of the symptoms of old age. One such drug is sulphadiazine, which is claimed to combat senility, lack of luster, graying of hair, and general lack of interest and vitality where such signs are due solely to old age. There is also a range of anabolic hormones that encourage tissue building, oppose wastage of bodily protein, speed the

It can be useful to restrain a cat by wrapping it in a blanket or towel.

healing processes, and generally increase appetite, alertness, and activity. The vet must decide whether your cat is suitable for treatment with any of these compounds.

NURSING CARE

Whether your pet's ailment is mild or serious, you will normally have to be prepared to do some nursing. There are some essential nursing techniques to be learned.

Handling a cat for examination

1. Cradle it in your arms if the animal is quiet and not in pain.
2. Place the cat prone on the table, holding all four legs so that it can't use its claws.
3. Hold by the scruff and press down firmly onto a flat surface to restrict the scratching ability of the paws.
4. The perspex cylinder method.
5. For a head examination, wrap in a large strong cloth or blanket.

Administering medicinc

Although the vet will try to select drug preparations as attractive as possible to cats, liquids and crushed pills mixed with the food are usually detected quickly. Puss then marches off in high dudgeon, going without a meal rather than taking its medicine.

The key technique to master is how to hold the cat's head, by bending it back on the neck until the mouth automatically opens a fraction. Then keep the mouth open by pushing the lips on each side between the teeth with your index finger and thumb. If giving a pill, drop it accurately onto the groove at the back of the tongue. Give a quick poke with the index finger of the other hand (or carefully with a pencil if you feel uncertain about your finger's safety), pushing the pill over the back of the tongue. Close the mouth immediately.

With the same grip on the head, liquids can be dropped in slowly. Do not be impatient and flood your pet's mouth with fluid. The cat will only choke, panic, and splutter furiously.

Injections

These are given by the vet and are normally the quickest, easiest means of giving drugs to cats.

Pre-tranquilizing

If your cat is as wild as a mountain lion but has to be taken to the vet's surgery for some reason, it is often possible to make things easier for all concerned by giving Valium or some other sedative under the vet's instructions before leaving home.

Taking temperatures

The accepted method of taking a temperature is by inserting a thermometer into the rectum. Generally, this is not worthwhile as most cats object to an undignified intrusion, become excited, and cause the temperature to climb. If you want to try, the normal temperature is 100.5 °F (38°C) — 101.5°F (39°C).

FIRST AID

Cats do occasionally appear to have nine lives. Their bodies are so elastic and wiry that they often survive being run over by a car tire without suffering fractures or serious damage. Nevertheless, hit by cars, airgun pellets, stones, falling masonry, or drunkards' boots, trapped in doors, falling from great heights, or savaged by dogs, Puss sometimes seems to need every life it can lay claim to. These serious crises produce skeletal and soft-tissue damage, which the vet will have to treat in the operating room. It is important to know how to give useful first aid emergency treatment until the animal can be taken to the vet.

Collapse and accident

If the cat is injured or unconscious, do not move it unless it is in danger. If you have to move an injured cat, slip a sheet under it and carry it as in a hammock, or with one hand grasping the scruff of the neck. Lay the cat down in a quiet, warm place indoors and cover it with a blanket. Place a hot water bottle, wrapped in a cloth, next to it. Don't give it anything to eat, but you may try to spoon in a few teaspoonsful of warm sweet tea. Don't give alcoholic stimulants or aspirin.

Check the cat's pulse, which can be felt on the inside of the thigh, where the leg joins the body. If the breathing is irregular or nonexistent, loosen the collar, open the mouth and remove any foreign body or saliva, blood, or vomit. In extreme cases, give artificial respiration.

Bleeding

If something is bleeding badly, slap a thick pad of cotton, lint, or a folded handkerchief on the place and press firmly — if necessary until the vet arrives.

Drowning and choking

In life-or-death cases of drowning or choking, where you cannot easily remove whatever is causing the obstruction, you must literally swing a cat. Pick it up by its two hind legs and whirl it round and round. This will cause centrifugal force to drive blockages from the airways. Do not be namby-pamby about this; swing the cat hard – it is difficult to dislocate a cat's legs. If this does not work, try artificial respiration.

First, make sure the tongue is not lying back in the mouth. Then place both palms on the chest over the ribs and push down firmly to expel air from the lungs. Do not press too hard, or you may cause injury. Alternatively use "mouth-to-mouth" respiration, by taking the whole of the cat's muzzle in your mouth and blowing in air steadily for three seconds, pausing for two, and then repeating the operation.

When it is necessary to provide heat for cats, a hot water bottle covered by a blanket fits the bill.

Reproduction

Everyone, well nearly everyone, loves babies, and few babies are more attractive than the cubs, or kittens, of cats, big or small. The successful breeding of, say, snow leopards or ocelots, is a notable and ever-welcome event — the more the merrier for such endangered species. With domestic cats however, the owner has a special responsibility. Pedigree kittens are usually in demand, and they sometimes sell for remarkably high prices; but crossbred animals are often regrettably a burden on the market.

Queens reproduce easily and fruitfully during most of their adult lives. With a relatively short gestation (pregnancy) period and an average litter size of almost four, cats can multiply almost as prodigiously as rabbits. It is gross irresponsibility to allow your cat, male or female, to produce unwanted kittens that end up being put down.

Unneutered toms run the risk of more fighting-wounds than their neutered colleagues, and for queens there are the stresses and strains, and possible complications, of repeated pregnancies. If you most definitely do not want your cat to have or to father a litter of kittens, or if you cannot be certain of finding good homes for any kittens born, make sure your queen is neutered (spayed) or your tom castrated (doctored), or talk to your vet about the Pill.

Reproduction in the cat follows the basic pattern of other mammals, but with certain interesting modifications, and owners of unneutered queens, pedigree or crossbred, should especially be acquainted with the basic biological facts of life, feline-style.

Sexual Behavior

A queen begins to rub and roll.

Queens reach sexual maturity between seven and twelve months of age. Do not breed a queen until she is at least one year old, at which age cats breed most easily. Toms mature sexually between ten and fourteen months of age.

The estrus cycle
Queens come into heat (estrus) according to a seasonal rhythm. The heat period lasts for two to four days and occurs at approximately two-week intervals. The cycle is usually repeated two or three times in spring (mainly March and April) and again in summer (mainly June and July), with sometimes a third period of activity in September. Not being machines some queens do their own thing and have heat cycles somewhat outside these main peaks.

When a queen is in heat she will adopt a characteristic posture: front end flat on the ground, rear end stuck in the air and hind legs "pedaling" an invisible bicycle.

Preventing pregnancy
A good time to have a female kitten neutered (spayed) if you do not intend to breed from her is when she reaches four months of age. This operation is done by a qualified vet under general anesthetic. It consists of removing both ovaries and part of the horns of the womb. The incision is usually made in one flank. There is very little risk of strain involved in the operation; the kitten is bouncing around again twenty-four hours after the operation. Sutures are generally removed seven to ten days after the operation and there are rarely any after-effects.

Tom kittens can be castrated when four months old. Personally I recommend waiting until they are a couple of months older. This allows the penis to grow in diameter and may avoid troublesome clogging up with urine sludge later in life. Castration is the painless removal of the testicles by a veterinarian.

Although it can be done under local anesthetic up to six months, after that age a full general anesthetic is used. "Doctored" toms do not necessarily become fat, sluggish and lazy, although their urine loses its pungent aroma and they become sweeter characters.

Some folk think spaying and castration are cruel, a denial of a cat's natural desires. In practice, a castrated tom is spared the bites, abscesses and other unfortunate consequences of midnight battles on the rooftops. And it is humane to save unwanted pregnancies.

Both spaying and castration can be carried out if necessary at any age, though a vet will not usually want to spay a queen who is more than a couple of weeks pregnant. If possible it is best to avoid operating on a queen that is "in heat"; at these times the high level of sex hormones in her blood slows the speed of clotting when the vet operates.

In females, an alternative to the surgical approach is the Pill. These contraceptive tablets, such as megestrol acetate, can be used in one of two ways: half a 5mg tablet daily for two months during the breeding season; or the same weekly for up to one-and-a-half years during the non-breeding season. Diabetic cats and certain others should not be put on the Pill, but discuss the best procedure with your veterinarian.

The classic position adopted by a queen ready for mating.

Mating

The cat, if you but singe her tabby skin,
The chimney keeps, and sits content within;
But once grown sleek, will from her corner run,
Sport with her tail and wanton in the sun:
She licks her fair round face, and frisks abroad
To show her fur, and to be catterwaw'd

Pope, *The Wife of Bath (Prologue)*

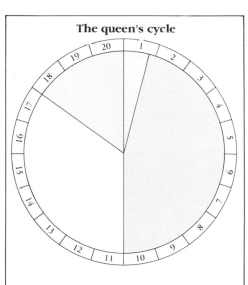

Initial contact between tom and queen.

Choosing a stud

If you plan to breed from your pedigree queen, you will, unless you also have a similarly blue-blooded tom, have to find a reputable breeder. Make enquiries at a cat club, cat show or your veterinarian's office. A first-class breeder of the kind you must seek, will have spacious, secure, hygienic and warm accommodation for the tom and queen. All the animals at the stud should be free of Feline Leukaemia virus. You should ask to see veterinary certificates verifying this and produce similar ones, together with vaccination certificates, for your cat. A stud fee will be payable, though if the first mating should not prove successful, a second attempt is normally granted free of charge.

Discuss with the breeder the approximate date (always impossible to predict with complete accuracy) when you should deliver your queen.

Recognizing estrus

So how do you know when a queen is ready to mate? Before the estrus (heat) begins in earnest she will be more affectionate than usual, rubbing and rolling with exaggerated enthusiasm. When heat sets in she will start to "call" — howl in a most imperious manner — and show marked restlessness and a longing to go out of doors so she can go in search of a feline Don Juan.

Her call may be a low, plaintive love song or, in the case of a Siamese, a powerful aria worthy of Callas. Most noticeable of all is the mating posture described and illustrated opposite. Once the queen begins to call, telephone the breeder and arrange to take your cat round. Do not go through with the lover's tryst if either of the cats is off-color.

The queen's cycle

If your queen becomes pregnant, the cycle from estrus through gestation, birth and lactation to the resumption of estrus lasts on average twenty weeks. Feline heat cycles are seasonal, and tend to start in January. Within any phase, two or three two-week cycles occur. Each estrus lasts two to four days.

Coitus

At the breeder's premises the queen will be placed in adjoining quarters to those of the tom, and separated by wire mesh. They will be allowed to mix when the female begins to make advances to the male. The couple will be allowed to mate three or four times and then perhaps left together for a further two to three days. You will then return to collect your hopefully pregnant animal.

When you arrive back home the queen may well still be in heat — do not let her go out of the house for a few days. It is not unknown for superfecundation to occur — a condition in which offspring from two toms, one of them perhaps the crossbred and cross-eyed tom that ruled the neighborhood, are conceived contemporaneously. In such cases the litter will consist of a mixture of pedigree and non-pedigree kittens.

Once a queen is with a tom — whether it is in the breeder's carefully supervised cattery or up on the roof — like many mammals the cats' rituals of courtship and mating progress through a series of clearly defined phases, as described on the following page.

Mating

1 The provocative rolling of the queen stimulates the tom's interest.

2 The queen goes into the typical mating position. Her body is pressed to the ground, back hollowed and hindquarters raised.

3 The tom mounts the queen and seizes the scruff of her neck between his teeth.

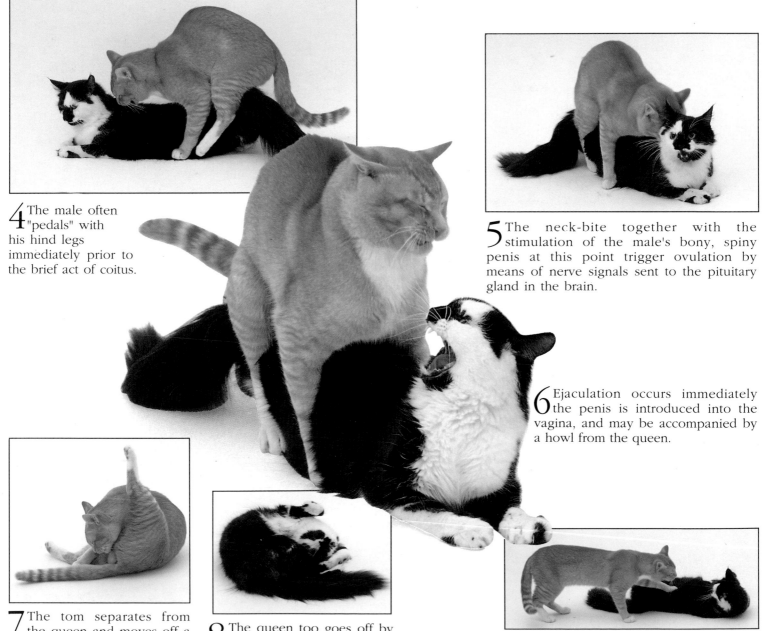

4 The male often "pedals" with his hind legs immediately prior to the brief act of coitus.

5 The neck-bite together with the stimulation of the male's bony, spiny penis at this point trigger ovulation by means of nerve signals sent to the pituitary gland in the brain.

6 Ejaculation occurs immediately the penis is introduced into the vagina, and may be accompanied by a howl from the queen.

7 The tom separates from the queen and moves off a little way. Sometimes he will sit or lie watching her. Here, he is grooming himself.

8 The queen too goes off by herself. She may give a luxurious display of rolling, rubbing and stretching.

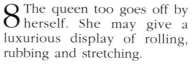

9 The above sequence is repeated after five to ten minutes, and then may occur many more times.

Pregnancy

The length of pregnancy in the cat is between fifty-six and seventy-one days, but the average length is sixty-five days. The mean litter size of the domestic cat in the United States is 3.88 kittens (only statisticians have ever seen 0.88 of a kitten!). Larger cats tend to have more kittens in a litter.

It is known that more eggs are ovulated and probably fertilized than kittens are born. The reason for this is that death and resorption of the early fetus is common in the cat. It occurs without producing any noticeable symptoms in the queen.

Kittens born earlier than fifty-eight days tend to be delivered dead or very weak and those born later than seventy-one days are generally bigger than normal and may also be dead. Such late, big kittens can cause birth problems – consult your vet if the seventy-first day of pregnancy arrives without any sign of labor beginning. Older queens tend to have smaller litters and toward the end of their lives may only produce a single, often quite big, kitten. Such mature mums may also have difficult births.

The largest litter on record was one of fourteen kittens born to a Persian queen in Wellington, South Africa, in 1974. Two years before that a Calico queen in Seneca, Missouri, USA, also produced fourteen, but of these five were born

Picking up a heavily pregnant queen should be done even more carefully than usual with minimum pressure on the tummy.

dead. An ideal litter size, with which the mother can comfortably cope, is three to four. Some queens cannot rear five or six kittens unaided.

Signs of pregnancy

If mating is successful the queen does not usually return into estrus. If it is not, estrus will recur in two to three weeks time. Occasionally a pregnant queen will show some signs of estrus and mating behavior at about the twenty-first and forty-second days — times which would have corresponded to heat periods in the absence of mating.

Points to watch for

• Reddening nipples — this is known as "pinking-up" and occurs around the third week of pregnancy.

• Gradual weight gain — two to four pounds (one to two kilograms) depending on the litter size.

• A swelling abdomen — don't prod and poke the abdomen to feel the developing kittens as you could cause serious damage.

• Behavioral changes — the queen tends to become "maternal".

What to do before the birth

• Discuss the birth with your vet.

• Obtain some safe worming drugs from the vet and give them to the pregnant queen.

• Provide a good, well-balanced diet with some extra vitamins and mineral supplements. Discuss this with your vet.

• In late pregnancy the presence of growing kittens in the womb can cause constipation. If this occurs, mix a few drops of liquid mineral oil with the queen's food.

• Prepare a kittening box for the queen in good time. This should be placed in a warm, quiet spot. It should be of wood or cardboard, open at the top and on one side. Line it with newspaper (easily changed when soiled and an efficient insulator). Blankets and sheets quickly become dirty and kittens can get lost in the fabric. Hang an infra-red lamp no lower than one yard (one meter) above the box. If the queen refuses to use the box you provide and picks her own place, put newspapers down there and hang the infra-red lamp above.

• Queens must be kept indoors during at least the last two weeks of pregnancy.

Predicting the birth date

If you know the date of mating, estimate nine weeks from then. If you don't know the date of mating, estimate six weeks after the first evidence of "pinking-up".

This pregnant queen shows a very distended abdomen and reddening of the nipples and will probably kitten in the next few days.

The Birth

Pregnancy ends when special hormones, sent out from the pituitary gland, set birth into motion.

Up to one-third of all kittens are born tail-end first. This is perfectly normal and these are *not* breech births. The term "breech birth" signifies a birth position where the kitten's bottom passes first through the vagina with its hind feet pointing towards its head. So pliable are kittens' bodies that even the occasional true breech birth usually occurs without causing difficulties.

The first stage of labor may last up to six hours. It begins when the cervix of the uterus opens up and a "wedge" of placental membranes enters it. As this happens, the involuntary contractions of the uterine muscles begin to push the kitten towards the outside world. When these contractions begin, the queen will probably make for her kittening bed. She may start breathing rapidly, panting and purring, but not in pain. A clear vaginal discharge may be seen.

The second stage should last around ten to thirty minutes but no longer than ninety minutes. It begins when the emerging fetus and its membranes stimulate the mother to aid the involuntary contractions with her own voluntary abdominal muscle contractions or straining ("bearing down"). At first, bearing down occurs once every fifteen to thirty minutes. Soon, a cloudy gray bubble, the first sign of the membrane that surrounds the kitten, appears at the vulval opening. The interval between bouts of bearing down decreases, until straining occurs once every fifteen to thirty seconds. The membrane protrusion increases in size, and part of the kitten may be glimpsed within it. With a few final contractions, the queen pushes out the kitten.

The third stage, following the birth, is the expulsion of the membranes and placenta. Each kitten has its own membranes and placenta, except in the case of identical twins, where they may share one set.

As soon as a kitten is born, the queen starts licking it, and she bites off the umbilical cord one to two inches (two to four centimeters) from its navel. Don't worry if she tries to eat the placenta when it emerges — this is instinctive in many mammals.

When all the kittens have been born, they should be ready to suckle. Make sure that they each latch on to a teat to receive their ration of first milk (colostrum) which contains important antibodies and nutrients.

The membrane around the kitten begins to appear.

1 After a period of straining ("bearing down") by the queen a cloudy bubble appears, which is the first sign of the emerging kitten.

2 The kitten is now visible within its membrane, and a few more contractions will complete the birth. In about one-third of cases the kitten will be born hind legs first, but this is rarely a problem.

The kitten can be seen within its bubble.

3 The kitten is born. The membranes and placenta will usually be delivered very quickly after this.

Tending a weak kitten

If a kitten is very cold and weak at birth, dunk it up to its neck in a bowl of water at blood temperature. Hold the kitten by its head and stroke and massage the body gently under the water. After two or three minutes it should become more vigorous. Remove the kitten from the water and dry it with warm towels.

Delays during delivery

The time between successive kitten births can vary between five minutes and two hours. Sometimes a queen will deliver half a litter and then rest for twelve to twenty-four hours before delivering the others.

If this happens, should you call the vet? If the first group of kittens were delivered normally and at short intervals, and the queen appears

A kitten is born.

content, suckles her kittens and accepts food, there may be no need to worry. However, unfortunately a delay of this type can be confused with "uterine inertia" where the contractions gradually fade and the queen tires of bearing down, eventually giving up. This condition is *not* normal and needs veterinary

4 The mother will lick clean the kitten, rupturing the semi-transparent sac, if still intact, and removing the amniotic fluid from its face. This persistent licking stimulates the kitten's breathing reflex.

By licking her kittens, the mother stimulates their breathing and circulation.

The queen chews through the umbilical cord of a newly born kitten.

5 Immediately after the kitten is born, the mother, with all the skill of the best obstetrician, will sever the umbilical cord with her teeth approximately one inch (two centimeters) from the kitten's body.

6 Almost immediately the kitten will reach out at a nipple and begin to suck. Just as quickly the mother's maternal instincts will surface and she will begin to make a fuss over her offspring.

The warmth, attention, and purring vibrations of the queen strongly attract her offspring.

attention. Queens with uterine inertia usually appear more fatigued and uninterested than a purely resting cat, but the difference may be difficult to judge. Therefore, if your queen clearly hasn't finished giving birth two hours after the last kitten was born, contact the vet.

When to help
If an inexperienced queen doesn't seem to know what to do with the new kittens, and doesn't break open the membranes as needed or sever the umbilical cord, you must play the part of the feline midwife.

• If the kitten is still draped in its membranes, simply strip them off with your fingers.

• Dry the kitten in warm toweling and make sure the nostrils and mouth are unobstructed.

• When the kitten is breathing, making faint squeaking noises and wriggling, deal with the umbilical cord. Sterilize a length of cotton and a pair of scissors in an antiseptic solution. Tie the cotton tightly around the umbilical cord about 2 inches (3cm) from the navel.

• Put a double knot in the cotton and then cut the umbilical cord 1/4 inch (0.5cm) beyond the knot on the *placental* side of the knot.

• Put the kitten in the kittening box beneath an infra-red lamp.

Labor problems
Labor problems are unusual, but if they do arise, arrange for the vet to make a house call, or take the cat to the surgery. Time is the vital factor. Don't try poking your finger inside the vagina of the queen. Put her into a well-padded box and take her to the vet in a warm car.

Contact the vet during birth

• When a queen has been bearing down for two hours without delivering a kitten.

• When no bearing down at all has been seen six hours after blood or any other colored discharge appeared from the vulva.

• When bearing down has stopped for more than two hours, although the queen is obviously still carrying a kitten or kittens.

Contact the vet after the birth

• If the queen bleeds significantly from the vagina (more than about two teaspoonsful).

• If you see a colored, white or foul-smelling vaginal discharge.

• If she seems lethargic or dull.

• If normal eating isn't resumed after the first twelve hours.

• If the queen is still straining after birth of the last kitten and the expulsion of its placenta.

• If the queen seems abnormally restless or feverish.

• If the queen shows no interest in her new kittens.

Maternal Behavior

The newborn kitten is eleven to fifteen centimeters (four to six inches) long and weighs between seventy and one-hundred-and-thirty-five grams (two and five ounces). It is a fairly helpless creature at this stage, unable to see because of closed eyelids, unable to hear with ears that are folded back, and capable of wiggling and squirming but not walking.

Over the next two to three months the mother cat gradually teaches her kittens all they need to know in order to look after themselves.

Brothers and sisters instinctively bunch together to conserve warmth.

Mother's grooming serves to stimulate the breathing, circulation, and muscles of her offspring.

Bonding

In the first few days of life, the queen is absolutely vital to the kittens' survival, not least in protecting them while they are physically so vulnerable. Instinctively, the queen knows what to do, even if it is her first litter. When she decides to carry a kitten, she does it by gently but firmly grasping the scruff of its neck.

A firm bond is established rapidly between mother and infants. Although shortly after birth a queen will accept kittens other than her own, once the bond is forged, strange kittens are not readily accepted. The sense of smell plays an important part in this bonding. Queen and litters recognize the "personalized" odor of the secretions of each other's skin glands, particularly those situated on the head. The pleasurable rubbing of heads transfers the characteristic scent.

In the first few days after giving birth, a queen may decide to move her kittens to a new "den." This often occurs with wild cats and is an instinctive act, designed to remove the babies from the liquids produced by the birth process which might attract predators. If your queen moves home like this, simply put her kittening box in a new spot.

Suckling

The kittens rely on their mother for their supply of milk. Each kitten adopts its own individual teat, and there is rarely much swapping of teats. By pushing with their forepaws against the mother's body as they suckle, the kittens trigger a nerve/hormone

Although the mother often grasps the kitten unceremoniously, she does it gently and never causes any harm.

This foster mother is taking as much care of the kittens as if they had been her own.

The cleaning of her kittens' rear ends encourages regular bowel movements and urination and keeps a delicate area clean.

reflex that initiates the "let-down" of milk. Restless, fretful kittens that cry a lot may indicate that the queen is failing to let down milk or, more rarely, that she simply cannot produce enough milk.

Where the "let-down" mechanism is faulty, a veterinarian may decide to give a pituitary gland hormone injection that almost instantly corrects the problem. If the queen simply cannot manufacture the necessary amount of milk, fostering or artificial rearing will be necessary.

Sometimes only one of the kittens appears to be short of milk and in this case the vet can examine it to see if it has a congenital condition such as cleft palate, or some other problem.

Communication

A mother licks her kittens often. This stimulates their breathing and the circulation of blood, and tones their infant muscles. Licking their bottoms is important in encouraging and teaching them to defecate and urinate regularly.

Communication between queen and kittens is mainly vocal at first. The mother produces a range of greetings, scolding, soothing, warning and "come-to-me" sounds. When the kittens are bigger and go on family walks, visual signals come into play. Everyone keeps together as the youngsters follow the "flag" made by the queen holding her tail high with the top bent backwards.

Gaining independence

Although the kittens learn by watching their mother and other cats, some things are instinctive. Even before their eyes are open they will react to certain stimuli — spitting or hissing if disturbed for example.

This litter of kittens is obviously well fed, well groomed and content.

They also tend only to rest when together as a litter. This instinctive habit serves to keep them warm and ensures that they do not become separated as a group. The snugness and the sound of their own heartbeats probably comfort them by reminding them of what life was like within their mother's womb.

The first major advance in independence is when their eyes begin to open at five to ten days of age. They are fully open at eight to twenty days. At sixteen to twenty days the kittens begin to crawl, at three to four weeks they start to take solid food and by two months of age they are usually fully weaned. When they begin to wean, the bond with their mother gradually weakens until she ceases to differentiate between her own and other kittens. At this stage they can fend for themselves.

Kitten Development

War games might as well begin with a toy bird.

Combat is practiced without inflicting damage.

The transformation of the kitten from its blind and helpless newborn state to full independence takes about six months. During that time physical and mental abilities mature steadily. The kitten's instinctive, inbuilt knowledge is progressively enhanced by a process of learning by observation, imitation, and practice through play. Play is the vehicle of the feline learning process — the life of the specialized natural hunter-killer is rehearsed and perfected in the theater of the game.

A lone, artificially reared kitten with no role models around to copy and emulate will never learn much of the repertoire of feline hunting skills. What is not learned during the formative first few weeks of life, cannot be acquired later. Kittens that watch, and are in a real sense taught by their mothers, learn more quickly than they would by watching some unrelated adult.

It is therefore nothing to worry about when your young kittens indulge in regular rough bouts of fighting. Play "combat" of this kind almost never results in any wounds, or the loss of a single drop of blood. As well as refining physical and mental abilities that will serve the cat well in adult life, there is quite obviously lots of sheer fun in kittens' boisterous play. As with a human child, play with its peers increases the social skills and sociability of a kitten. The kitten that is denied the opportunity of play may grow up into a rather antisocial, insular, and perhaps neurotic adult.

Under normal conditions the kitten packs a lot of learning and physical growth into half a year, equivalent to about ten years in the human life span, and, as with humans, a perfect feline upbringing can best be achieved by a family environment (normally a one-parent family in the case of the domestic cat). In raising a strong and sensible cat, there is nothing to equal the natural milk and constant attention of the queen, the endless games and competition with siblings, and the opportunities to learn from, and inwardly digest the example of mother and other sophisticated adults.

The same applies to the young cubs of wild cats. I have attended hundreds of young lions, tigers, leopards, and other cat species in captivity that have had to be hand-reared by humans without the influence of feline kith and kin. Such animals are never, in my opinion, quite as well adjusted as naturally reared ones. Their reintroduction into a naturally reared pride or group is often difficult.

Techniques taught by mother are essential if a kitten is to develop natural hunting skills.

First day

Giving birth to a large litter of kittens can be exhausting for a queen, and she will need to rest for about twelve to twenty-four hours after her labors. Under normal circumstances the kittens should stay with her.

Newborn kittens are completely helpless.

Second day

By the second day the queen should be feeling much recovered, be eating and drinking normally, and happily getting down to the business of rearing her kittens.

Blind, two-day-old kittens respond to the touch, warmth, and purring vibrations of the mother.

Eighth day

The kittens now weigh, depending on their breed and the physical characteristics of their parents, between 4 and 9 oz (110 and 250 gm). The eyes may open at any time between now and twenty days.

Seeing the world for the first time, as the eyes open after the eighth day.

Sixteenth day

The kitten's weight is now between 6 and 12 oz (180 and 340 gm). and crawling will start within the next four days.

Just over two weeks old, and this kitten is about to become a rather wobbly crawler.

Twenty-first day

The weight is now somewhere between 8 and 15 oz (215 and 420 gm). This is the time that weaning after natural rearing can begin. Give powdered cat milk substitute, or canned milk diluted with water as for human babies, but at double strength. Offer the liquid on a teaspoon, four times a day.

Toilet training should also start now. Put a litter tray in a convenient, quiet, and easily reached spot. At the first sign of a kitten even looking as if

Toilet training should begin early, as with these three-week-old kittens.

it might be thinking of defecating or urinating, pop it on it. If you have more than one kitten make sure the tray is big enough for communal toilet sessions, and if you have a single, nervous kitten provide a covered litter tray.

Four weeks

A kitten one month old weighs 9 to 18 oz (250 to 500 gm) and is now making great strides — literally. It begins to run and play games between four and five weeks old, and at about the same time first washes itself. Toys should be provided, either special cat toys, or simple household objects such as empty thread spools, or ping-pong balls; but avoid giving balls of knitting wool to breeds such as Burmese and Siamese.

A little baby cereal, puréed, canned, or bottled baby food (fish, meat, or cheese varieties) can now be added to the milk mixture.

One month old and washing begins.

Five weeks

The weight is between 10 and 22 oz (290 and 620 gm), and it is time for you to register the kitten's pedigree with the breed authorities.

Finely ground best meat, finely chopped canned cat food, or chopped, boiled, or milk-poached fish should be substituted for one of the four milk feeds. Place in a shallow tray or saucer and give the kittens as much as they will eat once a day, but don't put too much down at once.

Four weeks: game playing begins around now.

At four weeks, it is time to provide toys.

Six weeks

The weight of the kitten has now reached between 11 and 25 oz (315 and 700 gm). The youngster makes its first attempts at hunting practice between six and eight weeks.

Although it is best if a kitten stays with its mother until it is fully weaned at about eight weeks old, it can be separated from six weeks onward.

Increase the amount of solid ground food in the diet by replacing two more of the milk feeds with a balanced canned cat food.

Eight weeks

Weighing 14 to 31 oz (400 to 900 gm), the kitten is now normally fully weaned and possesses all its milk teeth. Feeding should comprise two or three solid meals a day, and a saucer of cow's milk – which can be substituted with fresh water once the kittens are six months old. Milk or water should be available all the time, but change it at least twice a day.

At six weeks, hunting practice normally begins.

As kittens grow, their nutritional demands on the mother dramatically increase.

Nine weeks

At eight to nine weeks old, the kitten will receive its first vaccination against the virus diseases Feline Influenza and Feline Infectious Enteritis. This is followed by a second shot three to four weeks later. Never neglect to have kittens protected against these potentially lethal diseases and, when adult, ensure that they receive annual booster vaccinations. Although in special cases, when there is a high risk of infection, your veterinarian may recommend vaccination of a kitten younger than eight to nine weeks, it is not normally done before this age. This is because antibodies transferred by the mother to the kitten will still be circulating in its blood and may neutralize the effect of the vaccine.

Theodore's first nine weeks

Theodore is a typical kitten and a number of important occasions in his first nine weeks of life have been recorded.

One minute old.

Five days and increasingly noisy when hungry.

Fifteen days and Theo first tries to crawl.

Ten days, his eyes open.

This group, nine weeks old, have just had their first vaccinations.

Points to remember:

- Vaccination is not dangerous and very rarely produces any side-effects. Should these occur, they are easily countered by the veterinarian.

- Kittens are not protected by the vaccine until about ten days after the first vaccination. Keep them indoors during that period.

- Pregnant cats must be given dead or inactivated vaccines, never the live sort.

- Vaccination should only be given to a healthy kitten.

- Don't forget to return the kitten for its second vaccination on the date advised. Animals vaccinated on veterinary advice earlier than eight weeks will normally receive a second shot at twelve weeks, or repeated doses at three- to four-week intervals until they are twelve weeks of age; the veterinarian will advise you what is best for your particular kitten.

- Make sure you receive a signed veterinary vaccination certificate. Take it with you for endorsing when you go for the annual boosters and also when taking your cat to a breeder or boarding cattery.

- If in doubt as to whether a kitten you acquire has been vaccinated, play safe and have it re-vaccinated. An "extra" vaccination won't do it any harm at all.

Twelve weeks

About now, the kitten's eye color changes to its permanent shade, and the permanent teeth begin to push through during the next six weeks. Your kitten receives its second Influenza and Enteritis vaccination.

Sixteen weeks

If you are not planning to breed from a queen, make arrangements with your veterinarian to have it spayed. Spaying involves the removal of both ovaries and much of the uterus under general anesthetic. It is a very safe operation, is irreversible, and has no after-effects. Because a general anesthetic is used, you must keep the animal off food and drink for twelve hours before admission.

A spayed queen will have either dissolvable or non-dissolvable stitches in her small skin wound. Non-dissolvable stitches will be removed by the vet five to ten days after the operation.

Twenty-four weeks

By now the kitten is totally independent of its mother.

This sixteen-week-old queen has just been spayed.

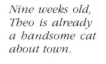

Thirty-six weeks

This is a good time to have tom kittens castrated. The operation is a safe, simple, and painless one carried out under general anesthetic. Keep the animal off food and drink for about twelve hours prior to admission. The cat will be ready for collection the same day and will require no nursing other than the provision of rest, warmth, light meals, and affection. There are normally no stiches to be removed.

Twenty-one days and he toddles towards his litter tray.

One month and he's ready to run.

Nine weeks old, Theo is already a handsome cat about town.

Raising and Fostering

There are occasions, such as the death of a queen or where she simply cannot produce a sufficient supply of milk, when you may be faced with the problem of rearing

If available, a foster mother is preferable to bottle rearing.

kittens in some other way. (If you decide to "destroy" the kittens, do not even consider drowning them. Animal euthanasia must always be carried out by a vet or clinic.)

You have two options — fostering and artificial rearing.

Fostering

A veterinarian, pet store, breeder or cat club may be able to put you in touch with somebody who has a newly kittened queen with spare teat capacity. Ideally any such adoption should be carried out as soon as possible after birth and before the queen has bonded too strongly to her own offspring.

To transfer a kitten, smear a little butter on it. The fostering queen will lick it off and in the process come to accept the newcomer as her own. To monitor a fostered kitten's progress and check that it really is getting enough warm milk, you should weigh it regularly. It should steadily gain some tens of ounces in weight every day.

Weighing a kitten to check on its progress is essential.

Artificial rearing

It isn't difficult to raise kittens on the bottle, but try to ensure they receive at least a few drops of the mother's first milk (colostrum). You should try to express a few drops of colostrum from her teats by gently squeezing and then give it to the babies by dropper. The colostrum gives the kittens some valuable antibodies against disease.

What artificial milk?

Pure cow's and goat's milk are too weak for kittens, and you should never give cow's milk to very young kittens. Instead you can use one of two alternatives: either a special cat milk powder available from the veterinarian or pet store, made up with water as directed on the container; or human baby milk-powder (or evaporated canned milk) made up to *double* human baby strength with water or lime water.

Equipment

Obviously, standard human baby equipment is much too big for kittens. Specially designed, curved kitten feeding bottles are available, but premature baby bottles serve just as well. Eye-droppers and 2ml - syringes without needles can also be

Young or weak kittens that don't suck well should be dropper fed.

Bottle fed kittens do best if they receive at least a few drops of their mother's first milk (colostrum).

used. All the equipment must be washed and sterilized between feeds.

Feeding methods

The bottle method is the best for most kittens, but with very weak ones or those that at first don't suck and swallow well, the dropper or syringe have advantages. A one-inch (2-cm) length of plastic tube attached to the syringe will deliver milk into the mouth, while a longer, two-inch (5-cm) tube would permit you to introduce milk directly into the stomach by sliding it gently over the back of the tongue and down the gullet. *Note:* This technique is very efficient, but should only be done after veterinary instruction. If the plastic tube is inserted wrongly and enters the windpipe, choking or a fatal milk-fat pneumonia may be the result. Never rush the feeding process, as it is easy to overwhelm the kitten's rate of sucking.

Whatever method you use, the milk should be at about blood heat 98.6°F (37°C). Up to seven days of age, give 3 to 6 ml every two hours. Between seven and fourteen days, increase to 6 to 8 ml every two hours during the day and every four hours during the night. Between fourteen and twenty-one days the quantity should be raised again to 8 to 10 ml given every two hours during the day and once at night between 11pm and 8am. When a kitten has fed it should be encouraged to urinate and defecate. To imitate the licking of the queen's tongue, use some cotton moistened in warm water to wipe the anal area and gently stroke the tummy with your fingers. When the kitten has responded, clean and dry the area beneath the tail and anoint it very lightly with diaper cream.

Between feeds keep the kittens warm in a clean box with disposable bedding, a heating pad or infra-red lamp, and a mother substitute such as a hot-water bottle wrapped in a woolly cover. The box temperature should be 77-86°F (25-30°) for the first two weeks, gradually reducing to 68°F (20°C) by the sixth week.

Weaning

Weaning of bottle-reared kittens begins when they are three weeks of age. Add about half a teaspoonful of the finest baby cereal, smoothly pureed baby food (meat, fish or cheese) or calves-foot jelly to the bottle feed for a few days. Thereafter wean the kittens in exactly the same way as naturally raised kittens.

General points on raising

• Don't pick up young kittens by the scruff of the neck.

• When kittens are three weeks old, discuss worming with your vet.

• Keep all kittens and their mothers indoors if possible until one week after they have been vaccinated at about nine weeks of age. Don't let the queen meet up with toms until after the kittens have been weaned, as many queens come into estrus a few days after giving birth.

• If kittens continue to pester their mother for milk after weaning fully she will start becoming thin and debilitated. Throughout the suckling period and for a while thereafter, make sure that the queen has ad-lib high-quality food. Discourage weaned kittens from suckling by smearing the queen's teats with a mixture of petroleum jelly and quinine, or by using a non-toxic repellent aerosol from the pet shop or a vet.

It isn't a good thing for kittens to pester their mother for food after they have been weaned.

Showing

The showing of pedigree cats has played the central role over the past century in creating the rich spectrum of breeds that delight cat lovers today. Through the shows, breeders have produced many new kinds of cats and had them recognized.

It must be said of course that the artificial selection carried out by breeders has been confined to the human ideal of a good-looking cat. Nobody bothered to ask a cat what it thought! In fashioning cats to charm the human eye, scant attention has been paid to the possible physical disadvantages. However, it is certainly true that genetic engineering has produced fewer harmful effects with pedigree cats than has been the case in some areas of dog breeding.

Should you decide to make a serious foray into cat shows, you must be prepared to spend a lot of time and money, but it will bring great fascination and excitement.

If you have a pedigree cat, or even if you do not, go along to a cat show or two. You will enjoy yourself immensely even though nothing there is likely to convince you that the faithful old tom you left behind snoozing by the fireside, isn't the most perfect cat on earth!

Heredity and Breeding

Basic mechanisms of heredity

Breeding for showing depends on the workings, be they calculated or accidental, of heredity. Every cell of an animal or plant contains structures called chromosomes. These look like microscopic strings of "beads" called genes. Each gene on a chromosome string carries details of the design of some particular part of the body. Some genes are concerned with eye color, others with coat color and so on. The genes are arranged in a fixed order along the length of the chromosome, so the chromosome contains a "blueprint" of the total make-up of an individual.

Domestic cats carry thirty-eight chromosomes arranged in pairs of nineteen. Eighteen of these pairs are virtually identical, but one pair differs slightly. This is the pair that decides the kitten's sex. Females carry a pair of so-called "XX" chromosomes, while males carry an "XY" pair. A kitten will inherit one of its mother's X chromosomes plus either the X or Y from its father, and thus its own sex will be determined.

Each kitten in a litter inherits genes from both father and mother in equal amounts but they will be arranged in a slightly different order along the chromosome bead chain. It is this new arrangement that gives each kitten its individuality.

Occasionally outside factors, such as X-rays, can alter the fundamental characters of genes, and the changes they induce are called "mutations." Sometimes, though very rarely, a gene mutation occurs spontaneously. Changes such as these result in the sudden popping up of new breeds, colors and types of cat.

Linked genes

Some genes tend to stick together and pass "arm in arm" from one generation to the next. These are "linked genes" and, where they are found on only one of the pair of chromosomes, are termed "sex-linked" genes. A good example of this in the cat is the fact that tortoiseshells are always female. A tortoiseshell coat is produced by a combination of genes linked to the female chromosome, and a male cannot therefore inherit it.

Dominant and recessive genes

Dominant genes are those which tend to get their own way, while recessive genes are shy and retiring types. When two color-carrying genes meet in a newly fertilized egg it is the dominant one that dictates the eventual color of the kitten that will be born. Tabby (agouti) colored genes, for example, are dominant, whereas solid (non-agouti) genes are recessive.

A noble feline lineage showing two generations in the family tree of a typical cat family where the father is ginger and the mother is tortie. Their offspring show the variety of colors that can result according to the rules of genetics.

Ginger

Tortoiseshell

Tortoiseshell

Colorpoint-and-White

Cream

Brown Tabby

Tortoiseshell Tabby

Blue Tabby-and-White

Brown Tabby

Cornish Rex

Devon Rex

Undesirable genetic effects

A dominant white gene frequently induces wasting away of the inner ear structures. This is why white cats, particularly ones with blue eyes, have a tendency to deafness.

The Manx gene, which causes taillessness, is similar to the condition of spina bifida in humans. If Manx genes are passed on by both parents, the kittens die in the uterus. Manx therefore aren't true-breeding cats. The fact that they survive at all means that they can only be carrying one Manx gene in each pair of chromosomes.

The Siamese gene may produce a defect in the optic nerve connecting the eye to the brain. This results in reduced binocular vision and a degree of double vision which the cat tries to correct by squinting.

Some other undesirable effects controlled by genes are hairlessness (sometimes allied to red genes), undescended testicles, badly positioned ear flaps, extra toes (polydactyly) and a cleft in the forefeet (splitfoot).

The Manx gene carries the inherited deformity of taillessness. Where kittens inherit Manx genes from both parents they usually die before birth.

Mimic genes: occasionally quite different genes can produce similar bodily effects. These are said to be "mimic" genes. There are two well-known feline mimic Rex genes — the Cornish and the Devon. These two breeds look similar, but genetically they have developed separately.

The squint of the Siamese is caused by an inherited fault in its vision.

Masking

A phenomenon known as masking occurs when some genes are so powerful that they swamp the characteristics produced by other genes. The best example of this is where the non-agouti gene masks the effects of the various tabby genes. This explains why a black cat with tabby genes usually has no tabby markings — the non-agouti gene

Extra toes are a genetic characteristic.

A British Cream kitten showing faint tabby markings from a "masked" gene.

has eliminated the agouti ticking of the hairs to produce a solid black appearance. Sometimes partial masking occurs, explaining why a faint tabby pattern is often seen in the coat of young, solid-colored kittens.

Selective breeding

The breeder of show cats has to operate within the labyrinth of miraculous natural processes I have just outlined. Little can be done yet by way of genetic engineering, although the day may come when we can actively make cats the way we want them. The breeder must select those characteristics that he wishes to promote, and enhance them by careful breeding plans. He can suppress unwanted features (cross-eyed Siamese have been quite successfully "bred-out") and experiment by crossing cats of different body type, color, hair length and so on.

Pedigree Birman kittens.

Of course, to win prizes at the cat show, the end product of all this considered breeding must resemble the ideal standard currently in vogue for a particular breed.

Cats for showing

In cat shows, pedigree cats are judged against a scale of points for their particular breed. The maximum number of points is one-hundred, with marks being deducted for features that do not match the breed standard. If your cat isn't up to scratch for showing, then consider buying a good pedigree kitten. Register it with the governing body or, if it is already registered, notify the change of ownership. In order to breed cats for shows it is best to start with one or two female kittens, rather than to buy an entire male (stud). Remember, however, that if you are going in for a rare breed, suitable studs may be difficult to find.

• Always consult an experienced breeder and join a cat club before you begin.

• Wait until your kitten is one year old before starting to breed.

• Compare the pedigrees of various studs and select the one most suited to your queen. Your aim should be to improve on her characteristics.

• Go to cat shows in order to study the potential stud's kittens and the judges' opinions of them.

If you haven't got a pedigree cat, don't worry. There is a "Household Pet" class at many shows in which prizes go to the prettiest or most characterful individuals.

The Show

The first cat show on record was held as part of an English fair in the year 1598, but serious showing really only began in 1871, with a large show at London's Crystal Palace for British Shorthair and Persian types. At about the same time, the first American cat show was held in New England for the Maine Coon breed. British cat shows are still run on the same lines as the early ones, with judges visiting each cat in its pen. Later, some shows had a ring class with cats on leads being paraded *en masse* around a ring by their owners — you can imagine the fracas that often ensued! Nowadays, cats in the American shows are taken from their pens to be examined in turn by a judge at a judging table, in full view of the public.

How shows are organized

Each country has a controlling authority for all the cat clubs and societies. In the US the largest body is the Cat Fanciers Association (CFA). Another important association is The International Cat Association (TICA), which has a genetic registry. These authorities lay down formally approved standards for all breeds, provide the registration of pedigrees and transfer of ownership, and

Mrs W Eame Colburn, America's most famous cat breeder, with her champion "Paris" in 1901.

approve show dates. There are many smaller cat clubs and societies, which often have slightly different breed standards.

In the US when you apply for a show, you will be sent an entry blank. Show rules are laid down to ensure fairness and to protect the interests of the cats. For example, all cats should be innoculated against the major feline infectious diseases. Also, after showing a cat you must wait at least a week before exhibiting it again. Another rule prohibits the use of any coloring matter that could alter a cat's appearance.

In the US entry forms for cat shows are obtainable from the entry clerk, who will be listed in the following publications: in "Cats On Show" in *Cat World ™ International* or in "To Show and Go" in *Cats* magazine; in the CFA's monthly periodical, *The Almanac*; and also in The Cat Fanciers' Newsletter, the TICA *Trend*, the CFF Newsletter, and the ACFA *Bulletin*. The entry clerk will mail a confirmation of receipt of your entry form, which carries the details of your entry as it will appear in the catalog. This should be checked and any errors notified to the entry clerk, if there is time before the catalog is printed, or to the master clerk at the show. Errors can result in the disqualification of winners.

Types and classes of show

In the US there are two types of show: the official Championship shows and the unofficial small shows held in conjunction with country fairs.

For Championship shows two or three clubs may combine so that several shows can take place in the hall at the same time. If an exhibitor is a member of the clubs concerned, the cat may be entered in each show. Such shows may last for one day only or may take up a weekend.

In American shows the classes are divided into Open, Champion, Grand Champion, and Household Pet categories. The neuter classes are the same, but the word Premier or Alter is used instead of Champion. A cat that wins the Open may enter the Champion class, and if it wins that class may be considered for Best Champion, as may Premiers under similar conditions.

A cat is usually entered in one basic color class for its breed according to its status, i.e. Open, Champion, Grand Champion. The cat is judged in this class, as well as in every allbreed (Longhairs versus Shorthairs) and specialty (Shorthairs versus Shorthairs or Longhairs versus

One of the early English cat shows, held in Richmond.

How a show cat is judged

Pedigree cats are judged against a scale of one-hundred points given for features matching the breed standard. Here are the marking systems used for champion Blue Persians and champion Siamese.

Blue Persian

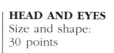

HEAD AND EYES
Size and shape:
30 points

EYE COLOR
10 points

TYPE
20 points

REFINEMENT
5 points

COAT
10 points

BALANCE
5 points

COLOR
20 points

Siamese

EYES
Type and shape:
10 points; color:
10 points

HEAD
Type and shape:
20 points

COAT
Texture: 10 points;
point color: 10 points;
body color: 10 points

EARS
Type and shape:
5 points

TAIL
Type and shape:
3 points

CONDITION
5 points

LEGS AND PAWS
Type and shape:
5 points

BODY
Type and shape:
22 points

Longhairs) competition for which it is eligible.

The Household Pet class has its own titles and awards. Some associations have a Novice class for first-time entries and entries that have been shown, but are not Champions in the Open class in other associations. There are also awards for kittens aged between four and eight months that are entered in their basic color class.

Preparing your cat for the show

• Make sure that your cat is vaccinated (or receives its annual booster) in good time before the show. Do not take your cat to a show if it is not in peak condition.

• Accustom your cat to being penned and handled. Put it into a pen for a few minutes a day to begin with and gradually extend the time. Let other members of the family and strangers handle the cat regularly in order to avoid embarrassing displays of aggression or panic when the show judge handles it.

• Accustom your cat to car travel.

Cat sickness can produce symptoms that mimic those of true illness and may make the cat most unwelcome at the show.

• Give the cat regular grooming sessions and inspections of eyes, ears, mouth, bottom, and feet.

Grooming

The coat of a Longhair should be full and "fluffed up" (see p. 154). Don't use grooming powder if the show is less than two days away as traces of powder in the coat will be penalized. If your cat's coat is white or has a lot of white patches in it, you can brush in a chalk-based powder to enhance the whiteness, but make sure you brush it all out. If your cat's coat is black, tortie, or any other dark color combination, don't use white powder as it is difficult to remove and flattens the colors. If you feel it necessary, use fullers earth then bay rum conditioner.

Groom shorthaired cats in the usual way (see p. 153), using bay rum conditioner instead of powder. To give the coat a final gloss, polish it with velvet or chamois-leather.

What to take

You will need the following:
Litter tray
Newspaper and litter for tray
Show blanket
Feeding dish
Water bowl
Bottle for carrying water
Cage drapes and floor covering
Clear plastic (to protect cage from overhead air-conditioning).
Carrier and carrier covers
Blanket for traveling
Cat food
Disinfectant and cloth
Brushes and combs
Grooming aids
First-aid kit
Confirmation of entry
Current vaccination certificate

Feeding

If you are showing a kitten, you would usually be best advised to feed it before you leave. Otherwise it is best to wait until after the show is over. If you do decide to feed your cat beforehand, give it meat or tinned cat food, not milky food that may precipitate an upset stomach.

BRITISH SHOWS

The first thing that happens at the show is vetting-in. The vet will give each cat a thorough health check, and if for some reason, such as runny eyes, fleas, or sore gums, the cat fails the examination, you will have to take it home and forfeit your entry fee. You may have to show your vaccination certificate to the vet, so have it ready.

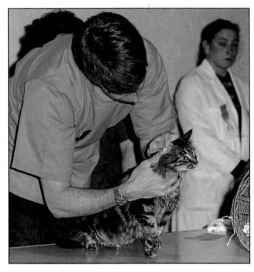

Vetting-in, a procedure generally discontinued in the USA.

Putting your cat in its pen

After vetting-in, you take your cat to its pen - a metal cage displaying the same number as that on the cat's tally. Although the show organizers will have checked that the cages are clean, it is best to play safe by wiping down the bars with some non-toxic disinfectant. Arrange the blanket, litter tray, and filled water bowl in the pen. In Britain, these are the only items allowed in with the cat.

Final checks

1. Check that the tally is securely tied around your cat's neck.

2. Give the cat its final grooming.

3. Check the corners of its eyes and clean them, if necessary.

4. If you have fed the cat in the pen, remove the bowl and change the litter in the tray.

5. Place the cat basket under the bench with the name tag hidden.

Judging

Before the judging, the steward will arrange the judge's mobile table, checking that it has a filled disinfectant spray bottle and paper towels. He or she will also check that all the cats are in the right pens.

When judging commences, the steward will take the first cat out of its pen, place it on the table, and allow the judge to make his or her assessment. Before the next cat appears, the table is disinfected.

For each of the pedigree breeds there is a standard of points against which the cat will be assessed (see p. 185). In the case of a household pet, where there is no scale of points, the cat will be judged on condition, grooming, coloring, attractive features, and temperament when handled.

After examining each cat, the judge will write his or her comments in a judging book. A judging slip is then placed on the award board. If a slip is marked with "CC", the cat has been awarded a challenge certificate. When all the entries have been assessed, each judge will nominate a best cat, neuter, and kitten from the exhibits he or she has judged. Then awards such as "Best Cat", "Best Neuter", "Best Kitten", and "Best in Show" are decided.

A winning cat has an award card placed on its cage. Prizes may be small amounts of money or rosettes.

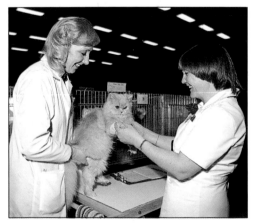

Individual examination of a handsome entrant at a British cat show.

Rosettes bedeck the cage of a feline winner in a British show.

AMERICAN SHOWS

While the British show organizers remain sticklers for caution, in North American shows vetting-in has generally been discontinued. Now, the exhibitor is trusted to bring only healthy cats. This is mainly because show organizers have found that the owners of pedigree breeds think far too much of their cats to enter an obviously sick individual. In any case, the veterinarian cannot detect infectious diseases in their early stages. Vaccination is the best safeguard against the spread of infection, although it remains true that wherever there is a high concentration of cats, the transmission of infectious diseases is made easier.

If a sick cat is brought, the show manager may tell the owner to leave the show and take the animal to a vet, together with all other entries from the same home. Such cats may be put back into the show if the owner can produce a certificate of fitness signed by a vet.

The judges do not visit the cats in their pens, and owners are permitted to furnish and decorate them. Some enthusiasts take the interior design of their cat's show-quarters to the ultimate extreme. It is possible to buy custom-made sets of pen linings in gold lamé, lace, satin, velvet, and even ostrich feathers, at prices of up to $300 or more.

To protect cats against damage or

even fatal injury by jealous competitors, some owners use security cages with built-in ventilation fans and air-filters.

Setting-up

When you arrive at the show the first thing to do is to check in at the table, which is usually set just by the show hall door. You will receive an envelope with your cat's cage/catalog number in it and a catalog. Sometimes these are free, but sometimes there is a charge of $2 to $4 per catalog. On a board you will find a benching chart — a plan showing the layout of the rows of benches with the owners' names inscribed on their positions. It is quite a good idea, particularly if you have lots of cat luggage and more than one cat, to move everything to your allotted space on a lightweight wheeled trolley.

The show is usually laid out so that all the Shorthairs are in one section and all the Persians are in another. Chairs are provided for exhibitors.

Judging

Now all you have to do is wait for the judging to start. By referring to the judging schedule, you will be able to calculate roughly when you will be

At the National Cat Club Show in Great Britain the judge moves from pen to pen, using a mobile table to examine each entrant. The results are then displayed on an award board.

An American judge uses a feather to encourage a cat to show off its best points.

called. Each judge has his or her own ring, with its own cages (often about ten), a table with a formica (or other washable) riser on it, to raise the standing cat up to a more convenient level, and a supply of paper towels, disinfectant, and show ribbons. Each judge also has a "Judge's Book", which lists the breed, sex, birth date, color class, color, and status (Open, Champion, Grand) of the cat.

At the side of the judge's table sits the clerk, often accompanied by an assistant or trainee clerk. It is their job to mark the catalog, which judges may not see until the show is over, take the appropriate numbers for each cat, and put them on the top of a ring cage in a slot provided, so that they stand up and are visible. The cats are benched so that male alternates with female, or that a space of at least one empty cage

separates adjacent males. Ring stewards wipe and disinfect cages between cats as the classes progress.

There is usually a microphone on each judge's table, which the clerk uses to call the cats to the ring. You must listen for your number; if you do not arrive after a third and final call, the number will be taken down and your cat marked "absent". When called you carry your cat to the ring, and place it in the cage above which its number is displayed. The judge is not supposed to know whose cat is whose, and owners should not speak to him. If you have something to convey, speak to the clerk or hand him a written note.

The cat is taken from its cage by the judge and placed on the riser on the table for evaluation. The animal will be picked up, turned around, and set down again. The judge often wields a feather in order to get the cat to show off its eye color, profile, etc. US judges do not open the cat's jaws in order to check bite (tooth alignment), and in some associations it is prohibited. Some judges call for the owner to take the cat out of the cage, place it on the table, and put it back, in order to avoid being bitten. Some judges, but by no means all, disqualify a cat (from that ring only) if they are bitten.

At an American show each cat is taken, when its number is called, to the ring of the judge concerned and the judging is done in public.

The Cat and the Law

It is a great privilege to be owned by a cat. Although many non-pedigree cats are unwanted, and considered by the uninitiated to be of little value, each and every one is worthy of the esteem due to all sentient living creatures, and we owners take on some responsibilities when cats come to share their lives with us.

In most states in the USA, because cats are not licensed, they have minimal legal protection.

Buying and selling cats
No license is at present needed for breeding, selling, or buying cats, but there are some restrictions on the sale of cats. Pedigree cats must be as described on their registration papers and must not have any serious illness at the time of their purchase, otherwise the purchaser may sue the vendor for compensation.

Damage caused by or to cats
You are not liable for acts of trespass by your cat, nor for any damage that it causes as a result of its normal feline inclinations, or if it is provoked.

In many states there are cruelty laws that ensure legal redress if, for example, your cat jumps a fence and your neighbor causes it bodily harm — even if the neighbor has enticed the cat over.

Road accidents
Under American law, it is not *always* mandatory to report an accident involving a cat; but in Massachusetts, to take but one example, you are legally obliged to do so.

Cat thieves
Cat theft and receiving stolen cats are both criminal offences. Cats are sometimes still snatched, perhaps for the value of their skins, or for medical research, or to be sold to raise money to support a drug habit. Even in areas where cats are not required to be licensed, adopting a seemingly stray cat can still be termed "stealing"; so beware if you decide to take in a cat that visits you regularly — it may well be the legal property of someone living nearby.

If you would like to be completely confident of your cat's safety, you may well be advised to confine your pet permanently inside or to choose a breed suited to the indoor life.

American laws
American laws governing cat ownership and treatment vary from state to state. In some cities, cats are only allowed out on a lead. Some states will prosecute for neglect or abandonment of a cat, but in other places there are no restrictions on abandoning pet cats and only "willful" cruelty is outlawed.

Useful addresses

American Cat Association,
8101 Katherine Ave.,
Panorama City, CA 91402
818-762-6080

American Cat Fanciers' Association, Inc.,
P.O. Box 203,
Point Lookout, MO 65726
417-334-5430

Canadian Cat Association,
52 Dean Street,
Brampton, Ontario,
Canada L6W 1M6
416-459-1481

The Cat Fanciers' Association Inc.,
1309 Allaire Avenue
Ocean NJ 07712
201-531-2390

Cat Fanciers' Federation,
9509 Montgomery Road,
Cincinnati, OH 45242
513-984-1841

The International Cat Association,
P.O. Box 2684
Harlingen TX 78551
512-428-8046

United Cat Federation,
5510 Ptolemy Way
Mira Loma CA 91752
714-685-7896

Cat World ™ International,
P.O. Box 35635
Phoenix, AZ 85069

Cat Fancy,
P.O. Box 6050,
Mission Viejo CA 92690

The Cat Fanciers' Newsletter,
304 Hastings,
Redlands CA 92373

"I Love Cats"
950 Third Ave., 16th Floor,
New York, NY 10022

Cats Magazine,
P.O. Box 290037
Port Orange, FL 32029

Index

Acknowledgements

Author's acknowledgements

Many, many thanks are due to my Editor, Maria Pal, and Designer, Liz Black, and to the rest of the magnificent staff at Dorling Kindersley who must have all things feline engraved on their hearts after the past months labors. Also to: Diane Wilkins, my most excellent and long-suffering typist; my colleagues in the International Zoo Veterinary Group who have given me much valuable advice; and my family who put up with me working on the book in the early hours of the morning. Thanks are also due to all the lovers of cats that I know — and they number many hundreds — for encouraging me in what they insisted was a worthwhile task, and to all the cats I've had the pleasure of working with — from "Buck Tooth", who tragically died in a timber yard fire behind my old surgery in Rochdale, to the tigers of Windsor Safari Park and the Atlas lions of the Zoo de la Casa de Campo, Madrid, Spain.

Dorling Kindersley would like to thank:

Daphne Negus, Editor/Publisher of Cat World ™ International, who provided much expert advice on the US cat scene; Margaret Stephenson, Assistant Secretary of the Royal Agricultural Society Cat Control, who supplied information on the Australian cat scene; Karen Tanner, of Intellectual Animals, for locating the cats to be photographed in the studio and for her feline expertise; Jan Beaumont; Eileen Fryer; Kim Taylor; Carolyn Woods; Ann and Arabella Grinsted; Georgina Parker and Family; the Covent Garden Pet Centre and P E Hatch for supplying materials; Jan Croot and Anne Lyons for picture research; and Ella Skene for the index.

Photographic credits

KEY: *b* bottom; *c* center; *l* left; *r* right; *t* top

Agence Nature/NHPA: **p**13 *r*

Animals Unlimited/Paddy Cutts: **pp**17 *l*, 18 *r*, 21 *l*, 43 *br*, 50 *l*, 58 *t*, 61 *tr*, 62 *bl*, 65 *br*, 67 *br*, 72 *t*, 73 *cr*, 87 *br*, 107 *br*, 108 *tr*, 109 *tl*, 113 *tc*, 117 *tr*, 119 *t*, *br*, 131 *bl*, *tr*, 151 *t*, 186 *t*, *l*, *b*, 187 *bl*

Ardea London: **pp**146 *b*, 156 *l*, 159 *b*, *t*

By permission of the British Library: **p**184

Jane Burton: **pp**5, 6, 7, 10 *l*, *t*, *b*, 11 *tr*, 12, 13 *l*, *b*, 14, 15, 17 *r*, *b*, 18 *t*, *l*, 19 *l*, 20 *bl*, *br*, 21 *b*, 22 *t*, 23, 25, 26, 27 *t*, 136-140, 144, 145 *b*, 146 *t*, 148 *t*, 152 *tr*, 156 *r*, 157 *b*, 158 *t*, 160, 164-182, 183 *b*

Chanan Photography: **p**133 *tl*, *tr*

Bruce Coleman: **pp**8 (except *bc*), 118 *bl*; Jane Burton/Bruce Coleman: **pp**11 *tl*, 16 *t*, 24 *l*, 147 *b*, 157 *t*, 162 *b*; Hans Reinhard/Bruce Coleman: **pp**22 *b*, 24 *r*, 26 *t*, 53 *tr*, 76 *cr*, *t*, 84 *br*, 129 *c*, 149 *br*, 161 *b*; Kim Taylor and Jane Burton/Bruce Coleman: **p**16 *r*

Geoscience Features Picture Library: **p**148 *b*

Marc Henrie ASC (London): **pp**26 *l*, 47 *bl*, 49 *cr*, 61 *br*, 64 *bl*, 65 *tr*, 66 *bl*, 70 *br*, 76 *tr*, 79 *br*, 90 *t*, 91 *br*, 95 *br*, 97 *tl*, 99 *br*, 101 *tr*, 108 *bl*, 113 *tl*, 117 *cr*, 124 *bl*, *c*, 125 *tl*, 161 *t*, 162 *t*, 183 *c*

Dorothy Holby: **pp**40 *t*, 103 *b*, 104 *bl*, 105 *cr*, *br*, 120 *br*, 121 *br*, 130 *c*, 134 *tr*

Pete Turner/Image Bank: **p**27 *b*

Vicky Jackson: **pp**104 *r*, 105 *tl*, *tr*

Eric Jenkins: **pp**47 *c*, 68 *bl*, *br*, 116 *bl*

Larry Johnson: **pp**123 *bl*, 187 *t*, *br*

Dave King: **pp**1, 2, 3, 8 *bc*, 16 *r*, 19 *r*, 25 *tr*, 28-39, 40 *c*, *b*, 41, 42, 43 *l*, *tr*, 44, 45, 46 *l*, *b*, 47 *t*, *l*, 48, 49 *t*, *bl*, 50 *r*, 51, 52, 53 *l*, 54-57, 59, 60, 61 *tl*, 62 *r*, 63, 64 *l*, 65 *l*, 66 *t*, 67 *l*, *tr*, 68 *t*, 69, 70 *l*, *bl*, 71, 72 *b*, 73 *t*, *b*, 74, 75 *tl*, 77 *t*, *b*, 79 *l*, *tr*, 80-83, 84 *t*, *bl*, 85, 86, 87 *t*, 88, 89, 90 *b*, 91 *t*, 92-94, 95 *tr*, 96, 97 *c*, *r*, 98, 99 *t*, *bl*, 100, 101 *tl*, *b*, 102, 106, 107 *t*, *bl*, 108 *cr*, 109 *tr*, 110-112, 113 *b*, *tr*, 114, 115 *t*, *br*, 116, 117 *tl*, 120 *l*, *tr*, 121 *bl*, *tr*, 122, 123, 124 *tr*, *br*, 125 *tr*, *cr*, *br*, 126-128, 129 *tl*, 130 *tr*, *b*, 134 *b*, 135, 141, 142, 143, 145 *t*, 146 *c*, 147 *t*, 149 *bl*, 150 *l*, 151 *b*, 152 *tc*, *tl*, *b*, 153-155, 183 *t*, *l*, 185

Robert Pearcy: **pp**79 *cr*, 87 *c*, 103 *t*, 115 *bl*, 117 *br*, 118 *tl*, *br*, 131 *c*, *cr*, 133 *cr*, *b*

Spectrum Colour Library: **pp**148 *l*, 150 *r*

Carol Thompson: **p**119 *bl*

Carl J Widmar: **p**132

Zefa: **pp**20 *t*, 46 *c*, 78 *t*, 118 *tr*, 129 *tr*

Cover: Dave King

Map: Swanston Graphics, Derby

Line drawings: Sandra Pond

Artwork services: Fred'k Ford and Mike Pilley of Radius

ACKNOWLEDGEMENTS

Studio cats

p1
Birman kittens
Litter of Kamasaki Midnight's Child
owned by Karen Tanner

p3
Burmilla with Birman kittens
Penric Quaker Girl
owned by Karen Tanner

pp28-29
Clockwise from top:
Doleygate Clarino, Grand Premier Doleygate Pacesetter, Doleygate Chaconne, Premier Downswood Red Baron, Samoto Louise
owned by Fred and Freda Greenhill

pp34-35
Black Persian
Ryshworth Inky Dink
owned by Rose Cook

p36
White Persians
Doleygate Clarino and Doleygate Chaconne
owned by Fred and Freda Greenhill

p37
Cream Persian
Downswood Emily
owned by Coral Allam

pp38-39
Blue Persian
Grand Premier Doleygate Pacesetter
owned by Fred and Freda Greenhill

p40
Red Persian
Premier Downswood Red Baron
owned by Fred and Freda Greenhill

p41
Blue-Cream Persian
Gablemist Ophelia
owned by Janet Fagg

pp42-43
Chinchilla Persian
Ginaliza Eaton Princess
owned by Mrs E Charles

pp44-45
Cream Cameo Persian
Premier Jandora Casino Royale
Tortie Cameo Persian
Jandora Caleidoscope
owned by Mrs Jan Beaumont

p46
Black Smoke Persian
Nosredna Excalibur
owned by Mrs P Craven

p47
Black-and-White Bicolour Persian
Amilynd Eastend Wicksie
owned by Janet Fagg

pp48-49
Blue Tabby Persian
Jindivik Ferniste
owned by Mrs Burgess
Brown Tabby Persian
Jindivik Cala Manda
owned by Mrs H Howe

pp50-51
Tortoiseshell Persian
Llegamos Dixie
owned by Mrs Burgess

pp52-53
Calico Persian
Pergoda Lotus Blossom
owned by Rose Cook and Gordon Cady

pp54-55
Seal-point Himalayan
Samoto Louise
owned by Fred and Freda Greenhill
Blue-point Himalayan
Grand Premier Omicron Prima Donna
owned by Eileen Fryer
Seal Lynx-point Himalayan
Zibaroue Gizzamo
owned by Janet Fagg

pp56-57
Pewter Persian
Premier Jandora Silver Crusader
owned by Mrs Anna Lodwig

pp58-59
Lilac Persian
Champion Catricat Lilac Limerick
owned by Mrs Carol Noel

pp60-61
Golden Chinchilla
Catricat Golden Charm
owned by Mrs Carol Noel

pp62-63
Blue-point Birman
Gazella Everso Chumley
owned by Karen Tanner
Birman Kittens
Litter of Kamasaki Midnight's Child
owned by Karen Tanner

pp64-65
Seal-point Ragdoll
Grand Champion Pandapaws Rag Fearless Fred
owned by Mrs Sue Warde-Smith

pp66-67
Frost Tabby-point Balinese
Northstar Minkey
owned by Anne Heslop

pp68-69
Turkish Van
Champion Cheratons Antigone
owned by Mr and Mrs Brett Hassel

p70
Chocolate Tabby Angora
Rocques Wotinelizat
owned by Mrs R Beauhill

p71
Tiffany
Kartush Abeche
owned by Mrs Southwell

pp72-73
Silver Sorrel Somali
Pandapaws Peach Melba
Mrs Dawn Lingley

pp74-75
Brown Tabby Maine Coon
Majanco Moshatel
owned by Mr and Mrs Tex Morgan

pp76-77
Blue Smoke Norwegian Forest Cat
Saqqara Fleur
owned by Mrs Pamela Wallsgrove

pp78-79
Non-pedigree Tabby Persian
Suki
owned by Mrs Melanie Munns

pp82-83
British Black Shorthair
Tapestry Moon Shadow
owned by Mrs Julie Avery

p84
British White Shorthair
Cherubin Snowberry
owned by Mrs J Avery

p85
British Cream Shorthair
Millcoombe New Moon Rits
owned by Mrs Pat Richards
British Cream Shorthair kitten
Cherubin Honey
owned by Mrs J Avery

pp86-87
British Blue Shorthair
Adiuesh Malletts Mallett
owned by Mrs Christine Mainstone

pp88-89
British Blue-Cream Shorthair
Camille
owned by Mrs J Avery

pp90-91
British Red Tabby Shorthair
Dubolly Raymor Red
owned by Miss E Button

pp92-93
British Tortoiseshell Shorthair
Champion and Grand Premier Czarist Cascade
owned by Mrs Joan Walls

pp94-95
British Silver Spotted Shorthairs
Premier Khaffra Silver Bojangles Khaffra Burlington Bertie
both owned by Mrs Rosemary Evans

pp96-97
British Blue-and-White Bicolour Shorthair
Champion Cherubin Arlene
British Cream-and-White Bicolour kitten
Cherubin Sherlock
British Blue-and-White Bicolour kitten
Cherubin Sugarberry
all owned by Mrs J Avery

p98
British Black Smoke Shorthair
Premier Tolray Phoenix
owned by Mrs Joan Carthy

p99
British Black-tipped Shorthair
Champion Brocton's Macgowan
owned by Mr and Mrs Tex Morgan

pp100-101
Calico Manx
Grand champion Jindivik Rainbow's End
owned by Mrs Burgess
Manx kitten
Manninagh King
owned by Melinda Rowe

pp102-103
Van Pattern American Shorthair
Linkret Tequila Sunrise
owned by Mrs Maureen Trompetto

pp106-107
Blue Tabby Exotic Shorthair
Jindivik Davallia
owned by Mr and Mrs McGuire
Colourpoint Exotic Shorthair
Boadicat Gypsy Love
owned by Mrs J Avery

pp108-109
Lilac-point Siamese
Tsuchiya Kumo
owned by Sue Roy

pp110-111
Russian Blue
Mirakhan Afternoon Delight
owned by Karen Tanner

pp112-113
Abyssinian
Grand Champion Iolas Akhenaten
Abyssinian kitten
Iolas Iolana
owned by Angel and John Wolfenden

p114
Korats
*Keiko Acrabat
Keiko Elvis*
owned by Sandra Collicot

p115
Havanna
Khaffra Chocolate Truffle
owned by Mr and Mrs Morris Dean

pp116-117
Burmese
Grand Champion Rumba Edelweiss
owned by Karen Tanner

pp120-121
Red-point Tonkinese
Windermere High Noon
owned by Cherry Young

p122
Bombay
Astahazy Prospero
owned by Billie Davis

p123
Snowshoe
Linkret Arctic Slippers
owned by Mrs Trompetto

pp124-125
Oriental Lilac Shorthair
Premier Khaffra Silveroberon
owned by Mrs Caroleen Iremonger
Oriental Chocolate Tabby Shorthair
Chocind Marbled Solitaire
owned by Mrs P Wallsgrove
Oriental Blue Tabby Shorthair
Khaffra Blueberry Pi
owned by P Wallsgrove

pp126-127
Black-tipped Burmilla
Astahazy Jacynth of Kartush
owned by Karen Tanner
Brown-tipped Burmilla
Kamasaki Nice Nigel
owned by Mrs Nicola Cane

pp128-129
Chocolate Tortoiseshell Cornish Rex
Lohteyn Swansong
owned by Mrs Leo Heath
White Devon Rex
Grand Champion Chantrymere Lotus
owned by Mr and Mrs Morris Dean

p130
Egyptian Mau
Khaffra Con Amore
owned by Mrs P Wallsgrove

pp134-135
British Non-pedigree Ginger-and-White Shorthair
Baldrick
owned by Mrs Trompetto
British Non-pedigree Tabby Shorthair
Kremlin
owned by Lucy Alexander

p152
British Blue-Cream Shorthair
Pretty Paws Crystal
owned by Mrs Eileen Fryer

p154
Blue Persian
Champion Sapajou Jolee
owned by Mrs Eileen Fryer

p155
Cream Persian
Champion Pretty Paws Candy Kisses
owned by Mrs Eileen Fryer

pp180-181
Seal-point Birman
Champion Jandora Jillyflower
owned by Anna Lodwig